GCSE

BIOLOGY

Julian Ford-Robertson
and
Tony Mays

EDUCATIONAL

Letts Educational
Aldine House
Aldine Place
London W12 8AW

Tel: 0181 740 2266
Fax: 0181 743 8451
E-mail: mail@ lettsed.co.uk

First published 1979
Revised 1981, 1987, 1989, 1994, 1997
Reprinted 1991, 1993, 1995, 1996, 1998

Text: © Julian Ford-Robertson and Tony Mays 1997
Design and illustrations: © BPP (Letts Educational) Ltd 1994, 1997

British Library Cataloguing in Publication Data
A CIP record for this book is available from the British Library.

ISBN 1 85758 575 5

Acknowledgements
The authors would like to acknowledge gratefully the expertise and help of many people,
including friends and patient wives and family, in the production of this book. Pam Dryden
and Alex Ford-Robertson made essential contributions behind the word processor.

Julian Ford-Robertson
Tony Mays

Printed in Great Britain by WM Print Limited, Walsall, West Midlands WS2 9NE

Letts Educational is the trading name of BPP (Letts Educational) Ltd

Contents

Introduction

How to use this book

GCSE Biology is written especially for those who need help in preparing for the GCSE or the Scottish Standard Grade examinations. It provides:

- advice on **what your syllabus requires**: a table of syllabus analysis.

- advice on **how to learn**: learning made easier.

- **what to learn** in readily revisable form: information, lavishly illustrated.

- advice on how to **show the examiner** that you know what he is asking for: an outline of good examination technique.

- **practice in answering** examination questions.

If you follow this sequence in the use of this book, you will have a good chance of success.

Using the syllabus analysis

Turn to pages 5–15 and select your own Examination Group and syllabus. For each syllabus details are provided on:
(*a*) the number of theory papers and their length;
(*b*) the 'tiers' of entry and the grades attainable.
  To help you use your *Study Guide* effectively the syllabus has been matched to the chapters of the book. This will help you to find the relevant sections to revise.

- Go through the book and highlight the sections for your syllabus.

- Make a note of the relevant *Study Guide* pages in your exercise book as you do the work in class.

- Follow the cross-references from one section of the book to another if they are needed for your syllabus.

- If you have obtained the official syllabus of your examination board, keep it handy so that you can see how much detail from each section your syllabus requires.

- You may need to select parts of some sections in the *Study Guide* when you know whether you are going to enter for the Higher or Foundation GCSE papers.

- Your teacher will also give you advice.

  Before using the subject material, first take care to understand *how* you should revise (see 'Studying and revising', pp. 16–19). Do not exceed your 'concentration time' (see pp. 18–19).

Using the subject material

Work through only the units that you have selected (see above). Use every memory aid that you can (see 'Studying and revising'). Remember that 75% of the marks that decide your grade in GCSE (or equivalent) can come from **your efforts on paper in the examination room**.

  The other 25% of your marks can come from practical work **in the laboratory** (Coursework Assessment). So remind yourself of the practical techniques that you should have used throughout the course.

Examination technique for biology examinations

Turn to page 210. The advice given ranges from tips on organizing what to take into the examination room to how to use your time well. Then build up your confidence by trying to answer the questions on pages 213–24.

The National Curriculum and GCSE

Science

Science is a compulsory part of the National Curriculum and may be studied as either

1. **Science: Single Award** *or* **Science: Double Award** – both of which include Biology, Chemistry and Physics – or

2. **Science: Biology** *and* **Science: Chemistry** *and* **Science: Physics**, i.e. a suite of three subjects. This method has the advantage of giving those who are more scientifically interested, wider opportunities in their subjects. It gives them three GCSE passes (instead of the two or one awarded in Science). It also prepares them better for Science A levels and the competition that ensues for University places.

Aims of the National Curriculum Biology course for GCSE

- To acquire a systematic body of scientific knowledge and develop an understanding of science including its power and limitations.

- To develop experimental and investigative abilities.

- To develop an understanding of the nature of scientific ideas and activity and the basis for scientific claims.

- To develop an understanding of the technological and environmental applications of science and of the economic, ethical and social implications of these.

How you get a Biology GCSE

There are two parts to getting a pass: Coursework (25%) and written Exams (75%).

- **Coursework**, also known as Science 1, is compulsory for all science courses. This is the programme of practical investigation continuously assessed by teachers in the laboratory or through fieldwork, throughout the course.

- **Written exams** in Biology are known as Science 2 from the double award syllabus with extension material (Chemistry and Physics are Sciences 3 and 4, respectively). All questions are compulsory. The exams are taken at the end of the course.

- **Grades:** After the examination a grade A★ to G is awarded, which is entered on your Certificate.

- **Entry tiers:** Your teacher, on the basis of your performance, enters you for exams at one of two tiers. The six different Exam Boards have their own names for these tiers, but they amount to Higher and Foundation tier. The Higher tier covers GCSE grades A★ to D and the Foundation tier covers GCSE grades C to G. You cannot be awarded a grade outside these boundaries so you must enter for the correct paper.

- **English:** Marks are awarded for quality of spelling, punctuation, grammar and for the precise use of specialist terms in coursework only.

The Scottish Certificate of Education (SCE)

The principles of the SCE are similar to those of GCSE.

Students are tested by teachers on their **Practical Abilities** during the course. At the end of the course, written examinations test **Knowledge and Understanding** and **Problem Solving**. A grade is awarded for each of these three 'elements' on the certificate, along with an overall grade.

- **Aims:** The aims of SCE are much the same as in GCSE. They add that pupils should appreciate the employment opportunities in biology and see its application to leisure pursuits. They also stress that 'positive attitudes' such as open-mindedness should be fostered but without sacrificing the ability to take decisions affecting the well-being of themselves, others and the environment.

- **Entry:** Biology is one of the few subjects that is only offered at Credit and General levels – there is no Foundation level. (All three levels do, however, exist for Science, which includes Biology, Chemistry and Physics.) Students can take either Credit or General level exams or, if teachers think it wise, both. If both are taken, the better of the two grades is awarded. Students can take Biology (or any other science subject) on its own.

- **Grades:** Credit level gives grades 1 and 2, General level gives grades 3 and 4 (with a possibility of grade 5 for work below the expected lowest mark. Grade 7 is reserved for those who have completed the course but fallen below the standard of grade 5. The overall grade 3 is equivalent to grade C in GCSE.

- **Syllabus:** There are seven topics
  The biosphere
  The world of plants
  Animal survival
  Investigating cells
  The body in action
  Inheritance
  Biotechnology

For details, see the Syllabus analysis (pages 5–15).

Practical abilities (SCE)

There are two categories of ability tested: (1) **Carrying Out Techniques** and (2) **Designing and Carrying Out Investigations**.

1 Carrying Out Techniques

This specifies ten tasks, which include sampling techniques in an ecosystem, measuring two abiotic factors and using a biological key for identifying specimens; preparing a wet mount on a microscope slide, using a simple microscope and drawing a biological specimen; performing the chemical tests for starch and reducing sugar; and setting up a choice chamber.

Repetition of the task to achieve full competence is permitted.

2 Designing and Carrying Out Investigations

During the course students are helped by teachers to appreciate four skill areas subdivided into 14 objectives. The assessment is on the *best two* complete investigations which are entirely the student's own work. Help given by teachers affects the marking. The four skill areas are:

1. **Generative skills** (G): identifying a problem, forming a hypothesis and stating an aim and a broad idea for action.

2. **Experimentation skills** (E): identifying the variables, setting up a controlled experiment, safely, and measuring accurately and repeatedly.

③ **Evaluation skills** (Ev): making valid conclusions, relevant to the hypothesis, including, perhaps, that the results were inconclusive.

④ **Recording and reporting skills** (RR): description of the experiment by diagram and by words and of how measurements were taken and variables controlled.

For fuller details on Practical Abilities consult your syllabus or teacher.

Assessment objectives

It is very easy to concentrate your revision on learning facts. Factual recall and understanding are very important aspects of GCSE Biology examinations and are probably the best starting place for all students. But you should be aware that factual recall and understanding only account for 60% of the marks. There are other skills to be tested and you should prepare yourself to answer questions testing these other skills.

Below is a list of Assessment Objectives. These are the intellectual and practical skills which you are asked to demonstrate. They are the same in all syllabuses, although they may be numbered differently.

You should be able to:

① Carry out experimental and investigative work in which you plan procedures, use precise and systematic ways of making measurements and observations, analyse and evaluate evidence, and relate this to biological knowledge and understanding.

② Recall, understand, use and apply the knowledge of biology set out in the syllabus.

③ Communicate biological observations, ideas and arguments using a range of scientific and technical vocabulary and appropriate scientific and mathematical conventions.

④ Evaluate relevant biological information and make informed judgements from it.

Of these Assessment Objectives the first is assessed in your Coursework (refer to pages 234–8). The second refers to recall and understanding, which is the area most teachers and students concentrate on when organizing revision.

You will find examples of questions testing Assessment Objectives 2 to 4 in the question section of this book, but perhaps one or two points should be made at this stage.

Assessment Objective 3 requires you to communicate scientific information effectively. It usually requires some extended writing. You could be asked, for instance, to explain the process of genetic engineering or how factories in the United Kingdom may cause acid rain in Scandinavia. Often some information will be given to you. It is essential that you make a rough draft of your answer before you write it. Try to make different points and not the same ones over and over again, and try to get these points in some logical sequence. You could be given information in a table and be asked to display it in a graph or be given information in a pie diagram and be required to use it in some other form. These skills will be practised during Coursework and so you should be able to carry them out correctly on written papers.

Assessment Objective 4 will require you to use information given in the question to make some kind of interpretation, evaluation or conclusion. You will probably not have carried out identical processes before, but you are expected to use your experience in similar situations. Make sure that the information is in a logical order and check at the end that your comments are reasonable and do fit the information you were given.

Analysis of Biology syllabuses

Find your Examining Group and syllabus in the following tables. The relevant table lists the topics you will need to know and understand. It also gives details of the papers you will have to sit, such as their length.

MEG

Midland Examining Group

1 Hills Road, Cambridge CB1 2EU
Tel: 01223 553311

Science – Biology – Syllabus A 1780

The content of the syllabus is shown below:

Syllabus topic	Covered in Unit No.	Units containing only Higher tier material	✓
1. Introducing biological principles	1.1, 1.2, 1.3, 1.7, 1.8, 5.1, 8.1	8.2, 8.3, 8.4, 8.5	
2. Diet, digestion and absorption	5.1, 5.4, 5.5, 5.6, 5.7, 7.1, 7.2, 7.3, 7.8, 9.5	7.4	
3. Respiration	4.5, 10.1, 10.2, 10.3, 10.4, 10.5, 10.13	4.6	
4. Breathing	10.6, 10.8, 10.10, 10.11, 10.12	10.9	
5. Photosynthesis	6.1, 6.2, 6.3, 6.4, 6.6, 6.7, 6.8, 6.10, 8.9, 8.10, 10.7, 17.1	6.5	
6. Circulation and transport	5.3, 6.6, 6.9, 8.5, 8.7, 8.8, 9.1, 9.2, 9.5, 9.6, 14.2, 23.2, 23.5	8.6, 8.10, 9.3, 9.4, 22.1, 23.6	
7. Communication and control	10.10, 10.12, 11.1, 11.2, 11.4, 11.6, 11.7, 11.9, 12.1, 12.2, 12.3, 13.1, 13.2, 13.4, 13.7, 13.8, 13.9, 13.10, 13.11, 13.12, 13.14, 13.17, 14.1, 14.3, 14.4, 14.5, 14.6, 14.7, 14.8, 15.3, 16.3, 16.4, 16.5, 23.7	11.3, 11.5, 13.3, 13.15, 13.16	
8. Energy flow and the cycling of elements	20.1, 20.2, 20.3, 20.4, 20.6, 20.9, 20.10, 20.13, 20.14,	20.5, 20.12, 22.1, 22.2, 22.5, 22.6	
9. Inheritance and evolution	1.5, 15.1, 15.2, 15.3, 15.6, 16.1, 18.1, 18.2, 18.3, 18.8, 18.15, 18.16, 19.1, 19.5, 19.6	1.4, 15.5, 18.4, 18.5, 18.6, 18.7, 18.9, 18.10, 18.11, 18.12, 18.13, 18.14, 18.17, 19.2, 19.3, 19.4, 19.7	
10. Diversity and adaptation	2.1, 2.2, 2.3, 2.5, 2.6, 2.7, 2.8, 2.9, 3.2, 3.5, 10.8, 13.13, 15.9, 20.1, 20.6, 20.7, 20.11, 21.1, 21.2, 21.3, 21.4, 21.5, 21.8	11.8	
11. Microorganisms and food	1.7, 3.3, 3.4, 3.6, 4.1, 4.5, 4.6, 4.7, 4.8, 4.9, 4.10	4.13, 18.17	
12. Infectious diseases	22.1, 22.2, 22.3, 23.1, 23.2, 23.3, 23.5, 23.7, 23.8		

All candidates complete a Coursework Assessment on Sc1   25%

Foundation tier – Two written papers of structured questions. No choice of question. Targeted at grades C–G.

Paper 1	1 hr 30 mins	50%
Paper 3	45 mins	25%

Higher tier – Two written papers of structured questions. No choice of question. Targeted at grades A★–D.

Paper 2	1 hr 45 mins	50%
Paper 4	1 hr	25%

Science – Biology – Syllabus C (Salters) 1790

The content of the syllabus is shown below:

Syllabus topic	Covered in Unit No.	Units containing only Higher tier material	✓
1. Life processes and cell activity	1.1, 1.2, 1.3, 1.8, 8.2, 8.3, 8.4, 8.5, 13.2, 14.2, 16.1, 18.1, 18.2, 18.10, 18.11, 18.12, 18.13, 18.14		
2. Humans as organisms			
Nutrition	1.7, 5.5, 7.1, 7.2, 7.3, 7.4, 7.5, 7.6		
Circulation	9.1, 9.2, 9.3, 9.4, 9.5, 9.6, 23.5		
Breathing	10.1, 10.6, 10.8, 10.10, 10.11	10.9	
Respiration	10.1, 10.2, 10.3, 10.4, 10.5		
Nervous system	12.1, 12.2, 12.3, 13.1, 13.2, 13.6	13.3, 13.4	
Hormones	13.9, 13.10, 13.11, 13.12, 16.3, 16.4, 16.5		
Homeostasis	5.7, 10.6, 10.11, 11.1,11.2, 11.4, 11.6, 11.7, 11.9	11.3, 11.5	
Health	3.1, 3.2, 3.5, 10.12, 11.10, 13.7, 13.8, 23.1, 23.2, 23.3, 23.5, 23.6, 23.7		
3. Green plants as organisms			
Nutrition	5.3, 6.1, 6.2, 6.3, 6.4, 22.1	6.5	
Hormones	12.1, 13.14	13.15, 13.16, 13.17, 15.3	
Transport and water relations	8.1, 8.6, 8.7, 8.8, 8.9, 8.10	8.4, 8.5	
4. Variation, inheritance and evolution			
Variation	11.8, 15.1, 15.2, 18.1, 18.2, 18.10, 18.11, 18.12, 18.13, 18.14, 18.15	18.16	
Inheritance	18.1, 18.2, 18.8	1.5, 15.3, 15.4, 15.5, 15.6, 18.4, 18.5, 18.6, 18.7, 18.9, 18.17, 19.5	
Evolution	11.8, 18.16, 19.1, 19.2, 19.3, 19.4, 19.6	18.15	
5. Living things in their environment			
Adaptation and competition	3.2, 3.6, 4.4, 11.8, 17.1, 17.2, 20.6, 20.8, 20.10, 21.1, 21.2, 21.3, 21.5, 21.8, 21.11, 21.12, 22.1, 22.2, 23.3		
Energy and nutrient transfer	3.3, 3.6, 4.3, 4.4, 20.1, 20.2, 20.3, 20.4, 20.6, 21.11	20.5, 20.12, 20.13, 21.4, 22.1, 22.2, 22.5, 22.6	
Off the blocks	1.3, 5.5, 7.1, 7.2, 7.4, 9.3, 9.4, 9.5, 10.1, 10.2, 10.4, 10.6, 10.8, 10.9, 10.10, 14.1, 14.3, 14.5, 14.6, 14.7, 14.8, 14.10, 23.7	10.3, 14.4	
Growing crops	15.1, 15.7, 15.8, 15.9, 15.10, 15.11, 18.2, 18.4, 18.5, 18.6, 18.7, 19.5, 22.1, 22.2, 22.5, 22.6	18.17	
The ploughman's lunch	3.2, 3.4, 3.5, 3.6, 3.7, 4.1, 4.5, 4.6, 4.7, 4.8, 4.9		
Industrious microbes		4.2, 4.10, 4.11, 4.12, 4.13, 15.6, 18.17	

All candidates complete a Coursework Assessment on Sc1   25%

Foundation tier – One written paper of structured questions. No choice of question. Targeted at grades C–G.

     Paper 1   2 hrs   75%

Higher tier – One written paper of structured questions. No choice of question. Targeted at grades A★–D.

     Paper 2   2 hrs 15 mins   75%

Science – Biology – Syllabus D (Nuffield) 1785

The content of the syllabus is shown below:

Syllabus topic	Covered in Unit No.	Units containing only Higher tier material	✓
B1. Life processes: an overview	1.1, 1.7		
B2. Levels of organization	1.2, 1.3, 1.8, 7.3		
B3. Nutrition in plants and animals	5.1, 6.1, 6.2, 6.3, 6.4, 6.6, 6.7, 6.8, 6.9, 6.10, 7.1, 7.2, 7.3, 7.4, 7.5, 7.6, 8.9	6.5	
B4. Transport in plants and animals	5.3, 8.1, 8.2, 8.6, 8.7, 8.8, 8.10, 9.1, 9.2, 9.5, 9.6	6.9, 8.3, 8.4, 8.5, 9.3, 9.4 22.1	
B5. Respiration (illustrated by humans as organisms)	4.5, 4.6, 4.7, 10.1, 10.2, 10.3, 10.4, 10.5, 10.6, 10.8, 10.9, 10.10, 10.11, 10.12, 10.13		
B6. Energy and nutrient transfer	20.1, 20.2, 20.3, 20.4, 20.6, 20.13, 20.14, 22.1	20.5, 20.12, 22.2, 22.3, 22.4, 22.5, 22.6	
B7. Health	9.5, 10.12, 13.7, 13.8, 23.2, 23.5, 23.6		
B8. The nervous system and hormones	12.1, 12.2, 12.3, 13.1, 13.2, 13.4, 13.9, 13.10, 13.11, 13.12, 13.14, 13.15, 13.16, 13.17, 15.3, 16.4	13.3, 16.3	
B9. Homeostasis	10.6, 11.1, 11.2, 11.4, 11.6, 11.7, 11.9, 11.10	11.3	
B10. Cell division	1.3	1.5, 18.10, 18.11, 18.12, 18.13	
B11. Variation	2.1, 2.4, 2.5, 2.6, 2.7, 2.9, 15.1, 15.2, 17.1, 18.2, 18.15, 18.16, 20.11	18.10, 18.14	
B12. Inheritance (Mendelian genetics)	15.3, 16.1, 18.1, 18.8, 19.5	1.5, 1.6, 15.4, 15.5, 15.6, 18.2, 18.4, 18.5, 18.6, 18.7, 18.9, 18.17	
B13. Evolution	19.6	19.1, 19.2, 19.3, 19.4,	
B14. The impact of human activities	20.1, 20.6, 20.7, 20.8, 21.1, 21.2, 21.3, 21.4, 21.5, 21.8	11.8, 22.2	
Microbiology 1: Helpful organisms	3.1, 3.2, 3.3, 3.5, 4.1, 4.2, 4.5, 4.6, 4.9, 4.10, 5.2, 20.12	4.12, 4.13	
Microbiology 2: Harmful organisms	3.4, 3.6, 9.5, 23.1, 23.2, 23.5, 23.6	23.4	
Microbiology 3: Vaccines and antibiotics	23.6, 23.7	4.12, 23.3	
Genetics 1: Applied genetics		18.2, 18.3, 18.4, 18.5, 18.6, 18.7, 18.8, 18.9	
Genetics 2: Genetic engineering		1.4, 1.5, 1.6, 1.7, 4.12, 18.16, 18.17, 18.18	
Environmental biology 1: Conservation	20.9, 20.10, 21.2, 21.12		
Environmental biology 2: Pollution	4.4, 21.3, 21.4, 21.5, 21.6, 21.7, 21.8, 21.9, 21.10, 22.1		

All candidates complete a Coursework Assessment on Sc1   25%

Foundation tier – Two written papers of structured questions. No choice of question. Targeted at grades C–G.

     Paper 1   1 hr 30 mins   50%   Paper 3   45 mins   25%

Higher tier – Two written papers of structured questions. No choice of question. Targeted at grades A★–D.

     Paper 2   1 hr 45 mins   50%   Paper 4   1 hr   25%

SEG

Southern Examining Group

Stag Hill House, Guildford, Surrey GU2 5XJ
Tel: 01483 506506

Science – Biology – 2640

The content of the syllabus is shown below:

Syllabus topic	Covered in Unit No.	Units containing only Higher tier material	✓
1. Life processes and cell activity			
1.1 Life processes	1.1, 1.8		
1.2 Cells	1.2, 1.3, 8.1, 8.2,	8.3, 8.4, 8.5	
2. Humans as organisms			
2.1 Nutrition	1.7, 5.5, 7.1, 7.2, 7.3, 7.4, 7.5, 7.7	7.6	
2.2 Circulation	9.1, 9.2, 9.3, 9.4, 9.5, 9.6		
2.3 Breathing	10.1, 10.6, 10.8, 10.9, 10.10, 10.11, 10.12		
2.4 Respiration	10.1, 10.2, 10.3, 10.4, 10.5		
2.5 Nervous system	12.1, 12.2, 12.3, 13.1, 13.2, 13.4	13.3	
2.6 Health	10.12, 13.7, 13.8, 23.7		
2.7 Hormones	13.9, 13.10, 13.11, 13.12	16.4	
2.8 Homeostasis	11.1, 11.2, 11.4, 11.6, 11.7, 11.9, 11.10	11.3, 11.5, 13.10	
3. Green plants as organisms			
3.1 Photosynthesis	6.1, 6.2, 6.3, 6.4, 6.5, 6.6, 6.7, 8.7	6.8	
3.2 Water and mineral salts	5.3, 6.9, 8.1, 8.2, 8.6, 8.8, 8.9, 8.10, 14.2	8.3, 8.4, 8.5	
3.3 Plant hormones	13.14, 13.17		
4. Variation, inheritance and evolution			
4.1 Growth	1.5, 17.1, 18.1, 18.2	18.11	
4.2 Reproduction	15.1, 15.5, 15.6, 18.2, 18.10, 18.15, 18.16	18.12, 18.13, 18.14	
4.3 Inheritance	18.8	4.12, 18.2, 18.4, 18.5, 18.6, 18.17, 19.5	
4.4 Evolution	2.1, 19.6	19.1, 19.2, 19.3, 19.4, 19.8	
5. Living things in their environment			
5.1 Adaptation and competition	11.8, 20.1, 20.7, 20.8		
5.2 Energy flow and cycles in ecosystems	20.2, 20.3, 20.4, 20.9, 20.10, 20.13	20.5, 20.12	
5.3 Humans and the environment	21.1, 21.2, 21.3, 21.4, 21.5, 21.6, 21.8, 21.12, 22.1, 22.2		
6. Patterns of feeding			
6.1 Feeding adaptations in invertebrates	22.4, 23.3		
6.2 Feeding in mammals	7.7		
6.3 Other methods of obtaining food		3.5, 20.6, 23.4	
7. Patterns of support and movement			
7.1 Skeletons and muscles	14.1, 14.3, 14.4, 14.5, 14.6, 14.7, 14.8, 14.9		
7.2 Adaptations in animals for locomotion	19.7		
7.3 Plant movement		13.14, 13.15, 13.16	

Syllabus topic	Covered in Unit No.	Units containing only Higher tier material	✓
8. Microorganisms			
8.1 Characteristics and use of microorganisms	2.4, 3.1, 3.2, 3.4, 3.5, 3.6, 10.3		
8.2 Economic importance of microorganisms	3.3, 4.1, 4.2, 4.4, 4.5, 4.6, 4.8, 4.9, 4.10, 4.11, 4.12, 21.11		
9. Controlling the spread of disease			
9.1 Disease and immunity	23.1, 23.2, 23.5	23.6	
9.2 Environmental health	3.4, 4.4, 23.2, 23.4, 23.7		

All candidates complete a Coursework Assessment on Sc1   25%

Foundation tier – Two written papers of structured questions some with extended prose writing. No choice of questions. Targeted at grades C–G.

    Paper 1 2640/2   1 hr 30 mins   50%
    Paper 2 2640/3   1 hr   25%

Higher tier – Two written papers of structured questions some with extended prose writing. No choice of questions. Targeted at grades A★–D.

    Paper 1 2640/4   1 hr 30 mins   50%
    Paper 2 2640/5   1 hr   25%

NEAB

Northern Examination and Assessment Board

Devas Street, Manchester, M15 6EX
Tel: 0161 953 1180

Science – Biology

The content of the syllabus is shown below:

Syllabus topic	Covered in Unit No.	Units containing only Higher tier material	✓
1. Life processes and cell activity			
1.1 Basic principles	1.1, 1.2, 1.3, 1.7, 1.8	6.6, 7.4, 8.4, 10.8	
1.2 Transport across boundaries	8.2	8.3, 8.4	
1.3 Cell division	18.1, 18.2, 18.10	18.11, 18.12, 18.13	
2. Humans as organisms			
2.1 Nutrition and health	5.1, 5.4, 5.5, 5.6, 5.7, 7.1, 7.2, 7.3, 7.4, 7.5, 9.5	7.6	
2.2 Circulation	9.1, 9.2, 9.3, 9.4, 9.5, 9.6, 9.7, 23.5		
2.3 Breathing	10.8	10.6, 10.9, 10.10, 10.11	
2.4 Respiration	10.1, 10.2, 10.4, 10.5	8.3, 10.3	
2.5 Nervous system	12.1, 12.2, 12.3, 13.1	13.2, 13.3, 13.4	
2.6 Hormones	13.9, 13.10, 13.12, 16.3	16.4, 16.5	
2.7 Homeostasis	8.1, 11.1, 11.6, 11.7, 11.9, 11.10	11.2, 11.3, 11.4	
2.8 Exercise and health	14.5, 14.6, 14.7, 14.8, 14.10		
2.9 Disease	3.1, 3.2, 23.1, 23.2, 23.4, 23.5, 23.6		
2.10 Biotechnology and disease	23.7	11.5, 14.7, 18.3, 23.1, 23.6	
2.11 Drugs	10.12, 13.7, 13.8		
3. Green plants as organisms			
3.1 Plant nutrition	2.6, 6.1, 6.2	5.3, 6.3, 6.4, 6.5, 6.8	
3.2 Plant hormones	13.14, 13.15, 13.16, 13.17, 15.3, 15.5		
3.3 Transport and water relations	8.1, 8.4, 8.6, 8.7, 8.8, 8.9, 8.10, 14.2	8.5	

Syllabus topic	Covered in Unit No.	Units containing only Higher tier material	✓
4. Variation, inheritance and evolution			
4.1 Variation	15.1, 16.1, 17.1, 18.1, 18.2, 18.15	17.6, 18.10, 18.11, 18.12, 18.13, 18.16	
4.2 Genetics and DNA	1.3, 1.4, 1.5, 1.6, 18.2, 18.8	18.4, 18.5, 18.6, 18.7	
4.3 Controlling inheritance	15.3, 19.5	4.1, 4.2, 4.12, 15.4, 15.5, 15.6, 18.17	
4.4 Evolution	19.1, 19.6	19.2, 19.3, 19.4	
5. Living things and their environment			
5.1 Adaptation and competition	11.8, 20.1, 20.7, 20.8		
5.2 Human impact on the environment	21.1, 21.2, 21.3, 21.5, 21.6, 21.7, 21.8, 22.1, 22.2	21.4	
5.3 Energy and nutrient transfer	20.2, 20.3, 20.4, 20.6	6.10, 20.5, 22.5, 22.6,	
5.4 Nutrient cycles	4.4, 20.13, 21.11	20.12	
6. Applied microbiology			
6.1 Using microbes to make useful substances	2.4, 3.1, 3.2, 3.3, 3.4, 3.5, 3.6, 3.7, 4.2, 4.5, 4.6, 4.7, 4.8	4.3, 4.4, 4.11	
6.2 Enzymes in home and industry	1.7, 4.13	4.2	

All candidates complete a Coursework Assessment on Sc1   25%

Foundation tier – One written paper of structured questions some with extended prose writing. No choice of question. Targeted at grades C–G.

     Paper F   2 hrs 15 mins   75%

Higher tier – One written paper of structured questions some with extended prose writing. No choice of question. Targeted at grades A★–D.

     Paper H   2 hrs 15 mins   75%

EDEXCEL (London Examinations)

London Examinations – Edexcel Foundation (formerly ULEAC)

Stewart House, 32 Russell Square, London WC1B 5DN
Tel: 0171 331 4000

Science – Biology – 1026

The content of the syllabus is shown below:

Syllabus topic	Covered in Unit No.	Units containing only Higher tier material	✓
Life processes and cell activity			
Life processes	1.1, 2.6, 7.3, 9.6, 10.8, 11.2, 12.2		
Cell activity	1.2, 1.3, 6.6, 8.2, 8.5, 13.2, 16.2, 18.1, 18.2,	8.3, 8.4, 18.10, 18.11, 18.12, 18.13	
Humans as organisms			
Nutrition	1.7, 5.1, 5.4, 5.5, 5.6, 5.7, 7.1, 7.2, 7.3, 7.4		
Circulation	9.1, 9.2, 9.3, 9.4, 9.5, 9.6, 23.5		
Breathing and respiration	10.1, 10.2, 10.3, 10.4, 10.5, 10.6, 10.7, 10.8, 10.9, 10.10, 10.11		
Nervous coordination	12.1, 12.2, 12.3, 13.1	13.2, 13.3, 13.4	
Hormonal coordination	11.5, 13.9, 13.10, 13.11, 13.12	16.3, 16.4, 16.5	

Syllabus topic	Covered in Unit No.	Units containing only Higher tier material	✓
Humans as organisms (contd.)			
Maintaining the internal environment	10.12, 11.1, 11.2, 11.4, 11.5, 11.6, 11.7, 11.9, 13.7, 13.8, 13.9, 16.2, 23.2, 23.7	11.3, 23.6	
Green plants as organisms			
Nutrition	5.3, 6.1, 6.2, 6.3, 6.5, 6.7, 6.8, 6.9, 20.13	6.4	
Water relations and transport	6.6, 6.9, 8.1, 8.5, 8.6, 8.7, 8.8, 8.9, 8.10	8.3, 8.4	
Control of growth	17.1	13.14, 13.15, 13.16, 13.17	
Variation, Inheritance and Evolution			
Variation	2.7, 2.9, 15.1, 18.1, 18.2, 18.3, 18.10, 18.11, 18.12, 18.15, 20.11	15.5, 18.16	
Inheritance	18.2, 18.3, 18.4, 18.5, 18.6, 18.7, 18.8	18.9	
DNA and its manipulation	19.5	1.5, 15.3, 15.4, 15.5, 15.6, 18.1, 18.17	
Evolution	19.1, 19.6	19.2, 19.3, 19.4	
Living organisms in their environment			
Humans and their environment	4.4, 20.1, 20.7, 20.8, 20.9, 20.10, 21.1, 21.2, 21.3, 21.4, 21.5, 21.7, 21.8, 21.9, 21.10, 22.1,	21.6	
Ecosystems	6.10, 20.2, 20.4, 20.6, 20.13, 21.11	20.3, 20.5, 20.12, 22.1, 22.2, 22.5, 22.6	
Microorganisms and disease in humans			
Structure and reproduction of microorganisms	2.4, 3.1, 3.2, 3.5		
The spread and control of disease	3.4, 3.6, 7.8, 23.1, 23.2, 23.3, 23.4, 23.6, 23.7		
Safe food and water	3.3, 3.4, 3.6, 4.4, 23.4		
Combating infection	4.1, 4.2, 4.11, 4.12, 23.7	23.5, 23.6	
Biotechnology in food preservation			
Fermentation using yeast	4.1, 4.2, 4.6, 4.7, 10.2, 10.3		
Fermentation using other microorganisms	4.1, 4.2, 4.3, 4.8, 4.10, 4.13		
Gene technology		4.2, 15.6, 16.4, 18.17	

All candidates complete a Coursework Assessment on Sc1   25%

Foundation tier – Two written papers of structured questions some with extended prose writing. No choice of question. Targeted at grades C–G.

Paper 1F	1 hr 30 mins	45%
Paper 2F	1 hr 30 mins	30%

Higher tier – Two written papers of structured questions some with extended prose writing. No choice of question. Targeted at grades A★–D.

Paper 3H	1 hr 45 mins	45%
Paper 4H	1 hr 30 mins	30%

WJEC

Welsh Joint Education Committee

245 Western Avenue, Cardiff CF5 2YX
Tel: 01222 265000

Science – Biology

The content of the syllabus is shown on page 12.

Syllabus topic	Covered in Unit No.	Units containing only Higher tier material	✓
B1 Basic organization of animals and plants	1.1, 1.2, 1.6, 2.6, 7.3, 9.6, 10.8, 11.2		
B2 Trapping and transfer of energy	6.1, 6.2, 6.3, 6.4, 6.5, 6.6, 6.7, 6.10, 20.2, 20.3, 20.4	19.5, 20.5, 22.1, 22.2, 22.3, 22.4, 22.5, 22.6	
B3 Release of energy by living organisms	1.7, 5.1, 5.2, 5.4, 5.5, 5.6, 5.7, 6.1, 6.2, 7.1, 7.2, 7.3, 10.1, 10.2, 10.4, 20.1, 20.2, 20.4, 20.5, 20.13	6.8, 10.3, 20.12	
B4 Transfer of materials in living organisms	8.1, 8.2, 8.7, 8.8, 8.9, 8.10, 9.1, 9.2, 9.3, 9.4, 9.5, 9.6, 10.6, 10.8, 10.10	6.9, 8.3, 8.4, 8.5, 8.6, 10.9	
B5 Transfer of information	12.2, 12.3, 13.1, 13.2, 13.9, 13.10, 13.11, 13.12, 13.14, 13.15, 13.16, 13.17, 16.3	13.4	
B6 Genetics	18.1, 18.2, 18.8,	1.5, 17.1, 17.2, 18.4, 18.5, 18.6, 18.7, 18.10, 18.11, 18.12, 18.13	
B7 Variation and evolution	15.1, 17.6, 18.10, 18.15, 18.16, 19.5, 19.6	4.1, 4.2, 4.12, 15.3, 15.5, 15.6, 18.17, 19.1, 19.2, 19.3, 19.4	
B8 The impact of human activity on the environment	20.7, 20.8, 21.1, 21.2, 21.3, 21.4, 21.5, 21.7, 21.8, 22.1, 22.2		
B9 Maintenance of a steady/ healthy state	5.3, 10.1, 10.5, 10.11, 10.12, 11.1, 11.2, 11.3, 11.5, 11.6, 11.7, 11.9, 11.10, 13.7, 13.8, 13.9, 13.10, 16.4, 16.5, 18.2, 18.4, 18.5, 18.7, 23.1, 23.2	11.4, 23.5, 23.6	
B10 Technology and life processes	1.7, 2.4, 3.1, 3.2, 3.3, 3.5, 3.6, 3.7, 4.1, 4.3, 4.4, 4.5, 4.6, 4.7, 4.8, 4.11, 4.13, 7.2, 23.7	4.12, 11.5, 23.6	

All candidates complete a Coursework Assessment on Sc1   25%

Foundation tier – One written paper of structured questions some with extended prose writing. No choice of question. Targeted at grades C–G.

    Paper F   2 hrs   75%

Higher tier – One written paper of structured questions some with extended prose writing. No choice of question. Targeted at grades A★–D.

    Paper H   2 hrs 30 mins   75%

CCEA

Northern Ireland Council for the Curriculum Examinations and Assessment

Clarendon Dock, 29 Clarendon Road, Belfast BT1 3BG
Tel: 01232 261200

Science – Biology

The content of the syllabus is shown on page 13.

Syllabus topic	Covered in Unit No.	Units containing only Higher tier material	✓
1. Living organisms and life processes			
Life processes	1.1		
Organ systems	1.8, 2.6, 7.1, 9.1, 10.1, 11.1, 15.1, 16.1		
Nutrition	5.1, 5.3, 5.4, 5.5, 5.6, 5.7, 6.1, 6.2, 6.3, 6.6, 7.1, 7.2, 7.3, 7.4, 7.5, 7.8, 8.1, 9.5, 10.13, 22.4	1.7, 6.4, 6.5, 6.8, 7.6, 22.1, 22.5	
Respiration	6.7, 8.7, 10.1, 10.2, 10.6, 10.7, 10.8, 10.9, 10.10, 10.11, 10.12	10.3, 10.4, 10.5	
Transport	5.7, 6.6, 8.1, 8.2, 8.4, 8.5, 8.6, 8.9, 8.10, 9.2, 9.3, 9.4, 9.5, 9.6, 23.2, 23.5, 23.6	8.3, 8.8, 9.7	
Reproduction	10.12, 13.7, 13.8, 13.11, 15.2, 15.3, 15.6, 15.7, 15.8, 15.9, 15.11, 16.1, 16.2, 16.3, 16.5, 16.6, 17.3, 17.4, 23.5, 23.6	15.10, 16.4	
Excretion	11.1, 11.2, 11.4	7.6, 11.3, 11.5	
Sensitivity and response	11.6, 11.7, 11.9, 12.3, 13.1, 13.2, 13.7, 13.8, 13.12, 13.15, 14.4, 14.7, 14.8	12.1, 12.2, 13.4, 13.5, 13.9, 13.10, 13.11, 13.17	
2. Environment			
Habitat study	20.1, 20.9, 20.10		
Classification	2.5, 2.6, 2.7, 2.8, 2.9, 3.5, 3.7, 20.11		
Life cycles			
Sampling	20.9, 20.10		
Adaptation	11.8, 20.2, 20.4, 20.5		
Cycles	4.4, 20.13, 21.11	20.12, 22.1	
Pollution	21.3, 21.5, 21.7, 21.8, 21.11		
Conservation	20.3, 20.7, 20.8, 21.1, 21.2, 21.8, 21.12, 22.2	20.4, 20.5, 21.4, 21.5, 21.6, 22.1, 22.2, 22.6	
3. Variation			
The cell	1.2, 1.3		
Specialization	8.4, 10.12, 16.2		
Levels of organization	1.8		
Genetics	18.1, 18.2, 18.4, 18.5, 18.6, 18.7, 18.8, 18.16	1.4, 1.5, 1.6, 4.12, 18.9, 18.10, 18.11, 18.12, 18.13	
Selection	15.1, 18.2, 18.15	15.2, 15.3, 15.5, 19.1, 19.2, 19.3, 19.4, 19.5, 22.1	
Growth	17.1, 17.5		
Cancer	17.6		
4. Microbiology	3.3, 3.4, 3.6, 4.1, 4.5, 4.6, 4.7, 4.8, 21.11, 23.1, 23.2, 23.5, 23.6, 23.7	4.2, 4.11	

All candidates complete a Coursework Assessment on Sc1   25%

Foundation tier – Two written papers – Paper 1 contains short answer questions; Paper 2 contains structured questions. Targeted at grades C–G.

Paper 1   1 hr   30%   Paper 2   1 hr 30 mins   45%

Higher tier – Two written papers – Paper 1 contains short answer questions; Paper 2 contains structured questions. Targeted at grades A★–D.

Paper 1   1 hr 30 mins   32%   Paper 2   2 hrs   43%

SQA

Scottish Qualifications Authority (formerly SEB)

Ironmills Road, Dalkeith, Midlothian EH22 1LE
Tel: 0131 663 6601

Biology at General and Credit Level

The content of the syllabus is shown on page 14.

Syllabus topic	Covered in Unit No.	Units containing only Credit level material	✓
Topic 1: The Biosphere			
a Investigating an ecosystem	20.1, 20.8, 20.9, 20.10, 20.11		
b How it works	17.2, 20.1, 20.2, 20.5, 20.6, 20.7, 20.8, 20.13	20.3, 20.12	
c Control and management	21.1, 21.2, 21.3, 21.4, 21.6, 21.7, 21.8, 21.9, 21.10, 21.11, 21.12	21.5, 22.1, 22.2, 22.5, 22.6	
Topic 2 The World of Plants			
a Introducing plants	2.4, 2.5, 2.6, 3.5, 3.7	4.7, 21.2, 21.12	
b Growing plants	15.1, 15.2, 15.3, 15.4, 15.7, 15.8, 15.9, 15.11, 17.3, 17.4	15.5, 15.10	
c Making food	6.1, 6.2, 6.3, 6.7, 8.6, 8.7, 8.8, 8.9, 10.7	6.4, 6.5, 6.6, 8.10	
Topic 3 Animal Survival			
a The need for food	5.1, 7.1, 7.2, 7.3, 7.4, 7.7	5.5	
b Reproduction	2.9, 16.1	16.2	
c Water and waste	11.1, 11.2, 11.3, 11.4, 11.5	7.6	
d Responding to the environment	13.13		
Topic 4 Investigating Cells			
a Investigating living cells	1.2, 1.3		
b Investigating diffusion	8.1, 8.2, 8.4	8.5, 14.2	
c Investigating cell division	1.4, 17.1, 18.1, 18.10, 18.11		
d Investigating enzymes	1.7, 7.2		
e Investigating aerobic respiration	10.1, 10.4, 10.5	10.2, 10.13	
Topic 5 The Body in Action			
a Movement	14.1, 14.3, 14.4, 14.5, 14.6, 14.7, 14.8, 14.9		
b The need for energy	9.1, 9.2, 9.3, 9.4, 9.5, 9.6, 10.6, 10.8, 10.9, 10.10, 10.11, 10.13		
c Coordination	12.1, 12.2, 12.3, 13.1, 13.2	13.4, 13.5, 13.6	
d Changing levels of performance	10.2, 10.3		
Topic 6 Inheritance			
a Variation	2.1, 18.1, 18.2, 18.15		
b What is inheritance?	18.1, 18.2, 18.4, 18.5, 18.6, 18.7, 18.8, 18.10		
c Genetics and society	16.2, 18.16, 19.5, 22.1		
Topic 7 Biotechnology			
a Living factories	3.3, 3.5, 4.5, 4.8, 4.9	4.1, 4.2, 4.3, 4.6, 4.7, 10.2, 10.3	
b Problems and profit with waste	3.5, 3.6, 4.2, 4.3, 4.4, 4.10, 21.3, 23.2	4.13, 20.12, 20.13, 21.11	
c Reprogramming microbes	3.2, 4.11, 4,12, 4.13, 23.7	1.7, 3.6, 4.2, 13.10, 18.17, 19.5	

All candidates are assessed on Practical Abilities (33%): on 10 compulsory techniques and on the best of two Investigations independently carried out by candidates.

Written papers – multiple choice items, short answer questions and extended answer questions.

Candidates can attempt both levels. They will be awarded the better of the two grades achieved.

General level paper – assessing grades 4 and 3

> One paper 1 hr 30 mins

Credit level paper – assessing grades 2 and 1

> One paper 1 hr 30 mins

Candidates will be awarded a grade on a scale of 5 to 1. Grade 5 will be awarded to candidates who narrowly fail to meet the criteria for General level. A grade 7 will be awarded if the candidate has completed the course but not fulfilled the requirements for grade 5.

IGCSE

International General Certificate of Secondary Education

University of Cambridge Local Examinations Syndicate, Syndicate Buildings,
1 Hills Road, Cambridge, CB1 2EU   Tel: 01223 553311

Biology 0610   The content of the syllabus is shown below.

Syllabus topic	Covered in Unit No.	Units containing only Higher tier material	✓
Section I Characteristics and Classification of Living Organisms			
1 Characteristics of living things	1.1		
2 Classification of living organisms	2.1, 2.2, 2.3, 2.9		
3 Diversity of organisms		2.4, 2.5 2.6, 2.7, 2.8, 3.1, 3.2, 3.5	
4 Simple keys	20.11		
Section II Organization and Maintenance of the Organism			
1 Cell structure and organization	1.2, 1.3		
2 Levels of organization	1.8, 8.4, 8.10, 9.2, 10.8		
3 Diffusion	8.1, 8.2	6.9, 8.3	
4 Osmosis	8.4, 8.5		
5 Enzymes	1.7	4.13, 17.3	
6 Nutrition	5.1, 5.2, 5.3, 5.4, 5.5, 5.6, 5.7, 6.1, 6.2, 6.6, 6.7, 6.8, 7.1, 7.2, 7.3, 7.4, 7.5, 7.6, 7.7, 7.8, 8.9, 8.10, 13.8, 21.3, 22.1	4.5, 4.8, 4.10, 6.3, 6.4, 6.5, 21.1, 21.2, 22.5	
7 Transportation	8.4, 8.6, 8.7, 8.8, 8.9, 8.10, 9.1, 9.2, 9.3, 9.4, 9.5, 9.6, 23.5	9.7, 11.8, 23.6	
8 Respiration	4.6, 4.7, 10.1, 10.2, 10.3, 10.4, 10.5, 10.6, 10.11, 10.12	10.9	
9 Excretion and homeostasis in humans	7.6, 11.1, 11.2, 11.4, 11.6, 11.7, 11.9	11.5, 13.10	
10 Coordination and response	10.12, 12.1, 12.2, 12.3, 13.1, 13.2, 13.4, 13.7, 13.10, 13.14, 13.15, 13.16, 13.17, 14.8	13.5, 13.12, 13.13	
Section III Development of the Organism and the Continuity of Life			
1 Reproduction	3.2, 3.5, 13.11, 15.1, 15.2, 15.7, 15.8, 15.9, 15.10,15.11,16.1, 16.2, 16.3, 16.5, 16.6, 17.3, 23.2	16.4	
2 Growth and development	17.1, 17.2, 17.4, 17.5		
3 Inheritance	18.1, 18.2, 18.4, 18.5, 18.6, 18.7, 18.8, 18.10, 18.11, 18.12, 18.15, 18.16, 19.5	18.3, 19.1, 19.2, 19.3, 19.4	
Section IV Relationships of Organisms with One Another and with Their Environment			
1 Energy flow	20.1, 20.5		
2 Food chains and food webs	20.2, 20.4, 20.5	20.3	
3 Nutrient cycles	20.12, 20.13, 20.14	21.4	
4 Population size	20.8, 21.1, 21.2, 21.3		
5 Human influences on the environment	21.3, 21.5, 21.7, 21.8, 21.10, 21.12, 22.1, 22.2, 22.5, 22.6	4.4, 21.11	

All candidates complete Coursework Assessment (Paper 4) or Practical Test (Paper 5) or an Alternative to Practical (Paper 6)   20%

Core curriculum – Two written papers – Paper 1 contains multiple choice questions. Paper 2 contains short answer and structured questions. Targeted at grades C–G.

Paper 1   45 mins   40%   Paper 2   1 hr   40%

Higher tier – Three written papers – Paper 1 contains multiple choice questions. Paper 2 contains short answer and structured questions. Paper 3 contains structured and free response questions. Targeted at grades A–G. Paper 1 and 2 are only used to award a grade up to D if the performance on Paper 3 is too low.

Paper 1   45 mins   40%   Paper 2   1 hr   40%
Paper 3   1 hr 15 mins   80%

Studying and revising

Successful students are those who can organize their work. In particular, they must be able to work effectively on their own. If you are to be successful you need determination to succeed, a work plan fitted to a time schedule and determination to keep to that schedule. Unfortunately, few students are told *how* to devise that plan and carry it out – that is where this book comes in.

This section contains some advice that will help you to succeed in school. It also gives reasons for this advice. The rest of the book concerns itself with presenting biological facts, and how to deduce them by experiment, in a form that makes it easy to revise.

The first three steps in the learning process (see Fig. A) are planned by your teacher, who knows the sort of examination you will be sitting (stage 5) and plans accordingly. Where so many students fail, needlessly, is at stage 4 (revision) – because they do not know how to go about it. **Revision** is what this book is all about – leave out stage 4 in the diagram below and you have F for failure.

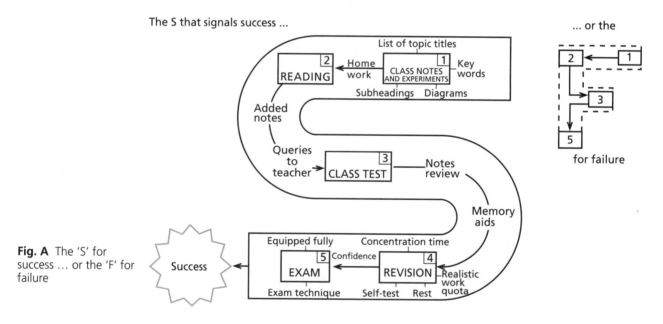

Fig. A The 'S' for success ... or the 'F' for failure

The learning process

In science subjects you learn from experiments – your own or those reported by others. It is well known that students tend to remember far better the 'facts' they have learned by doing experiments themselves. Unfortunately there is not enough time to learn everything this way, so that the rest has to be learned by reading, listening and seeing visual aids.

Why is learning through reading and listening harder than learning by experiment? Why are good annotated diagrams often so much easier to learn than line upon line of words? Why is a good teacher such a help in learning?

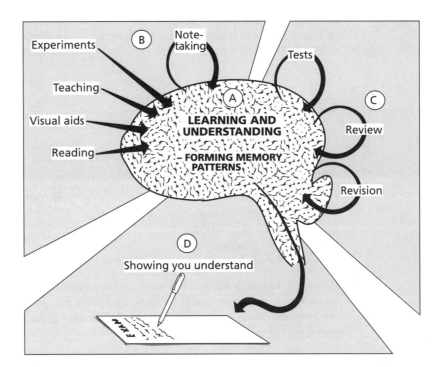

Fig. B From learning to showing you understand

Experiments: Doing these needs personal involvement and the use of several senses. Then, at the end of the experiment, one must arrive at a conclusion – which requires some reasoning. In a word, the whole process requires *understanding* – understanding the **aim** of the experiment, the **method** to be used and how to record the **results** in a meaningful way. And the final step, the **conclusion**, requires reasoning from what you have already understood. If there is any doubt about the conclusion this should be explained.

During this process you will notice that you have built up a pattern of knowledge – like a jig-saw – lacking just one piece to complete it (the conclusion). In other words, **learning is a process requiring patterns to be built up in the mind**: relate what you have just learned to what you already know and the facts will stick – because you *understand*.

Reading: In contrast to experimenting, when reading you are using only one of your senses – sight – and you are not *involved*, as you are in an experiment, unless you make a mental effort. Nor do you feel the same sense of discovery. Worst of all, the information is presented as a series of facts. In well-written books the facts *are* written to form patterns; but it is you, the reader, who has to concentrate hard enough to pick them out. Do this by use of a highlight pen or make summary notes as you go. This is initially much harder to do than learning by experiment.

Pictures and diagrams: One method of learning from books goes halfway towards experimental learning. Do you enjoy strip cartoons? At any rate you will agree that they are easy reading and convey much more than the few words appearing with the pictures. Pictures and diagrams, like words, require eyes alone to see them. But, unlike words, pictures build up patterns in the brain more readily and understanding is more immediate. So, well-constructed diagrams are an invaluable learning aid. If you learn the art of diagram-drawing you will reinforce both your memory and your understanding. Ultimately you should be able to construct your own original topic-summary diagrams, and there is a definite stage in the learning process when you should do this (see 'Retaining facts').

Teachers: Have you ever thought about the role of teachers in the learning process? They attempt to activate more senses in you than just your hearing. By showing films and slides, by drawing diagrams or asking your opinions and by giving you definite learning objectives, they try to keep you personally involved. It is for you to respond – if you are going to learn. Amidst it all you must carefully latch onto the *pattern* of facts that the teacher explains. A teacher usually explains what the *whole* lesson is to be about during the first few minutes. Listen hard to that outline and the rest of the lesson will be easier to absorb. The outline is the basic skeleton upon which the teacher will build up the flesh and features of the subject, as the lesson proceeds. If you miss the description of the skeleton, the subject may turn out to be a monster for you!

Capturing facts

Class notes: Your teacher has probably advised you on how to make these. For easy revision it is essential that they include:

(*a*) a topic list referring to numbered pages in your notebook;
(*b*) clear, underlined topic titles and subtitles;
(*c*) underlined 'key words';
(*d*) clear diagrams with titles;
(*e*) space for topic-summary diagrams made during revision.

Reading texts: Your teacher may advise you what to read. Realize too that a text has an index at the back; use it to look up things for yourself. At this stage many students get bogged down because they read slowly and give up. If you are someone with this problem, try this:

The cat sat on the mat.

Because of the way you were taught to read, for example 'c-a-t' or 'cat', you have been 'brainwashed' into thinking that you can only read one word at a time. Now bring your head back further from the page. Notice that now you can have more than one word in focus at a time – without having to move your eyes at all. With practice you will find that not only 'cat' is in focus but also 'The' and perhaps even 'sat' as well. It does need practice but soon you will find that the whole of 'The cat sat on' is in focus at one glance and that you can take it *all* in. Four words instead of one at each glance – four times your original reading speed!

Time how long it takes you to read a page now. Repeat the test after each week of practising the new method. Some people can read 800 words per minute with ease, understanding as they go. No wonder this method is called speed-reading! Reading the text should be done after you have been taught the topic – say during homework. Your reading:

(*a*) reinforces in your mind the facts recorded in class notes;
(*b*) allows you to add extra bits to your notes;
(*c*) should clear up misunderstandings.

Ask your teacher if you still do not understand something.

Class tests: These are designed to help you to recall facts and to reason from them. In this process you and the teacher are on the *same* side; together you will succeed. The teacher is *not* putting you to the torture. Tests:

(*a*) help you to assess your progress (should you work harder?);
(*b*) help the teacher to clear up your difficulties (adjust your notes?);
(*c*) help you focus on the key parts of each topic;
(*d*) help you to remember facts better;
(*e*) give you exam practice.

Retaining facts

Revision: This is the vital last stage in the learning process, the stage when you are finally on your own.

All of us have different '**concentration times**'. How long is yours? Go to a quiet working place indoors, without distractions, and note the time. Read a part of your textbook that is new to you, making a determined effort to take in all you read. When your mind begins to wander, look again at your watch; you are at the end of your concentration time. It should be around 20–40 minutes and will differ according to the amount of sleep you have had, what else is on your mind, and even on the subject matter. Never revise for longer than your concentration time. If you do, you will waste your time. You may still be reading but you will not understand. So **rest** for five minutes.

After the rest, surprisingly enough, the facts you read in the textbook will come back to you more easily still. During the rest, your brain was 'organizing' the facts you took in. Note-taking would have assisted this organizing process. Unfortunately most of these facts go into what is called your 'short-term memory'. Within 48 hours you will retain as little as 10% of what you thought you knew so well. Don't be depressed. You can push these facts into your 'long-term memory', which is essential for examination purposes, by **reviewing**.

Reviewing: This is a *quick* reread of your notes, taking only a few minutes. If your notes are disorganized you will not gain much. But with clear summaries, such as you will find in this book, you should dramatically increase the number of facts going into your long-term memory. Do this rereading after a week and then again two weeks later after having learned the topic for the first time in class.

Revision is just an extension of reviewing. If you have followed the learning plan so far, there will be relatively little to do. During revision whole chunks of your notes will not need to be read because subtitles and key words alone will trigger off a mass of facts already in your long-term memory. For the rest of the plan, follow these principles:

(i) Months ahead of the examinations plan how much to revise each week.

(ii) Have a regular time for work and stick to it. Avoid distractions: no TV or pets.

(iii) With your concentration time in mind, plan a *realistic* amount of work for each 20–40 minute session. You must get up from your task with a sense of achievement, i.e. that you have completed what you set out to do. Otherwise you will get depressed 'at the hopelessness of it all'.

(iv) Take those 5-minute breaks. But do not exceed them.

(v) Use the memory aids and summary diagrams in this book to help you.

Memory aids:

(i) Repetition   (ii) Mnemonics   (iii) Pattern-diagrams

(i) **Repetition:** By chanting something over and over again you can learn it 'parrot-fashion'. Many people learn their times-tables or poetry in this way. The method has its uses. But though you can remember in this way you do not necessarily *understand*.

(ii) **Mnemonics:** These are words, sentences or little rhymes chosen from everyday language to help you to remember technical words that you find difficult to memorize. This book provides you with a few examples; but you may be able to do better. Make your own mnemonics funny, outrageously absurd – even rude – if you are going to remember them. Dull mnemonics are difficult to remember. The words you choose must be sufficiently similar to the technical words to remind you of them. For example:

'How can I remember the characteristics of living things – which I *do* understand but may not be able to remember fully in an exam?' Try **Germs in our seas** and turn to Unit 1.1. This example uses initial letters of the key words only. You will find another mnemonic in Unit 2.2.

(iii) **Pattern-diagrams:** these are important or 'key' words written down and joined up with lines according to their connections with each other. You have already seen two examples (Figs. A and B). When you have finished revising a topic always try to summarize it in this way. You will be surprised how easy it is. And why? Because your mind thinks in patterns and not in lists. When you come to the examination you will be able to remember your pattern-diagrams and even create new ones when planning your answers to essay questions.

Chapter 1
Life

1.1 Characteristics of organisms

Living things are called **organisms**. Two large groups of organisms are the **plants**, e.g. grass, and the **animals** (see Units 2.5, 2.7 and 2.9). All organisms perform *all* the seven 'vital functions' (growth, excretion, respiration, movement, sensitivity, nutrition, reproduction) at some time during their existence and their bodies are made of cells. Some organisms remain, for a time, **dormant** (inactive), e.g. as seeds, spores or cysts. These bodies appear not to perform vital functions but they can be activated by suitable stimulation to do so, e.g. by germinating.

Eight characteristics of organisms (*Mnemonic:* GERMS NR Cs 'germs in our seas')
Growth
Excretion
Respiration
Movement
Sensitivity
Nutrition
Reproduction
Cells

G **Growth:** cells divide and then get larger again by adding more living material (made from their food) until they repeat the process. (See Unit 17.1.)

E **Excretion:** removal of waste products from **metabolism** (all the chemical reactions within the body). (See Chapter 11.)

N.B. Do not confuse this with 'egestion' (removal of **indigestible** matter – which has thus never entered cells to be metabolized) (Fig. 1.1).

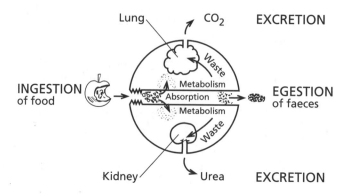

Fig. 1.1 The distinction between excretion and egestion

R **Respiration:** release of energy within cells from food so as to power other vital functions. In most organisms this requires oxygen and releases carbon dioxide and heat. (See Chapter 10.)

M **Movement:** an animal moves its whole body, using limbs or their equivalent. A plant 'moves' only by *growing* parts of itself towards or away from influences important to it. (See Units 13.13 and 13.14.)

S **Sensitivity and response:** influences (**stimuli**) in the surroundings (**environment**) stimulate certain areas of an organism so that they send messages to other parts which respond, e.g. by movement, growth or secretion. (See Chapter 12.)

N **Nutrition:** intake of food materials from the environment for building up and maintaining living matter. (See Unit 5.2.)

R **Reproduction:** formation of more individuals either from one parent (**asexually**) or two (**sexually**). (See Unit 15.1.)

All organisms eventually die. **Death** is when metabolism ceases completely.

1.2 Cells: plant and animal

C **Cells:** the simplest units of life. All cells, when young, have at the very least three parts: *a membrane* enclosing jelly-like *cytoplasm*, in which lies a *nucleus* which controls their life. (See Unit 1.3.) These three parts make up *protoplasm* (living matter). The cell wall secreted outside the protoplasm, by plant cells only, is non-living. Cells cannot live without supplies of energy, food, water and O_2 and a suitable environmental temperature and pH.

Cells from animals and plants show differences, as seen in Fig. 1.2.

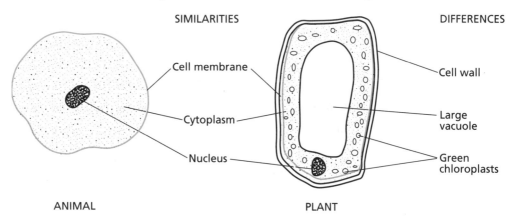

Fig. 1.2 Generalized animal and green plant cells as viewed through a light microscope

Other cells you should know about are root hair, sperm, ovum and neurone – use the index.

Observing

Cells need to be stained to show up their parts better under the light microscope.

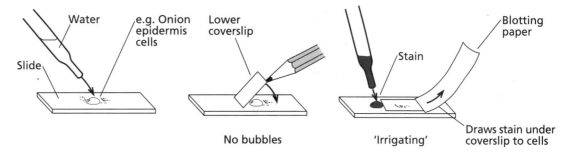

Fig. 1.3 Mounting and staining cells for microscopic examination

The *coverslip* delays water drying up around cells and permits viewing under high power without distortion under the light microscope.

1.3 Parts of cells and their functions

Only certain organelles (parts of the cell with special functions) can be seen under the light microscope's magnification. Even smaller organelles can be examined with an electron microscope.

①   Cell wall
Made of cellulose.
Freely permeable (porous) to all kinds of molecules.
Supports and protects the cell.
Supports non-woody plant organs, e.g. leaves, by water pressure within vacuole distending the cell wall. (See Unit 8.5)
Osmoregulates by resisting entry of excess water into cell. (See Fig. 8.6C.)

②   Cell membrane
Exterior of all protoplasm.
Very thin layer of protein and oil.
Freely permeable to water and gases only.
Selectively permeable to other molecules (e.g. allows foods in but keeps unwanted molecules out).

③   Vacuoles
Spaces for various functions, e.g. food storage, osmoregulation.
Plant cell vacuoles contain 'cell sap' (a weak solution of sugar and salts) inside a membrane.

④   Cytoplasmic matrix
Consistency of raw egg-white: supports organelles.
Up to 80% water; remainder mainly protein.
Often contains grains of stored food: starch (plants); glycogen (animals).

⑤   Nucleus
Stores 'information' which controls chemical activities in the cytoplasm.
Contains many long strands of DNA (invisible by light microscope).
When a cell divides, the DNA coils up to form chromosomes (visible). (See Unit 18.1.)
Segments of DNA are called **genes**.
Genes are responsible for characteristics of organisms, e.g. blood group and eye colour. (See Unit 1.4.)

⑥   Chloroplasts (for photosynthesis)
Large bodies containing chlorophyll (green).
Chlorophyll converts sunlight energy into chemical energy (ATP).
ATP is used to combine CO_2 with H_2O making glucose – which stores the energy in its bonds.

Examiner's tip

Notice how both organelles are involved in 'feeding' each other; both transform energy for life.

Fig. 1.4 The roles of chloroplasts and mitochondria in transforming energy

⑦ **Mitochondria** (for cell respiration)
Just specks (2 μm) in the cytoplasm under the light microscope.
Absorb O_2 and glucose.
Break down glucose to CO_2 and H_2O. This releases energy from glucose bonds to form ATP.
ATP is chemical energy a cell can use – for *any* vital function.

⑧ **Ribosomes** (protein factories)
Invisible (20 nm) without the electron microscope.
Minute bodies in thousands in cytoplasm.
Assemble amino acids into proteins, each different according to purpose (see Unit 5.5.) Instructions for assembly come from nucleus.

1.4 How the nucleus 'controls' the cell

Every gene is a recipe for a different protein.
Required recipes are 'copied' and passed to ribosomes.
Ribosomes assemble amino acids in a special order – according to recipe – to make proteins.
Thus DNA makes RNA and RNA makes proteins (Fig. 1.5)
These different proteins are either

① *secreted* by gland cells, e.g. digestive enzymes, hormones, or

② *retained* within cells for metabolism, e.g. enzymes for photosynthesis, respiration; and haemoglobin in red blood cells.

In both cases the proteins determine what each cell can do. So the nucleus, through the proteins it determines, controls what cells can do.

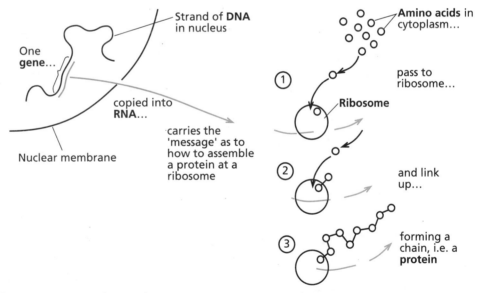

Fig. 1.5 From genes to proteins

1.5 DNA structure and function

DNA is a huge ladder-like molecule made up of sugar ▮, phosphate ● and four organic bases called **A**denine, **G**uanine, **C**ytosine and **T**hymine (Fig. 1.6). The bases will only join up in the pairs A to T and G to C (base pairing).

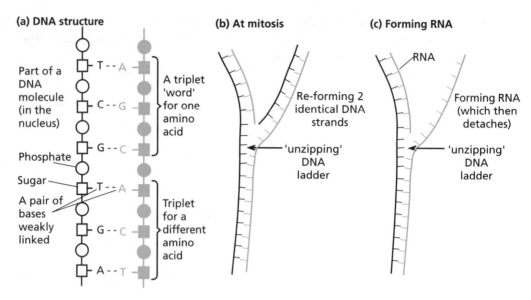

Fig. 1.6 (a) DNA structure; (b) duplicating itself; (c) passing its 'message' to ribosomes

The two halves of the ladder can also *un-zip* between the pairs of bases. They do this:
(a) **At mitosis**: each half ladder forms the other half on itself. So *two* ladders, which are identical, result. This is the reason why a chromosome that splits in mitosis forms two identical chromosomes (see Unit 18.11).

(b) **When genes make proteins**: each half ladder forms a related substance, RNA, (very similar to DNA) on it. This then detaches, passing to the ribosomes (see Fig. 1.5). RNA carries the sequence of bases that were in the DNA. Each three-letter 'word' (triplet), e.g. AGC, attracts a particular amino acid to the ribosome.

So the *sequence* of the hundreds of DNA triplets is what determines the *sequence* of the hundreds of amino acids in each protein. Each protein arises from its own *unique* DNA sequence.

Thus a length of DNA with its own unique sequence is a gene; and a gene is what is used to make its own, unique, protein by linking a particular sequence of amino acids together at a ribosome.

The 'ladder' structure of DNA is in fact turned into a spiral (double helix) thread, with 10 base pairs per complete 360° turn. This has little to do with the function of DNA but it was a crucial fact, discovered by Franklin, Wilkins, Watson and Crick, in determining its structure.

1.6 RNA and protein synthesis

There are two kinds of RNA:

1 **m-RNA** is a copy of the *message* of a gene (see Fig. 1.5).

2 **t-RNA** (not shown in Fig. 1.5) *transfers* amino acids to the ribosome ensuring that they arrive in the correct sequence to form the exact protein that the DNA requires.

t-RNA comes in short lengths of different kinds. Each kind attracts only one kind of amino acid (of the 20 kinds used by cells) by one end. The other end has a triplet of bases that can only link, by 'base pairing', with certain sites on the m-RNA, where its triplets fit.

So the order of triplets of the m-RNA determines the order in which the t-RNAs arrive in the ribosome; which determines the order in which the 20 kinds of amino acids link up. Each particular order of amino acids determines a particular protein.

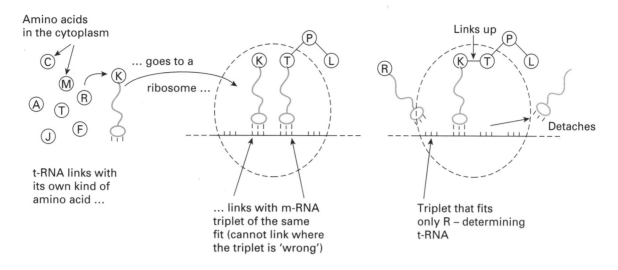

Fig. 1.7 How t-RNA helps to determine protein structure

1.7 Enzymes and metabolism

Enzymes are

1. **catalysts** – substances that speed up chemical reactions. These reactions do not change the catalyst, so even small amounts of enzyme can do a big job.

2. **protein** – whose chemical shape (see Fig. 1.8) is special to the substance it works on.

3. **specific** – starch alone fits into the special shape of the enzyme salivary amylase, not protein or anything else, so starch alone is digested by it.

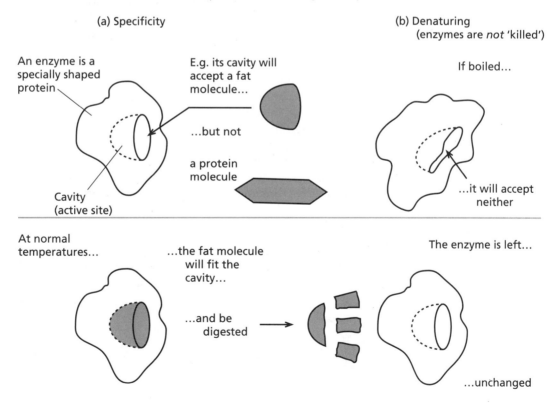

Fig. 1.8 Two features of enzymes dependent on their chemical shape: the 'lock and key' hypothesis

④ **temperature sensitive** – boiling denatures enzymes (by altering their shape); cooling only slows down their action. The rate of action increases with temperature. Best (i.e. 'optimum') for mammals is blood temperature.

⑤ **pH sensitive** – each enzyme has its own preferred (optimum) pH, e.g. optimum pH for pepsin is pH 2 (acid); for salivary amylase pH 6.8 (almost neutral); for lipase pH 9 (alkaline). (See Fig. 7.4.)

Enzymes catalyse all chemical reactions of the body (metabolism). Without enzymes, reactions would not go fast enough for life to exist.

Metabolism includes:

Anabolism: building up complex molecules as in photosynthesis, food storage, e.g.

(many) glucose-1-phosphate $\xrightarrow{\text{phosphorylase}}$ starch.

Catabolism: breaking down complex molecules, e.g. in respiration, digestion. It occurs both within cells (e.g. respiration) and outside them (digestion),

e.g. $2H_2O_2 \xrightarrow{\text{catalase}} 2H_2O + O_2$.

1.8 Units of life beyond the cell

Just as inorganic molecules are built up into organic molecules, which in turn are built into organelles (see Unit 1.3), so cells are subunits of organisms. There is a great variety of types of cell. (See Units 6.6, leaf cells; 8.4 and 17.1, root hair cell; 8.10, xylem and phloem; 9.2, blood cells; 13.2, neurones; 14.4, bone; 16.1, gametes.)

Tissues are groups of cells, usually of the same type, specialized to carry out certain functions, e.g. muscle for movement, nerves for sending 'messages', xylem for transport and support.

Organs are made up of tissues coordinated to perform certain functions, e.g. eye, leaf, kidney.

Organ systems are groups of organs which combine to perform their functions, e.g. digestive system, endocrine system, nervous system. The nervous system consists of brain, spinal cord and nerves.

Organisms, depending on their complexity, may each be just one cell, e.g. a bacterium or *Amoeba*, or millions of cells with a variety of functional units as above, e.g. an oak tree or Man. An organism which reproduces sexually is not much use on its own, unless it self-fertilizes. The basic unit of reproduction is thus usually a **breeding pair**. From this arise **populations** – as small as herds or as large as hundreds of herds occupying an island or a continent. All the populations of this type of organism form a **species** (see Fig. 1.9). Populations of different species living in balance in nature are called **communities**. Communities form part of **ecosystems** in the **biosphere**. (See Unit 20.1.)

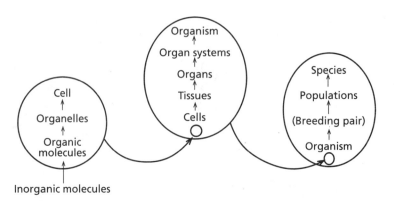

Fig. 1.9 Units of life

Summary

1 Organisms have seven vital functions in common; and they are made of cells.
2 Animal cells are made up of a nucleus, cytoplasm and a cell membrane.
3 In addition, plant cells have a cell wall of cellulose, a large central vacuole and, if green, chloroplasts.
4 Chloroplasts are the organelles of photosynthesis; they trap sunlight energy.
5 Mitochondria are the organelles of aerobic respiration; they release energy from molecules.
6 Ribosomes assemble amino acids to make proteins.
7 DNA is the chemical of genes and controls the making of proteins.
8 RNA is both the gene's messenger to ribosomes (m-RNA) and the transferrer of amino acids from the cytoplasmic matrix to the ribosome (t-RNA).
9 Enzymes are the protein catalysts of life, controlling every biochemical reaction of metabolism.
10 Cells of one type make up a tissue; various tissues make up organs and organ systems. Put together, these form organisms.

Quick test 1

1 What are the three main parts of living cells?
2 What is the difference between excretion and egestion?
3 In what form do chloroplasts receive energy and what do they do with it?
4 What do mitochondria do with the glucose they absorb?
5 What do most plant cells have that animal cells do not?
6 What are the two main functions of the nucleus?
7 What three kinds of chemical make up DNA?
8 How does a gene work in a cell?
9 What is an enzyme?
10 Arrange the following terms in order of simplest to most complex.

   A organ system   **B** organelle   **C** tissue   **D** cell   **E** organ   **F** organism

Chapter 2
Types of organisms

2.1 Naming species

Carl Linnaeus of Sweden in 1735 introduced the basis of modern **taxonomy** (classification). All species are given two names in Latin – the **binomial system** of naming:

1. genus name, written first, which starts with a *capital* letter, e.g. *Homo* (Man);

2. species name, written second, which starts with a *small* letter, e.g. *sapiens* (modern).

The binomial ought to be printed in italics but is underlined when handwritten or typed by scientists, e.g. <u>Panthera tigris</u> (tiger).

Species: a group of organisms capable of breeding to produce fertile offspring. They are very similar, but do show variety.

Genus: a group of organisms with a large number of similarities but whose different subgroups (species) are usually unable to interbreed successfully.

Examiner's tip

Write all scientific names this way. Know your own species name.

2.2 Groups and subgroups

Just as species are subgroups of genera, so Linnaeus grouped genera into larger and larger groups. Each group included as many *similarities* as possible. The largest group is a kingdom, the smallest a species. The lion can be classified as follows:

Kingdom	Animalia	– animals, as opposed to plants.
Phylum	Vertebrata	– animals with backbones (fish, amphibia, reptiles, birds and mammals).
Class	Mammalia	– hairy, warm blooded, suckle young on milk.
Order	Carnivora	– mainly flesh-eating group (cats, dogs, bears, seals).
Family	Felidae	– cats, large and small.
Genus	*Panthera*	– certain cats (includes tiger, *P. tigris;* leopard, *P. pardus*).
Species	*leo*	– lion only.

Mnemonic: **K**adet, **P.C.**, **OF**ficer, **G**eneral in**S**pector (promotion in the police force).

Advantages of the system

- **Universal:** Japanese, Bantu or Russian biologists all understand that *Panthera catus* means 'house cat' without having to resort to a dictionary.

- **Shorthand information:** one word, e.g. mammal, conveys a mass of information to all biologists.

- **Reflects evolutionary relationships:** e.g. the five classes of vertebrate are very different (see Unit 2.9), yet all have a common body plan. The basic plan (in Fish) was improved upon, allowing land colonization (Amphibia), its exploitation (Reptiles and Mammals), and even conquering of the air (Birds). The classification of vertebrates thus probably reflects the evolutionary process.

2.3 Modern classification

Most biologists favour the **Five Kingdom** classification.

Viruses are not included in this scheme since they lack many properties of living things: not cells, a very small piece of DNA or RNA inside a protein coat; parasitic inside cells when active. (See Unit 3.1.)

1. **Kingdom Prokaryotes:** bacteria – single, very small cell, no true nucleus (since no membrane around the DNA in the cytoplasm) but have cell wall. (See Unit 3.2.)

Organisms in the other four kingdoms have much larger cells and true nuclei:

2. **Kingdom Protoctista:** algae and protozoa (see Fig. 2.1) and slime moulds.
3. **Kingdom Fungi:** (see Fig. 2.1) usually made up of filaments of cells (hyphae); have no chlorophyll; absorb food they have digested from outside, through cell walls.
4. **Kingdom Plants:** all green plants in Fig. 2.2 except algae; they photosynthesize; have cellulose cell walls.
5. **Kingdom Animals:** organisms with no cell walls or chlorophyll in their cells; have nerve and muscle cells.

2.4 Microbes

See Fig. 2.1.

2.5 Plant kingdom

See Fig. 2.2.

2.6 Flowering plants

See Fig. 2.3.
See also Units 6.6 (leaf), 8.10 (stem and root), 15.7 (flowers), 15.11 (fruits) and 17.3 (seeds).

Fig. 2.1

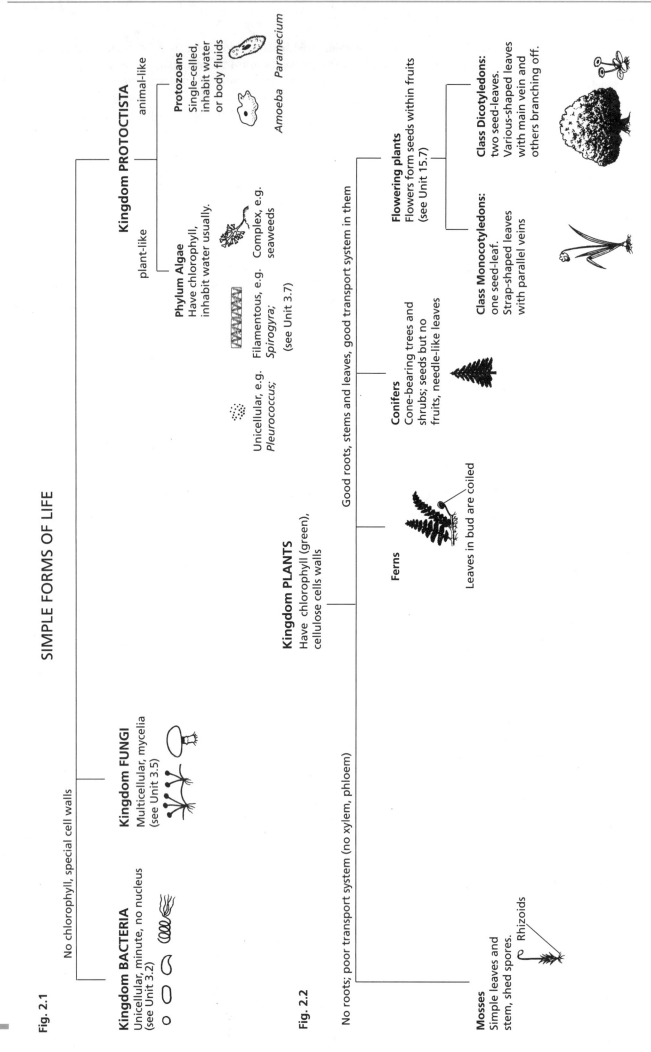

SIMPLE FORMS OF LIFE

No chlorophyll, special cell walls

Kingdom BACTERIA
Unicellular, minute, no nucleus
(see Unit 3.2)

Kingdom FUNGI
Multicellular, mycelia
(see Unit 3.5)

Kingdom PROTOCTISTA
animal-like

plant-like

Protozoans
Single-celled,
inhabit water
or body fluids

Amoeba   Paramecium

Phylum Algae
Have chlorophyll,
inhabit water usually.

Unicellular, e.g.
Pleurococcus;

Filamentous, e.g.
Spirogyra;

(see Unit 3.7)

Complex, e.g.
seaweeds

Fig. 2.2

Kingdom PLANTS
Have chlorophyll (green),
cellulose cells walls

No roots; poor transport system (no xylem, phloem)

Good roots, stems and leaves, good transport system in them

Mosses
Simple leaves and
stem, shed spores.

Rhizoids

Ferns

Leaves in bud are coiled

Conifers
Cone-bearing trees and
shrubs; seeds but no
fruits, needle-like leaves

Flowering plants
Flowers form seeds within fruits
(see Unit 15.7)

Class Monocotyledons:
one seed-leaf.
Strap-shaped leaves
with parallel veins

Class Dicotyledons:
two seed-leaves.
Various-shaped leaves
with main vein and
others branching off.

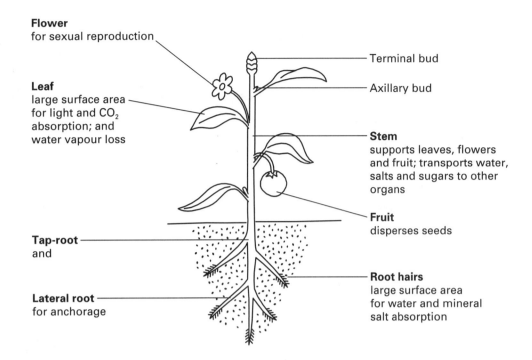

Flower
for sexual reproduction

Terminal bud

Axillary bud

Leaf
large surface area
for light and CO_2
absorption; and
water vapour loss

Stem
supports leaves, flowers
and fruit; transports water,
salts and sugars to other
organs

Fruit
disperses seeds

Tap-root
and

Lateral root
for anchorage

Root hairs
large surface area
for water and mineral
salt absorption

Fig. 2.3 General structure of a dicot plant

2.7 Invertebrate animals

Fig. 2.4
Some
invertebrate
animals

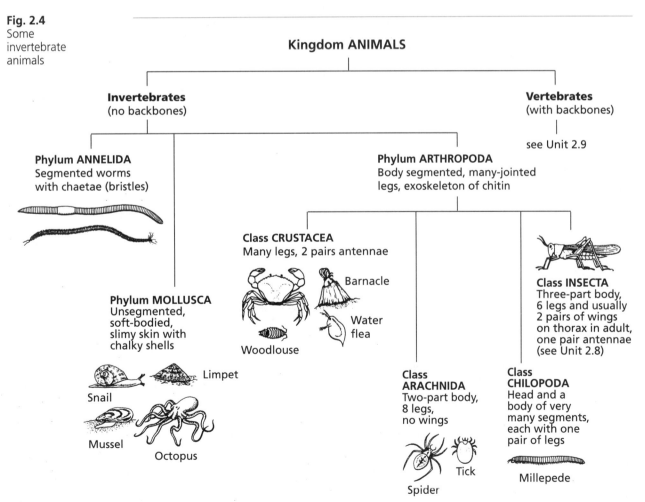

Kingdom ANIMALS

Invertebrates
(no backbones)

Vertebrates
(with backbones)

see Unit 2.9

Phylum ANNELIDA
Segmented worms
with chaetae (bristles)

Phylum ARTHROPODA
Body segmented, many-jointed
legs, exoskeleton of chitin

Class CRUSTACEA
Many legs, 2 pairs antennae

Barnacle

Water
flea

Woodlouse

Class INSECTA
Three-part body,
6 legs and usually
2 pairs of wings
on thorax in adult,
one pair antennae
(see Unit 2.8)

Phylum MOLLUSCA
Unsegmented,
soft-bodied,
slimy skin with
chalky shells

Limpet

Snail

Mussel

Octopus

**Class
ARACHNIDA**
Two-part body,
8 legs,
no wings

**Class
CHILOPODA**
Head and a
body of very
many segments,
each with one
pair of legs

Tick

Spider

Millepede

2.8 Insects

Insect characteristics
As insects are **Arthropods** (Unit 2.7), they also have:

1. an exoskeleton of chitin;
2. discontinuous growth – see below (compare humans: continuous growth);
3. many-jointed legs;
4. segmented body.

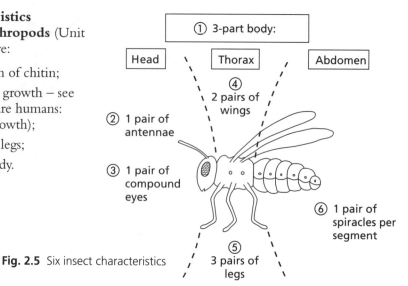

Fig. 2.5 Six insect characteristics

Growth is discontinuous. The exoskeleton does not grow. It has to be shed (**ecdysis**) from time to time.

To do this the old skeleton is partly digested away and finally split open. The insect emerges with a new soft exoskeleton, which it expands before it hardens at a larger size, within an hour. So the size of an insect increases in bursts (Fig. 2.6). Each stage between ecdyses is called an **instar**.

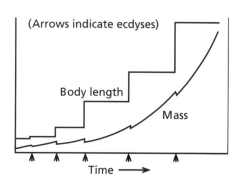

Fig. 2.6 Discontinuous growth pattern of an insect

Metamorphosis is the change from a young to an adult form. Young stages in insects have no *wings*, nor can they *reproduce*.

Two kinds of life cycle:

1 Incomplete metamorphosis	**2 Complete metamorphosis**
Examples: locust, cockroach, dragonfly	butterfly, bee (most insects)
Growing stage: **nymph** (similar to adult, lacking only wings and ability to reproduce). Last ecdysis gives adult.	**larvae** (so unlike adult that reorganization into an adult must be achieved as a **pupa**).

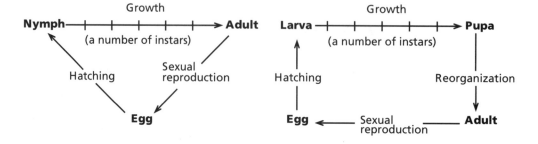

Fig. 2.7 Two kinds of life cycle in insects

2.9 Vertebrate animals

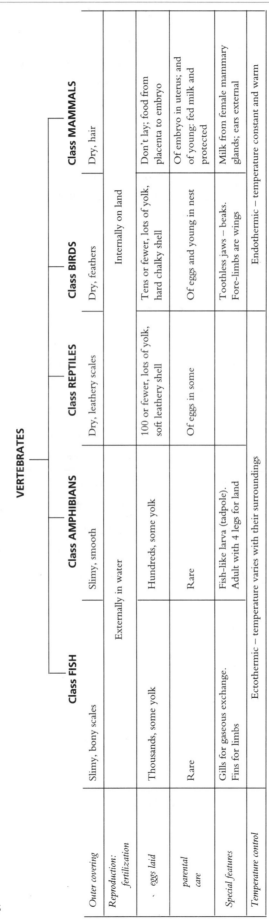

	Class FISH	Class AMPHIBIANS	Class REPTILES	Class BIRDS	Class MAMMALS
Outer covering	Slimy, bony scales	Slimy, smooth	Dry, leathery scales	Dry, feathers	Dry, hair
Reproduction: fertilization	Externally in water		Internally on land		
eggs laid	Thousands, some yolk	Hundreds, some yolk	100 or fewer, lots of yolk, soft leathery shell	Tens or fewer, lots of yolk, hard chalky shell	Don't lay; food from placenta to embryo
parental care	Rare	Rare	Of eggs in some	Of eggs and young in nest	Of embryo in uterus; and of young; fed milk and protected
Special features	Gills for gaseous exchange. Fins for limbs	Fish-like larva (tadpole). Adult with 4 legs for land		Toothless jaws – beaks. Fore-limbs are wings	Milk from female mammary glands; ears external
Temperature control	Ectothermic – temperature varies with their surroundings			Endothermic – temperature constant and warm	

VERTEBRATES

Fig. 2.8 Vertebrates

Summary

1   Linnaeus invented a method of classifying organisms and the binomial system for naming them, using Latin words.

2   Today, we classify organisms into five kingdoms: Prokaryotes (bacteria); Protoctista; Fungi, Plants and Animals.

3   Flowering plants have organs specialized for different functions.

4   Insects have three or four main stages in their life cycle, each adapted to different functions.

5   Insects often use different foods at larval and adult stages e.g. butterfly and blowfly.

6   Invertebrates (animals without backbones) have a great variety of body plans.

7   Vertebrates (animals with backbones) have a common body plan modified for life in water, on land and in the air – particularly their skin structures and reproductive lives.

Quick test 2

1   Write the name of your own species scientifically.

2   Why are viruses not regarded as organisms?

3   How do bacterial cells differ from all others?

4   What kinds of organisms carry out decay?

5   What groups of green multicell plants reproduce by spores?

6   What are the characteristics of arthropods?

7   In what three ways do insects differ from spiders?

8   Which groups of animals are warm blooded?

9   Which animal group has a fish-like larva but an adult with four legs?

10 What are the four stages, in sequence, in the life cycle of most insects?

Chapter 3
Viruses, microorganisms and fungi

3.1 Viruses

Size: between 30 and 300 nm (1/100 size of bacteria) – visible only with electron microscope.

Structure: protein coat around a DNA or RNA strand (a few genes) (Fig. 3.1).

Living?: no; are not cells, having no metabolism of their own. (See Unit 1.1.)

All are *parasites*, killing host cells as they reproduce within them, using the cell's energy and materials. This causes disease, e.g. rabies.

Disease transmission

1. by water, e.g. polio;
2. by droplet (sneezing), e.g. colds, 'flu;
3. by vector (carrier of disease), e.g. mosquito transmits yellow fever and greenfly transmits the TMV (Fig. 3.1).

Useful: for biological control of rabbits – myxomatosis virus.

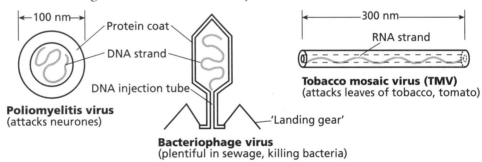

Fig. 3.1 Viruses

Fig. 3.2 Virus 'life cycle'

3.2 Bacteria

Size: between 0.1 and 10 μm (1/100 size of mammal cheek cell).
Structure: cell is unique in *not* having:

- nuclear membrane around its single loop chromosome, so there is no nucleus;
- mitochondria (cell membrane has the same function).

Cell is unlike a green plant cell in having *no*:

- chloroplasts (therefore bacteria are either saprophytes or parasites) (see Unit 5.2);
- cellulose in cell walls (made of nitrogenous compounds instead) (Fig. 3.3).

Reproduction

- asexually: by binary fission, every 20 minutes in suitable conditions.
- sexually: use a tube to transfer DNA from one bacterium to another.

Bacteria do *not* reproduce by forming spores. Some bacilli, only, form spores (endospores) for *survival* when conditions become unfavourable.

A generalized bacterium

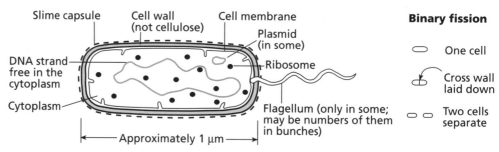

Bacterial shapes

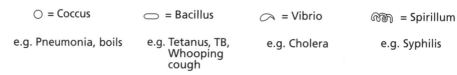

Fig. 3.3 Bacteria

Plasmids (small rings of DNA) give bacteria special properties, e.g. cholera bacteria become killers (normally harmless); and certain bacteria can fix nitrogen (otherwise cannot).

3.3 Importance of bacteria

Bacteria obtain both energy and materials from their food as we do. In doing so, their metabolism can help or harm Man. In some cases (see nos. 1a, 3a and 3b in Table 3.1), the *same* bacterium can be both helpful and harmful – according to what it is acting upon.

Table 3.1 The importance of bacteria to Man

Activity	Helpful	Harmful
1 Decomposing	(a) *Dead organisms*, litter, manure, into simple nutrients for green plants to use, e.g. CO_2, salts (see Unit 21.11) (b) *sewage*, so preventing water pollution	*Food*, e.g. putrefying meat, fish
2 Circulating nitrogen	(a) *Fixing nitrogen*, so increasing soil fertility (see Unit 20.12) (b) Converting ammonia (toxic) into nitrate for green plants, i.e. *nitrification*	*Denitrifying* the soil by converting nitrate to nitrogen gas, so reducing soil fertility
3 In industry	(a) *Dairy products*:* making yoghurt, butter, cheese (see Units 4.8, 4.9) (b) *Wineries:* making vinegar (c) Making biogas *fuel* (methane)	*Souring* milk Souring wine *Damaging oil* lubricating engines
4 Affecting health	(a) Producing *antibiotics*, e.g. *Streptomyces* gives over 50 of them (b) Producing human *hormones* by genetic engineering (see Unit 18.17)	Causing *disease* in Man and his animals (see Unit 3.2) Causing *food poisoning*, e.g. *Salmonella*

* Special bacteria turn milk sour, to form **yoghurt**; or turn cream sour, to make a lumpy product which when churned becomes unsalted **butter**.
   To make **cheese**: (a) milk is soured, (b) rennin (see Units 4.8 and 4.9) is added to clot it forming solid (curds) and juice (whey) which is removed, (c) the curds are 'ripened' by adding special bacteria or fungi which feed on it, giving it characteristic flavours (see Units 4.9 and 7.3).

3.4 Control of harmful bacteria

If the basic requirements of bacteria are removed, they die (Table 3.2).

Table 3.2 Control of harmful bacteria

Requirements of bacteria	Control measure, with examples
1 Moisture	**Dried foods:** peas, raisins, milk, meat – keep for ever **Salting:** e.g. ham, or *syruping*, e.g. peaches, plasmolyses (see Unit 8.5) bacteria, so killing them
2 Organic food	**Hygiene:** removal of bacterial foods by washing body, clothes, food utensils; by disposing of refuse, excreta and hospital dressings; cleaning homes
3 Suitable temperature (warmth)	**Temperature treatment** (a) *refrigeration:* deep-freeze ($-18\ °C$) suspends life; fridge ($+4\ °C$) slows rotting to acceptable level; (b) *boiling:* kills most, but not spores; (c) *pressure-cooking* ('sterilizing' or 'autoclaving') for 10 min at 100 kN/m² (15 lb/in²) kills all, including spores; (d) *pasteurization* (of milk): heat to 77 °C for seconds and rapidly cool to 4 °C Enclosing food from (b)–(d), by bottling, canning and vacuum packing, prevents access of bacteria to it
4 Suitable chemical environment	**Chemicals** are also used to kill bacteria: (a) *chlorine* in drinking water and swimming baths; (b) *disinfectants* in loos; (c) *medical use* of antiseptics, antibiotics, antibodies and drugs in or on Man's body (see Unit 23.7); (d) *vinegar* for pickling food (pH too acid for bacteria)
5 No ultraviolet light	**Irradiate with ultraviolet light** (thin sliced food, surgical instruments) and plan sunny homes (sunlight contains UV light)
6 No γ-rays	**Irradiate with radioactive source**

3.5 Fungi

Fungi consist of multicellular filaments called hyphae. Cells forming hyphae lack chloroplasts, cellulose and complete cross-walls – in contrast to green plants.
Nutrition: saprophytic – potato blight or parasitic (see Units 20.6 and 22.3).
Distribute themselves by spores, formed asexually.

(a) Moulds

Rhizopus (mould on bread) and *Mucor* (mould on dung) are both 'pin-moulds' (Fig. 3.4).

Structure: A continuous tube of chitin, the cell wall, contains the cytoplasm, with many nuclei in it. Inside the cytoplasm is a continuous vacuole. Threads of fungus (hyphae) make up a mycelium.

Nutrition: saprophytic (see Unit 5.2). Rootlet hyphae branch through the food, secreting digestive enzymes and absorbing the soluble products.

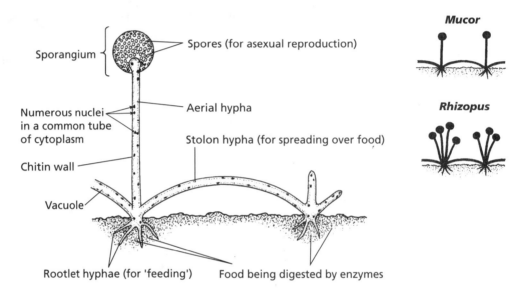

Fig. 3.4 Structure of a mould fungus

Reproduction:

1 **asexually** by hundreds of spores from each sporangium. In *Mucor*, the sporangium wall dissolves in moisture and spores are distributed in a slime-drop by rain or animals. In *Rhizopus*, the wall cracks open when dry and wind distributes dry spores.

2 **sexually** using special hyphae from two different strains to bring together gamete-nuclei. These gametes fuse and a tough zygospore is formed to survive unfavourable conditions, e.g. drought or the winter.

(b) Mushrooms and toadstools these exist unseen as a mycelium within soil, dead wood, etc. In damp cool conditions (e.g. October), hundreds of hyphae grow solidly up together, out of the soil, to form a toadstool (Fig. 3.5). On the underside this sheds millions of spores from 'gills' or pores. Such fungi are usually saprophytic; others are parasites and mutualists (see Unit 20.6). Growing mushrooms on waste straw avoids stubble burning – which pollutes the air – and provides useful garden mulch at the end.

(c) Yeasts Yeasts are exceptional among the Fungi in being single celled – no hyphae (Fig. 3.6). Natural yeasts on fruit skins ferment them to produce wine. Special yeasts are cultivated by Man for brewing, SCP (single cell protein), and baking (see Chapter 4).

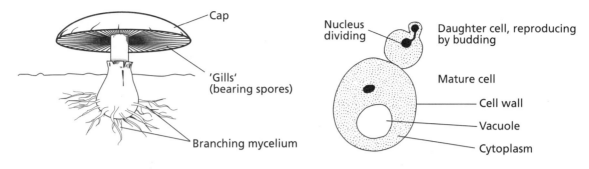

Fig. 3.5 Mushroom fungus

Fig. 3.6 Yeast cells

3.6 Growing bacteria and fungi

Culturing microbes safely

Golden rules:

① Do not culture microbes except under teacher supervision.

② Do not incubate them unless within taped petri dishes or stoppered test tubes, clearly marked with their source. Do not open them.

③ Dispose of unwanted cultures by autoclaving.

④ Take care not to eat during such classes, nor to inhale air close to cultures.

⑤ Bacterial 'loops' (of wire), used to transfer microbes, must be 'flamed' in a Bunsen burner after use.

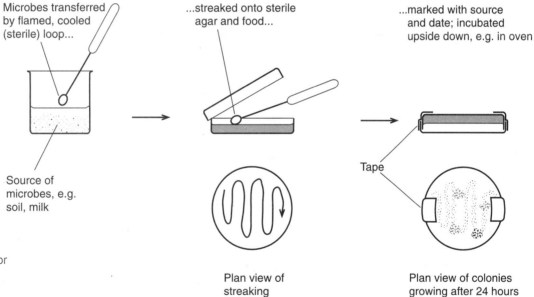

Fig. 3.7 Method for culturing microbes on agar jelly

Testing antibiotics (or antiseptics, mouthwashes)

- Particular microbe colonies may be transferred by means of a 'swab' of sterile wet cotton wool on a stick, and 'painted' onto fresh agar to spread it evenly.
- Discs of filter paper, soaked in antibiotic, are placed on the culture before incubation. The control disc contains no antibiotic.
- After incubation, clear zones indicate no microbial growth, i.e. antibiotic effective (Fig. 3.8).

A doctor may take a swab from an infection to discover, using the method above, which antibiotic is the best for curing it.

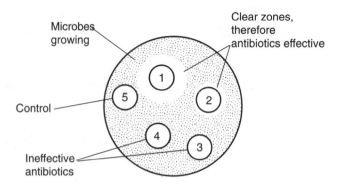

Fig. 3.8 Testing antibiotics

3.7 Algae

The Algae are green plants with no roots, stems or leaves (Fig. 3.9).
Their cells are little specialized — apart from gametes.
Nutrition is holophytic (see Unit 5.2).

Importance of algae

- **Diatoms** (unicellular algae) are the main plant component of plankton (phytoplankton). They
  - (a) provide the majority of the world's O_2;
  - (b) are at the base of most marine food chains.
- Some **seaweeds** are eaten, e.g. 'Irish moss'.
- **Extracts:** 'agar' for bacterial culture methods; 'alginates' for ice-cream.

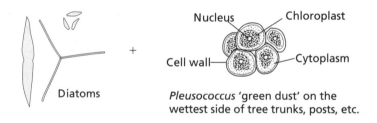

Examples of multicellular algae

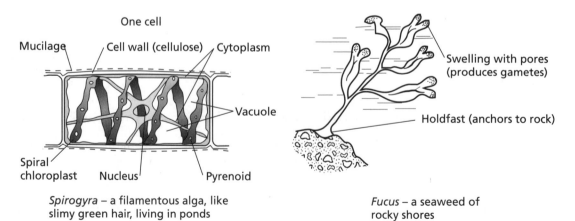

Fig. 3.9 Some algae

Summary

1 Viruses fall outside the description 'organisms', yet are immensely important parasites within cells.

2 Bacteria are uniquely tiny and simple cells, without a proper nucleus.

3 Bacteria are important in decay and animal disease.

4 Man has also harnessed bacteria to his own use in making many dairy products, fuel and antibiotics.

5 By genetic engineering, bacteria are used to make many useful products unnatural to them, e.g. hormones, enzymes.

6 Man has learned to control harmful bacteria by denying them the five vital conditions essential to their lives.

7 Fungi are also important in decay and plant disease. Man has learned to harness and control them.

8 Algae, though simple green organisms, are important, particularly in the sea, as they produce food and oxygen for the world.

Quick test 3

1 What chemicals make up a virus?

2 Where and how do viruses 'live'?

3 Name four conditions that bacteria need in order to multiply.

4 By what method do bacteria multiply?

5 What agents are used to control bacteria in:

   (a) swimming baths   (b) lavatories   (c) inside bodies

6 A sore throat bacterium has been spread, ready for culture, on an agar plate. How could you test for an effective antibiotic against it?

7 How do moulds feed?

8 What are the benefits of decay?

9 What are the characteristics of algae?

10 Why are algae important in the sea?

Chapter 4
Biotechnology

4.1 Biotechnology

Biotechnology is the application of biological processes of microorganisms to manufacturing industries, service industries and to the maintenance of a pollution-free environment. Biotechnology is not new. Humans have used microorganisms to produce their bread, wine, cheese, yoghurt and even biogas fuel for a long time. More recently they have disposed of sewage, produced antibiotics and obtained protein-rich foods using microorganisms.

The most recent advances result from understanding cell processes (dependent on enzymes), and from putting useful genes into microorganisms (genetic engineering) to do special jobs.

Biotechnology could transform our lives by providing efficient, low-cost solutions to many of the future problems of an overcrowded world, including shortage of energy and food.

4.2 Growing microbes in fermenters

The successful use of many microorganisms and their products can only be achieved if small scale trials in laboratories can be scaled up to make production economically viable. This usually means growing microorganisms in fermenters containing 10,000 litres of culture solution.

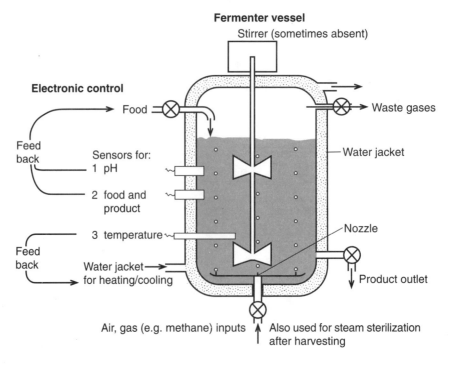

Fig. 4.1 A generalized fermenter

To achieve the desired pure product as cheaply and safely as possible the fermenting agent (microorganism or enzyme) must be studied carefully to achieve the best possible production levels. There are three main needs:

1. **Sterilization:** vessel must be sterilized by steam before use. During fermentation, food, air and other gases must also be sterile. The entry of unwanted organisms could spoil the product or poison or kill the consumer of it.

2. **Efficient contact** between the fermenting agent and the food and gases it needs. This maximizes production:

   (a) Stirrers or gases bubbling through the 'brew' continually supply the fermenting agents with fresh molecules to work on.

   (b) Organisms (e.g. yeast) or enzymes can be trapped ('immobilized') in jelly or acetate film, providing a huge surface area for reactions in the food flowing over them. This method also avoids the need to separate the product from the organisms at the end of the process.

3. **Temperature, pH, food and oxygen control:**

   Initially the fermenter may need warming; later, when microorganisms are multiplying, so much heat may be generated that cooling may be necessary. The pH may vary as food is used up or waste products are produced. The food will be used up as the microbes grow and reproduce. Oxygen may be necessary for some microbes to respire. Each of these factors is monitored by biosensors coupled to electronic control systems which automatically adjust the conditions in the fermenter.

   Fermenters are used either for a **batch process** where the conditions change in the fermenter and nothing is added or removed from the fermenter until the end of the process, e.g. beer brewing, or for a **continuous process** where new materials are constantly added and products are constantly removed from the fermenter, e.g. mycoprotein production. The sensors are particularly important in continuous processes to control the rate of flow of food in and product out.

4.3 Biological fuels

Some *anaerobic* microbes can be used to turn waste organic material into fuel.

Biogas (CO_2 and methane) is produced by bacteria in digesters supplied with faeces and vegetable waste. This gas is piped to burners for cooking, heating, or generating electricity (as in sewage works, see Unit 4.4).

Gasohol (ethanol brewed from waste sugar cane) fuels over a million vehicles in Brazil; methanol (at present produced chemically) fuels over 5000 vehicles in oil-rich California. Neither fuel provides the pollution hazards of petrol (see Unit 21.3).

Vegetable oils (sunflower, rape) are now being used by experimental buses as bio-diesel.

4.4 Sewage disposal

1. **Removes pathogens** from infected people, e.g. those suffering from cholera, typhoid and bacillary dysentery.

2. **Lowers biological oxygen demand** (BOD) which would kill organisms, especially fish, if raw sewage reached rivers or lakes. The bacteria and fungi in them would decompose the faeces, using up the oxygen needed by aquatic life.

3. **Removes mineral salts** which would cause algal 'blooms' that turn the water green (see eutrophication, Unit 22.1).

Faeces, urine and water from washing comprise sewage. Sewage treatment works use bacteria and fungi to decompose organic matter. The aerobic sprinkler or the activated sludge method is used to break down small organic particles in water that don't settle in the settlement tank. Both rely on a food web of invertebrates, which feed on the bacteria and fungi, and on algae which thrive on the CO_2 and mineral salts produced by decomposers. The remaining mineral salts are removed either chemically or by vegetation in large ponds before water is returned to rivers.

The sludge enters anaerobic digesters where bacteria break down the organic material. The methane provides fuel and the harmless waste sludge can be sprayed on fields as fertiliser.

Examiner's tip

Remember why sewage has to be treated and what the end products can be used for.

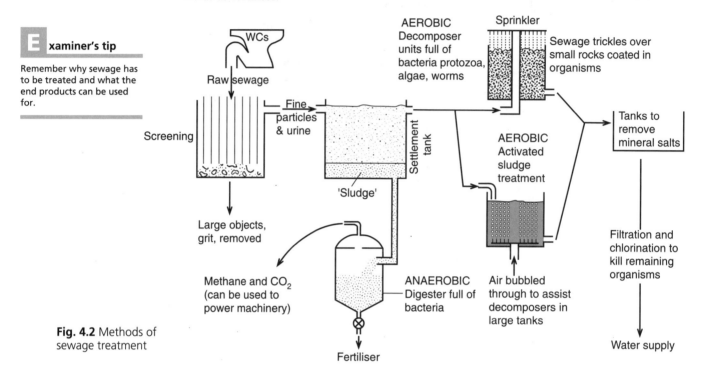

Fig. 4.2 Methods of sewage treatment

4.5 Bread

1. Wheat flour and a little sugar and yeast are mixed with water to form dough.
2. Within the dough the yeast respires the sugar anaerobically for 1 hour at 35°C;

$$\text{sugar} \longrightarrow \text{carbon dioxide and alcohol}$$

3. The risen dough is kneaded and cooked.
4. The heat expands the CO_2 to give the 'bubbles' within bread (its texture). The alcohol evaporates.

4.6 Wines and spirits

Wine is made from grapes.

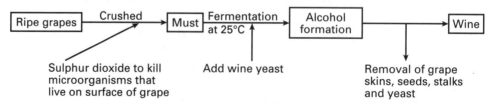

Fig. 4.3 Wine production

Yeast reproduces in the grape juice, respiring anaerobically:

$$\text{sugars} \longrightarrow \text{carbon dioxide and ethanol}$$

Ethanol extracts colour from grape skins; the CO_2 is lost. As ethanol concentration rises to 12–15% the yeast is killed; the yeast is filtered off.

Spirits are made by distilling wines to increase the alcohol concentration to 30% or higher.

4.7 Beer and lager

These are 3–6% alcoholic drinks produced by fermenting barley and flavouring it with hops. This is a batch fermentation (see Unit 4.2).

1. **Barley**, sprayed with water (assisted by gibberellins, see Unit 13.17) germinates over some days. Starch, digested by the seeds' amylases, is converted to maltose.
2. The seeds are **killed** by heat and dried to give malt.
3. Malt is turned into **mash** by addition of water; digestion of starch continues.
4. Straining off solids produces **wort**. This is boiled with hops for a few hours to **flavour** it and **sterilize** it.
5. Wort is **fermented** (lager is fermented at 10–15 °C whereas beer, using different yeasts, is fermented at 15–18 °C) by yeast for 8–10 days. Sugars are turned into ethanol and CO_2. When alcoholic content is correct, it is filtered to give:
6. **Green beer**, cooled to 0°C for a few weeks to mature.
7. Mature beer is filtered, pasteurized, carbonated and bottled or kegged.

4.8 Yoghurt

Yoghurt is produced by the fermentation of low fat milk using two species of *Streptococcus* and *Lactobacillus* bacteria. Other species of bacteria can grow in milk so they are killed by pasteurization before the cultures are added. The bacteria use the milk as a food source and lower the pH by producing lactic acid. The milk proteins coagulate when pH 4.4 is reached, so thickening yoghurt.

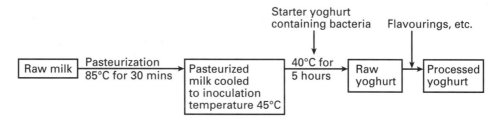

Fig. 4.4 Yoghurt production

4.9 Cheese and butter

Cheese can be made from the milk of goats, sheep and cows. The initial stages are very similar to those of yoghurt production.

1. Raw milk is pasteurized to kill unwanted microorganisms.
2. *Streptococcus* and *Lactobacillus* bacteria are added to respire lactose (sugar in milk) to lactic acid. This acidity and the action of rennin (enzyme) clots soluble milk protein to form solid curds and liquid whey.

③ The whey is drained off and dried for animal feed.

④ The curds are pressed to remove water. The greater the pressing the harder the cheese.

⑤ The cheese is then ripened to give flavour by microbes.

e.g. Cheddar (hard) – lactic acid bacteria in curds.
Camembert (soft) – *Penicillium camembertii* painted on surface.
Roquefort (medium) – *Penicillium roquefortii* mixed into curds.

Butter can be made in the following ways.

① By pasteurizing milk, churning it, draining, and then salting.

② By inoculating milk with a bacterial culture of *Streptococcus* and *Leuconostoc* (for flavours). This mixture is churned, drained, but not usually salted.

4.10 Mycoprotein

Mycoprotein is an example of a 'single cell protein' food (SCP) – whole dried filaments of the fungus *Fusarium graminearum*, produced in a '*continuous process*' fermenter (see Unit 4.2). It is marketed as Quorn, suitable as a meat substitute for humans. The hyphae have the same texture as meat fibres and are tasteless.

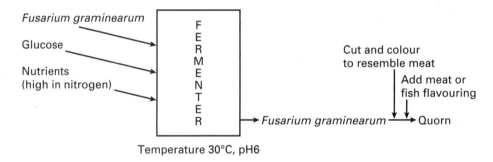

Fig. 4.5 Mycoprotein production

Advantages of mycoprotein

Fungus grows fast (doubles its mass every few hours). High in first class protein and fibre. Low in fat, with no cholesterol. A rich protein source for vegetarians and vegans.

Disadvantages of mycoprotein

Can be indigestible and taste 'different'. May cause gout due to the high RNA content. Costly at present.

4.11 Penicillin

The effects of the fungus *Penicillium notatum* were first observed by Alexander Fleming (see Unit 23.8). He noticed that bacteria in a Petri dish did not grow around an area of the dish contaminated with fungus. The active chemical, penicillin, which prevented growth was isolated and purified in 1940 by Florey and Chain. Penicillin is produced in a '*batch process*' fermenter (see Unit 4.2) because the conditions have to change for the fungus to begin to produce the antibiotic.

As the fungus grows aerobically in the fermenter (Fig. 4.6) it uses up the nutrients. Only when the nutrient level falls greatly does the fungus produce penicillin. Production of the antibiotic begins after about 40 hours in the fermenter and reaches its maximum after about seven days. Penicillin is effective against a wide range of pathogenic bacteria. It prevents them making their cells walls.

There are over 100 other antibiotics, e.g. streptomycin, erythromycin. If one is ineffective a different one will be used next time. To avoid bacteria becoming resistant to antibiotics it is important to finish a course of treatment totally.

Examiner's tip

emember to explain how a rmenter works and what onitoring will take place it.

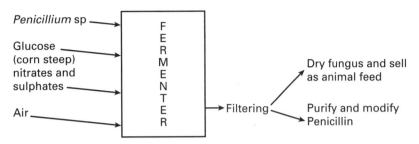

Fig. 4.6 Penicillin production

4.12 Hormones and antibodies

Insulin is one of the hormones in the body responsible for controlling blood glucose levels. Diabetics unable to synthesize the hormone themselves used to rely on insulin extracted from animals. Human insulin is now produced by bacteria in a fermentation tank. Using genetic engineering, a human insulin gene has been inserted into the bacterial genetic material.

Advantages
Relatively cheap. It is human (and not cow) insulin. No side effects. No immune response. Product more pure.

Disadvantages
There may be ethical objections to genetic engineering. Initial plant production and development costs high.

   Antibodies, apart from their natural role in defending the body from infection (see Unit 23.5) can be made artificially in culture ('monoclonal antibodies'). This is done by fusing white blood cells (lymphocytes) that have been stimulated to produce a useful antibody with cancer cells (which live for ever). These hybrid cells rapidly divide in culture producing antibodies that can be extracted. Useful antibodies are those that attach to harmful or diseased cells in the body or their products. Others are used to detect hormones, e.g. those in urine that confirm pregnancy. There is hope that drugs can be coupled to monoclonal antibodies to deliver a lethal dose only to harmful cells, e.g. cancer cells – so called 'magic bullets' – leaving other cells unharmed. Monoclonal antibodies are therefore useful in diagnosis and treatment of medical conditions.

4.13 Enzymes for industry

Enzymes (see Unit 1.7) have great advantages over inorganic catalysts.

1. Enormous variety of them, for every purpose.
2. Continuously produced (no shortages or great cost: compare platinum).
3. Work at low temperatures (not costly in energy).
4. Do a precise job, e.g. digesting the lignin of wood, leaving its cellulose intact for useful SCP microorganisms to use – as in the Pekilo process.

Enzymes *secreted* by microorganisms are easier to collect than those kept within their cells. Once extracted they store easily.

Enzymes are used either in solution, or trapped in polymer beads (where they are less easily destroyed) and can be used over and over again after each harvest of product. Many traditional processes can now be completed more quickly and with better control over the quality of the product using enzymes from microorganisms. Many enzymes produced by microorganisms work over a wide temperature and pH range, so suiting home and industry.

Table 4.1 The use of enzymes

Process	Enzymes from microorganisms used	Purpose
Washing clothes	Proteases Lipases	'Biological' washing powders remove stains, e.g. blood and fat
Washing dishes	Amylases	Dishwasher powders remove starch smears on plates
Cheese making	Rennin Lipases	Curdles milk Speed up ripening of Danish blue cheese
Leather making	Proteases	Make leather supple (replace use of enzymes in dog dung!) and remove hair from hides
Brewing	Carbohydrases Proteases	Split starch into maltose and proteins into amino acids in malting
Slimming foods	Isomerase	Converts glucose into fructose which is sweeter, so less is used
Baby foods	Proteases	Pre-digest protein in baby food
Fruit juices	Pectinases	Break down cell walls to release more juice
Meat tenderizing	Proteases	Begin breakdown of protein fibres

Examiner's tip

Look in your syllabus to see which of these enzymes you need to know.

Summary

1 Biotechnology is a fast growing science which, by manipulating microorganisms to our use, may provide solutions to major world problems, e.g. food supply. It also poses risk of mutant dangers.

2 Humans have harnessed bacteria to make many dairy products, fuels and antibiotics.

3 Microorganisms can be grown in fermenters using either batch or continuous processes.

4 Conditions in fermenters are constantly monitored and controlled to give maximum, uncontaminated yields.

5 Microorganisms can be used to break down organic waste, e.g. to produce Biogas and in sewage treatment.

6 Microorganisms are used to produce food and drink, e.g., bread, yoghurt, butter, cheese, mycoprotein, beer and wine.

7 Microorganisms are used to produce health products, antibiotics, hormones and antibodies.

8 Microorganisms are used to produce enzymes for industry, e.g. biological washing powders and meat tenderizers.

Quick test 4

1 What is the difference between fermentation by batch process and by continuous process?

2 What conditions are monitored in a fermenter?

3 Why is steam flushed through a fermenter before it is set up?

4 What are the main gases in Biogas?

5 In sewage treatment what is activated sludge?

6 Why are barley seeds allowed to germinate for a few days before they are killed to make malt for brewing?

7 In yoghurt production how is the milk pasteurized?

8 *Fusarium graminearum* can be grown in a fermenter to produce mycoprotein. Besides the fungus what else must be added to the fermenter?

9 Into what kind of organism has the human insulin gene been inserted to produce artificial insulin?

10 What are the two main kinds of enzyme in biological washing powders and what do they each achieve?

Chapter 5
Foods and feeding

5.1 Food

Food (material for building up protoplasm) is of two types:

1. **Inorganic:** (simple molecules common to nonliving matter) e.g. carbon dioxide, mineral salts and water.

2. **Organic:** (complex, carbon-containing compounds) e.g. carbohydrates, fats, proteins and vitamins. These classes of molecules are characteristic of living matter.

5.2 How plants, animals and decay organisms feed

There are two fundamentally different methods of nutrition:

1. **Autotrophic** organisms (plants containing green chlorophyll) need *only inorganic food* from which they synthesize organic molecules, using *energy trapped from sunlight* to drive the reactions.

2. **Heterotrophic** organisms (animals, fungi, bacteria) have to feed on ready made *organic food*. From this they derive their *energy, released by respiration*. They also need some inorganic food.

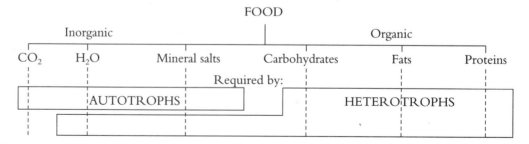

Organic food can be obtained from living organisms (**holozoic** nutrition) or from dead matter (**saprophytic** nutrition). (For other variations see Unit 20.6.)

Table 5.1 Comparison of types of nutrition

	Autotrophic	Heterotrophic	
	Holophytic	Holozoic	Saprophytic
Examples of organisms	Typical **green plants**, e.g. flowering plants	Typical **animals**, e.g. mammals	**Bacteria and fungi** of decay, e.g. *Mucor* and mushrooms (Unit 3.5)
Type of food	Inorganic only: CO_2, H_2O and mineral salts	Organic, H_2O and mineral salts	Dead organic, H_2O and mineral salts
How the food is used	**1** CO_2 and water are combined in **photosynthesis** to make carbohydrates **2** carbohydrates are modified and also often combined with salts to **form other organic molecules**, e.g. protein	Food organisms are killed; *ingested* into a **gut**; *digested* by enzymes secreted **internally**; soluble products *absorbed*; indigestible waste *egested* (eliminated)	Dead organisms or excreta are digested by enzymes secreted **externally** onto them; soluble products absorbed
Source of energy for vital functions	**Sunlight** – trapped by chlorophyll during photosynthesis	Cannot trap sunlight energy since they lack chlorophyll. Rely on **respiration** of organic molecules (the bonds of which contain energy)	

Thus the kinds of organisms practising these three forms of nutrition provide food for each other:

(For detail see Unit 20.4)

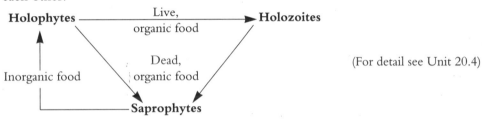

xaminer's tip

Notice how plants, animals and decay organisms rely on each other for their food in a kind of cycle.

INORGANIC FOOD

1 **Water** (see Unit 8.1).
2 **Mineral salts**

5.3 Mineral salts for flowering plants

Table 5.2 Flowering plant requirements (see Unit 6.9)

Element	Sources	Uses	Deficiency effects
N *(Nitrogen)*	Nitrates	Protein and DNA synthesis	Poor leaf growth – older leaves yellow
S *(Sulphur)*	Sulphates		
Ca *(Calcium)*	Lime ($CaCO_3$)	'Gum' (middle lamella) between adjacent cell walls	Faulty cell division
Fe *(Iron)*	Iron salts	Enzymes for making chlorophyll	Pale leaves (chlorosis)
Mg *(Magnesium)*	Magnesium salts	Part of chlorophyll molecule	
P *(Phosphorus)*	Phosphates	ATP (energy molecule) in photosynthesis and respiration; DNA synthesis; cell membranes	Poor root growth – purple younger leaves
K *(Potassium)*	Potassium salts	Help enzymes involved in photosynthesis and respiration to work	Poor growth – yellow leaves with dead patches

Trace elements include zinc (**Zn**), copper (**Cu**) and manganese (**Mn**). Required in very minute quantities for healthy growth (larger quantities are often poisonous).

Although green plants absorb mineral salts as ions, Man does not always give them to crops by way of inorganic fertilizers (see Unit 22.1). Organic fertilizers, such as dung, also yield salts, once they have been broken down by bacteria and fungi (see Units 3.3, 20.12).

5.4 Mineral salts for mammals

Table 5.3 Some mammal requirements (especially Man)

Element	Good sources	Uses	Deficiency effects
Ca (*Calcium*)	Cheese; milk; bread (chalk added by law)	Bones and teeth are over 70% calcium phosphate	Brittle bones and teeth
Fe (*Iron*)	Liver, egg yolk	Part of haemoglobin, the oxygen-carrying molecule	Anaemia (lack of red blood cells)
F (*Fluorine*)	Toothpaste or tap water that have been fluoridated	Ensures hard tooth enamel, therefore less tooth decay (caries)	Dental caries more likely (Unit 7.8)

ORGANIC FOOD

1 **Carbohydrates, fats and proteins**
2 **Vitamins**

5.5 Carbohydrates, fats and proteins

Table 5.4 Carbohydrates, fats and proteins

	Carbohydrates	Fats (*solids*), oils (*liquid*)	Proteins
Elements	C, H, O Ratio of H:O is 2:1 (as in H_2O)	C, H, O Ratio of H:O is very high, i.e. very little O	C, H, O, N, often S
Examples	Glucose $C_6H_{12}O_6$ Starch $(C_6H_{10}O_5)_n$	Mutton fat $C_{57}H_{110}O_6$	Haemoglobin, amylase, insulin $C_{254}H_{377}N_{65}O_{75}S_6$
Units	Monosaccharides (simple sugars, like glucose)	Glycerol + fatty acids	Amino acids
	These are the smallest units into which these three classes of food can be broken down by digestion (*hydrolysis*). The units can be reassembled into larger molecules again by *condensation*, e.g. when food needs to be stored (see Unit 7.5)		
Larger molecules	Disaccharides (2 units), e.g. sucrose, maltose		Dipeptides (*two* linked amino acids)
	Polysaccharides (thousands of units), e.g. starch, glycogen, cellulose		Polypeptides (*many*)

Table 5.4 *(continued)*

	Carbohydrates	Fats *(solids)*, oils *(liquid)*	Proteins
Chemical tests	**1** Blue **Benedict's** solution + **reducing sugar** $\xrightarrow{\text{brought to the boil}}$ *orange* precipitate **2** Brown **iodine** solution + **starch** $\xrightarrow{\text{must be cold}}$ *blue-black* **3** Clinistix + **glucose** $\xrightarrow{\text{cold}}$ mauve or *purple*	**1** The clear filtrate obtained from mixing **absolute ethanol** with crushed food, when added to an equal quantity of water, gives a *white emulsion* (cloudiness). **2 Translucency:** when warmed on paper, makes paper permanently translucent ('grease spot')	**1** Colourless 40% **NaOH** + protein extract, add 2 drops blue **CuSO₄** → *mauve* Biuret colour (**Biuret test**) **2 Albustix** and *some* proteins $\xrightarrow{\text{cold}}$ green or (usually) *blue-green*
Functions	**Energy supply** when respired: 17 kJ/g. Stored as *starch* (green plants) and *glycogen* (animals, fungi). Transported as sugars **Structural:** cellulose cell walls **Origin of other organic molecules:** e.g. sugar + nitrate → amino acid	**Energy supply** when respired: 39 kJ/g. (More energy per unit mass than glycogen) Important in flying, migrating and hibernating animals. **Heat insulation:** subcutaneous fat in mammals **Electrical insulation:** myelin sheathing nerve cell fibres **Waterproofing:** oils coat skin, fur, feathers **Buoyancy:** e.g. fish larvae in the sea	**Energy supply** when respired: 18 kJ/g. Important in carnivores, otherwise only respired extensively in starvation **Movement:** *muscles* contract; *tendons* connect muscles to bones; *ligaments* connect bone to bone at joints – all are protein **Catalysts:** *enzymes* make reactions of metabolism possible (see Unit 1.7) **Hormones** regulate metabolism (see Unit 13.9). Many, e.g. insulin, are protein

Examiner's tip

ne smallest units of each ood and their functions are ften asked about in exams.

5.6 Vitamins

Vitamins: organic substances (of a variety of kinds) required in *minute* amounts to maintain health of heterotrophs. Autotrophs make all they need.

Lack of a vitamin in the diet results in a *deficiency disease*, e.g. scurvy. A vitamin for one organism is not necessarily a vitamin for another, e.g. Man suffers scurvy from lack of vitamin C but rats do not because they synthesize their own.

Vitamins A and D are *fat soluble*, ingested in fats and oils.
Vitamin C is *water soluble* and present in other materials.

Table 5.5 Some vitamins

Vitamins	Good sources	Functions	Deficiency diseases
A	Vegetables, butter, egg yolk. Liver oils, e.g. cod-liver oil, contain both A and D	**1** Healthy epithelia **2** Part of 'visual purple' in rod cells of retina (Unit 12.3)	Susceptibility to *invasion by disease organisms* *Poor night vision*
D *'sunshine vitamin'*	Butter, egg yolk. (Can be synthesized in the skin from oils irradiated by ultraviolet light)	Regulation of calcium and phosphate absorption from gut and their deposition in bone	*Rickets:* poor bone formation, weak and often deformed, e.g. 'bow legs' in children
C	Citrus fruits, blackcurrants; fresh vegetables and milk	Healing of wounds; strong skin and capillaries	*Scurvy:* capillary bleeding; poor healing of wounds

Test for vitamin C: blue **DCPIP** solution is turned colourless by **vitamin C** solution (and by other reducing agents in foods as preservatives). DCPIP may turn red if acid foods are added but bleaching still occurs with vitamin C.

How much vitamin C in a food?
Find out the volume of liquidized food needed to decolourize a volume of DCPIP solution of known strength. Do the titration again with a standard vitamin C solution instead of food. By comparing the two volumes, the vitamin content of the liquid can be calculated.

5.7 Diet and health

A **balanced diet** is one that maintains health. It must provide enough of the following:

1. **Energy** from carbohydrates and fats when respired.
2. **Materials for growth and repair:**
   from proteins to make muscles, enzymes;
   from mineral salts to make bones, red blood cells.
3. **Vitamins** to help run metabolism.
4. **Water** to transport materials; provide a medium in which they react (see Unit 8.1).
5. **Fibre** (roughage) to help peristalsis (preventing constipation); helps prevent bowel cancer; and lowers cholesterol absorption.

Starvation refers to massive lack of food of all kinds.
Malnutrition refers to lack or excess of particular parts of the diet, e.g. *obesity* (fatness) results from excessive intake of energy foods – linked to heart disease. *Anorexia* (wasting away) results from not eating enough energy foods. See also mineral salt and vitamin deficiency diseases (Units 5.4, 5.6) and Kwashiorkor (lack of protein – see below).
Balanced diets differ according to *age* (the young require more protein and calcium), *occupation* (energy requirements and water intake to replace sweat differ), *climate* (less energy needed to keep body warm in tropics than in the Arctic) and *sex* (pregnant women need more iron and calcium for the baby's blood and bones). Males need more energy than women since they are usually larger.
Milk: Human milk supplies babies with enough water, protein, sugar (lactose), fat, minerals and vitamins. Cows' milk has much more protein (×3) and salts (×4) and less sugar. Young babies will vomit cows' milk if it has not been diluted and had sugar added. Some babies are allergic to cows' milk protein.

Quantity and quality of food is important for health:

1 Protein: made of 20 different amino acids, linked into chains. Of these 20, Man cannot make 8 and so must get them from food. Animal protein and SCP (see Unit 4.10) are rich in all of them: 'first class protein'. Plant protein is usually poor, deficient in some amino acids: 'second class protein'.
Kwashiorkor (wasting of limbs, puffiness of tissues and pot-belly full of fluid) results from lack of first class protein, e.g. in maize-eating Africans.
2 Fats: two kinds – saturated (plentiful in animal fats) and unsaturated (plentiful in plant oils). High intake of animal fats, e.g. butter, seems linked with *heart disease* (Unit 9.5). Margarines made from most plant oils seem safer.

Summary

1   Food can be simple (inorganic) or complex, containing carbon (organic).
2   Autotrophs (green plants) need only inorganic food, synthesizing it into organic compounds using sunlight energy trapped by chlorophyll.

3   Heterotrophs rely on organic compounds to provide their energy (by respiration).

4   Heterotrophs have two different ways of dealing with organic food – the animal (holozoic) way and the decay (saprophytic) way.

5   Water, carbon dioxide and various mineral salts are the food of plants (see also summary to Chapter 6).

6   Animals also need water, but a different range of mineral salts. However, their main requirements are carbohydrates, fats and proteins, with small amounts of vitamins.

7   Human diets are 'balanced' if they keep the person healthy.

8   The ideal diet changes with age, activity and climate.

Quick test 5

1   What is organic food?

2   What foods do autotrophs need?

3   Why cannot heterotrophs trap sunlight energy?

4   What metal is an important part of chlorophyll?

5   Where in a human would you expect to find (a) iron   (b) calcium (c) fluorine?

6   What human food gives most energy when respired?

7   What are vitamins?

8   What is kwashiorkor?

9   What chemical test identifies reducing sugars in food?

Chapter 6
Green plant nutrition

HOLOPHYTIC NUTRITION

Unique features: uses only inorganic food molecules to photosynthesize sugars and synthesize amino acids.

6.1 Photosynthesis

Photosynthesis makes sugars and the by-product oxygen from CO_2 and water, using the energy of sunlight, trapped by chlorophyll. Occurs in chloroplasts (see Unit 1.3). The simplest equation for photosynthesis is:

$$6CO_2 + 6H_2O \xrightarrow[\text{chlorophyll}]{\text{sunlight energy}} C_6H_{12}O_6 + 6O_2$$

carbon dioxide   water   glucose (energy-rich)   oxygen

Examiner's tip

This equation must be memorized.

6.2 Fate of glucose and oxygen

Glucose

(a) is converted to sucrose – for *transport* elsewhere

(b) is converted to starch – for *storage* in leaf (basis for leaf starch test). Starch is transported away by night as sucrose, for storage as starch in stems and roots. Being insoluble, starch does not cause swelling of storage cells by osmosis (as sugar storage would).

(c) is converted to cellulose of new *cell walls* at growing points

(d) is converted to oils for *storage* in some seeds

(e) is made into *amino acids*, then proteins (see Unit 6.8)

(f) is used in *respiration* to release energy for metabolism

Oxygen

Diffuses out of leaves to air or to water surrounding submerged plants. For evidence that it is oxygen see Fig. 6.1.

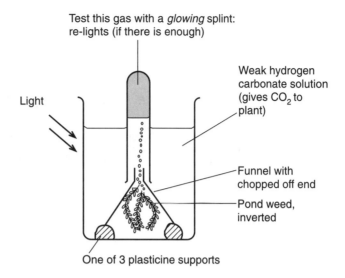

Fig. 6.1 Collecting and testing the gas from a pond weed

6.3 Factors necessary for photosynthesis

Evidence

Plant must be *de-starched* before any experiment by keeping it in the dark for 48 hours. A leaf must now be tested for starch (as a control). The presence of starch in the leaves at the end of the experiment is evidence of photosynthesis.

1 The starch test for leaves (Fig. 6.2)

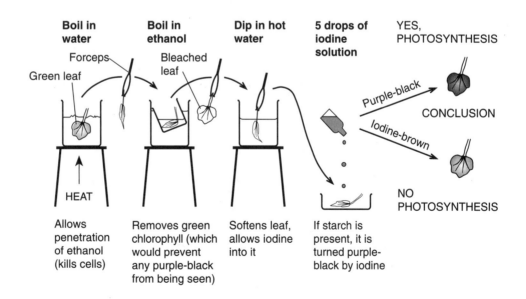

Fig. 6.2 Testing leaves for starch

2 Test the need for: ① Sunlight, ② Carbon dioxide, ③ Chlorophyll (Fig. 6.3)

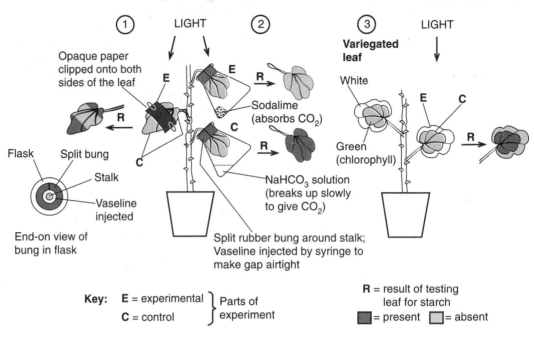

Fig. 6.3 Testing the need for ① sunlight, ② carbon dioxide, ③ chlorophyll in photosynthesis

3 Colour of light

If coloured light filters are placed over leaves (instead of opaque paper as in ①) and after some hours in light the leaves are starch-tested, only red and blue lights give starch. Chlorophyll can only use *red* and *blue* light in the spectrum – green is reflected: hence leaves are green. Less than 5% of the sun's energy is used in photosynthesis.

6.4 Rate of photosynthesis

Rate of photosynthesis in a water plant, e.g. *Elodea*, can be estimated by counting the *number of bubbles* per unit time coming from a cut stem. Alternatively, trap bubbles and measure *volume* per unit time in a capillary tube (see Fig. 6.4).

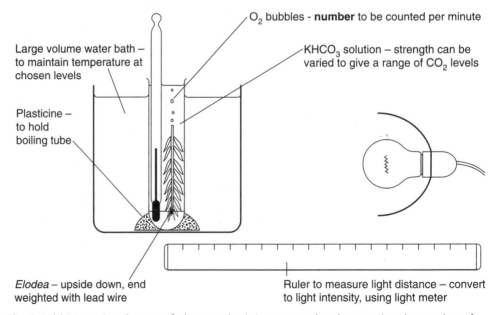

Fig. 6.4 (a) Measuring the rate of photosynthesis in a water plant by counting the number of bubbles released per minute

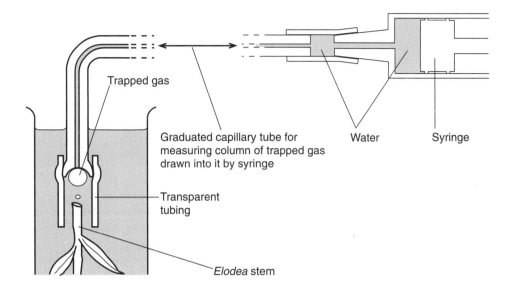

Fig. 6.4 (b) Measuring the rate of photosynthesis in a water plant by measuring the volume of gas evolved per minute

6.5 Limiting factors

In a physiological process (such as photosynthesis) any factor which is in short supply, so that it reduces the rate of the process from its possible maximum, is said to be the limiting factor. Thus with plants photosynthesizing outdoors, *light* is limiting at dusk; *carbon dioxide* (CO_2) during most of the day; *water* probably never. *Temperature* can also be limiting (too cold – reactions too slow; too hot – denatures enzymes). *Factors closing stomata* are limiting by reducing flow of CO_2 into leaf. *Lack of magnesium (Mg)* in soil limits the amount of chlorophyll made in the leaf (see Fig. 6.5). Crops grown in commercial greenhouses avoid natural limiting factors: extra lighting, controlled warmth and air enriched with extra CO_2 (See Unit 22.5)

On the graph below, at each plateau a factor is limiting photosynthesis.

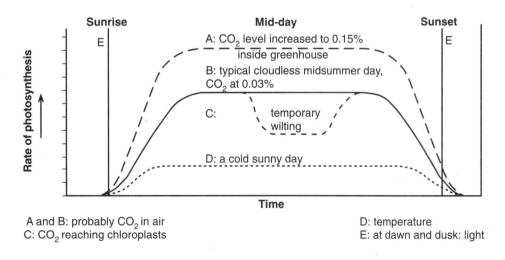

Fig. 6.5 Limiting factors for photosynthesis

6.6 Leaf structure and photosynthesis

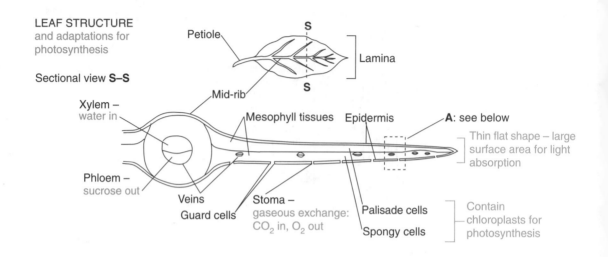

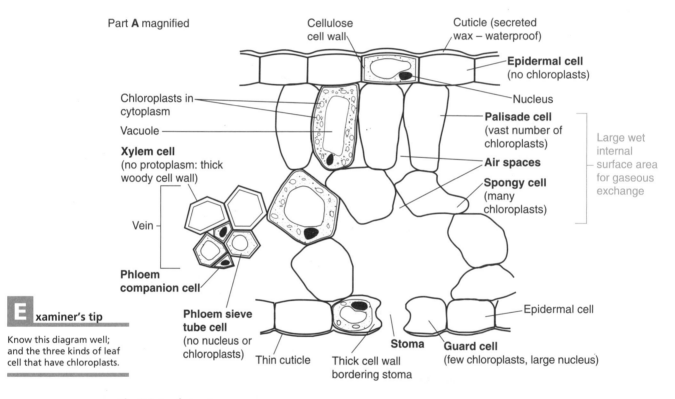

Fig 6.6 Leaf structure

6.7 Gaseous exchange in leaves

By night, leaves only respire: CO_2 out, O_2 in.

By day, they photosynthesize: CO_2 in, O_2 out. However, they also respire. But more sugars are made (by photosynthesis) than are broken down (by respiration).

At dawn and dusk (very little light) the two processes break even – the *compensation point*. This point can be determined by using the apparatus shown in Fig. 6.7, changing the distance of the light from the plant until the indicator remains orange – as in a corked control tube.

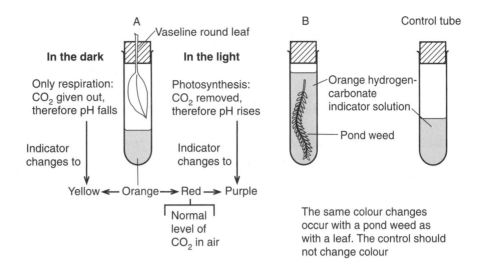

Fig. 6.7 Determining gaseous exchange: A in a leaf, B in a water plant using hydrogencarbonate indicator

6.8 Amino acid synthesis

Dependent on photosynthesis.
Nitrates combine with sugar products to form amino acids.
Green plants alone can do this, at root and shoot tips (growing regions).
Amino acids are converted to form protein (see Unit 7.1).
Chlorophyll is a protein with a magnesium compound linked to it.

6.9 Mineral salt uptake by roots

Absorption of salts
Mainly at root tips.
Partly at root hair region (see Fig. 17.1).
Mainly by active transport and thus oxygen is needed. Partly by diffusion (see Unit 8.2).
Quite independent of water uptake by osmosis (see Unit 8.4).

Evidence of need for salts
Plants are grown with roots in salt solutions ('water culture').
Control solution contains all salts needed (see Table 5.2).
Test solutions each omit one element, e.g. −N = omit nitrates; −S = omit sulphates.
Solutions aerated to allow efficient salt uptake.

In the experiment in Fig. 6.8, growth of test plants can be compared against control plants: harvest them, dry in oven at 110 °C, weigh. To avoid the possibility that some seedlings grow more vigorously than others because of *genetic* differences, the plants should be from the same clone, e.g. cuttings of the same plant.

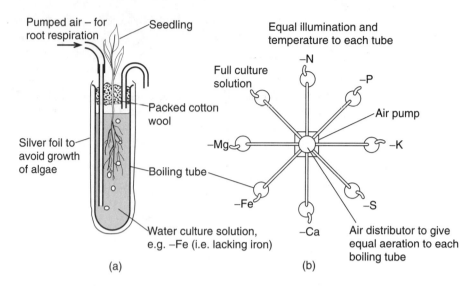

Fig. 6.8 Water culture experiment to determine the mineral salt requirements of a plant: (a) side view of one tube, (b) plan view of experiment

6.10 Energy and life

The sun radiates waves of energy to the earth. Some waves have a short wavelength, e.g. X-rays, others have a long wavelength, e.g. radio waves. This range of wavelengths is known as the **electromagnetic spectrum**. Only the shorter waves have any known biological importance (Table 6.1).

The *light* energy trapped by plants is stored as *chemical* energy in bonds of organic compounds, e.g. glucose and ATP. As glucose is broken down during respiration, energy is released for movement, so providing *mechanical* energy, but much is wasted as *heat*. Thus, energy that came into living things as light may be converted into a variety of other forms of energy.

Too much heat energy may kill organisms. It may be lost by *conduction, convection, radiation* and by *evaporation* of water. However, too little heat may also kill, so it may be kept in by *insulation* (see Units 11.6 and 11.7).

Table 6.1

Wavelength		700 nm				360 nm
Type of wave	Infrared		Visible light			Ionizing radiations
		Red Orange	Yellow Green	Blue Violet		Ultraviolet, X-rays, γ-rays
Effect	Heat		Trapped in photosynthesis			Can cause mutations
	(see Unit 11.6)		(see Unit 6.1)			(see Unit 18.16)

Summary

1   Green plants need carbon dioxide and water to make carbohydrate (initially sugars) and the by-product oxygen. This process, called photosynthesis, needs light.

2   Only red, (white) and blue lights can be used by chlorophyll for photosynthesis.

3   Sugars can be made into starch (for storage), cellulose (for cell walls) or be used in respiration (to provide energy).

4   Sugars can also be made into oils, or into amino acids and then proteins, with the help of mineral salts (especially nitrates).

5   Other substances can be made from sugars with the help of mineral salts, e.g. chlorophyll (needing magnesium) and DNA (needing phosphates and nitrates).

6   Any of the three factors light, temperature and carbon dioxide can become a limiting factor to photosynthesis – when its scarcity prevents a higher rate of photosynthesis. Water is usually not a limiting factor.

7   The starch test (iodine turns starch blue-black) is used to show whether photosynthesis has taken place in a leaf.

8   Hydrogencarbonate indicator solution can be used to show changes in the rate of both photosynthesis and respiration in living organisms, changing from red in ordinary air to yellow if carbon dioxide is being produced (respiration) and to purple if it is being removed (photosynthesis).

9   The leaf is a structure well adapted to photosynthesis by its shape, internal anatomy and the presence of chlorophyll.

10 The electromagnetic spectrum can be both helpful (light, heat) and harmful (UV and γ rays) to organisms.

Quick test 6

1   Write the equation for photosynthesis in words.

2   How is starch formed in leaves?

3   When a leaf is tested for starch, what reagent removes chlorophyll?

4   If you wanted to test whether chlorophyll is needed for photosynthesis, what kind of plant would you use?

5   Which colours of the spectrum are useful in photosynthesis?

6   What is a 'limiting factor' in photosynthesis?

7   Which cells in a leaf contain chloroplasts?

8   By what routes do the raw materials for photosynthesis reach the leaf?

9   What two chemicals are needed to make amino acids?

10 What processes obtain mineral salts for a plant from the soil?

Chapter 7
Animal nutrition

HOLOZOIC NUTRITION

Features: organic food is ingested into a gut, digested to form absorbable products and the wastes are egested.

7.1 Digestion and its consequences

Food is **ingested** via the mouth into a gut. Exceptions: parasites, e.g. tapeworm which bathes in food in the gut of its host absorbing it through its skin.

In the gut, food is **digested** in two ways:

(a) *physically* – by chewing or grinding (important in herbivores), stomach churning and peristalsis. This increases the surface area of food, making it easier for (b) below.

(b) *chemically* – by enzymes (see Unit 1.7) which hydrolyse large molecules into their small basic units (see Unit 5.5). Without this, large insoluble food molecules would not be small enough to be **absorbed** through the membranes of gut cells: e.g.

$$\text{starch} + \text{water} \xrightarrow[\text{enzymes}]{\text{carbohydrase}} \text{monosaccharides}$$
$$\text{fat} + \text{water} \xrightarrow[\text{enzymes}]{\text{lipase}} \text{fatty acids} + \text{glycerol}$$
$$\text{protein} + \text{water} \xrightarrow[\text{enzymes}]{\text{protease}} \text{amino acids}$$

$\left. \right\}$ these molecules are now soluble and small enough for absorption

Absorbed food is then **assimilated** (used or stored) into the body. Storage occurs when enzymes condense the small units of foods into large molecules (reverse of hydrolysis). For example:

$$\text{amino acids} \xrightarrow[\text{enzymes}]{\text{condensing}} \text{protein} + \text{water}$$

Indigestible food is **egested** (eliminated) through the anus or equivalent. Most animals have no enzymes to digest cellulose – hence special adaptations of herbivores. Mammal *faeces* include egested fibre, bacteria, mucus, dead cells and water, and excreted bile pigments (see Fig. 7.8).

A model of digestion and absorption is shown in Fig. 7.1. Four sacs of Visking containing different solutions are placed in distilled water (the saliva must not contain sugar from sweets.). After 30 minutes the water in the four tubes outside the Visking is tested for starch and for reducing sugar.

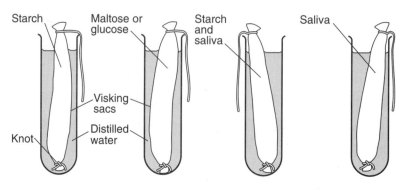

Fig. 7.1 A model of digestion and absorption

Results of tests on water outside the Visking in the 4 tubes in Fig. 7.1:

Benedict's test (Table 5.4)	−	+	+	−
Iodine test (Table 5.4)	−	−	−	−

The model 'gut' is Visking membrane, known to allow small molecules (sugar) but not large ones (starch) through its pores.

The enzyme in saliva turns starch into maltose. Maltose is turned into glucose in the gut (see 'villi', Fig. 7.6).

Conclusions: **1** Sugars, but not starch, pass through Visking pores
               2 Saliva turns starch into sugar

7.2 Experiments with digestive enzymes

Examiner's tip

Remember - enzymes are not living so they cannot be killed. They are destroyed or denatured.

Examiner's tip

This section may be useful to you when you are planning investigations.

Each enzyme works best at a certain temperature and pH (these are its 'optimum' conditions). Outside these conditions enzymes may cease to work or may even be destroyed.

Example 1: Investigating the effect of temperature on digestion of starch by salivary amylase

Method:
1 Add 5 cm^3 of 1% starch solution to each of 5 boiling tubes and 1 cm^3 of saliva diluted with water to 4 test-tubes as shown in Fig. 7.2.
2 Leave the starch and the enzyme for at least 2 minutes, to gain the temperature of the water bath.

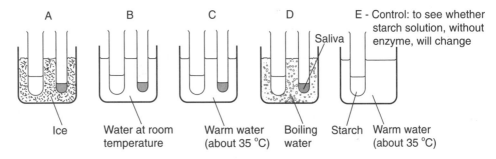

Fig. 7.2

3 Pour the saliva into the boiling tube next to it, so mixing it with the starch. Note the time immediately.
4 Using a separate dropper for each tube, test one drop from each boiling tube with iodine solution, as shown in Fig. 7.3.

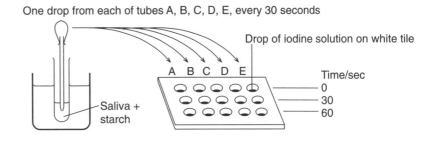

Fig. 7.3

5 Note the time when each drop no longer turns the iodine solution blue-black (i.e. starch is digested). Do not test for longer than 15 minutes.

Possible results:

A – still blue-black after 15 minutes   D – still blue-black after 15 minutes
B – changes to brown at 8 minutes   E – still blue-black after 15 minutes
C – changes to brown at 2 minutes

6 Now put the boiling tubes from A and D into the warm water bath C and test them with iodine solution after 5 minutes (once only).

Results:

A – brown colour   D – blue-black

Conclusions:

1 Digestion proceeds faster at warm temperatures than at cold (A, B, C).
2 At low temperatures, the enzyme is inactive but not destroyed (A, step **6**).
3 At water's boiling point, the enzyme is destroyed (D, step **6**).

Example 2: Investigating the effect of pH on digestion of egg albumen (protein) by pepsin

Method:

1 Put in each of 6 tubes a 5 mm cube of cooked egg white and a thymol crystal (to prevent bacteria digesting the egg). Then add 2 cm^3 of 0.1M solutions to affect the pH as shown in Fig. 7.4.

Fig. 7.4

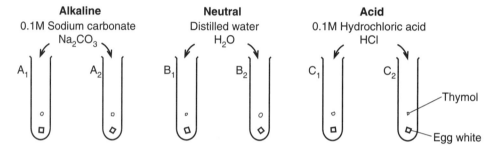

2 Add 2 cm^3 pepsin solution to A$_1$, B$_1$ and C$_1$, but not to A$_2$, B$_2$ and C$_2$ (which are controls used to see whether Na$_2$CO$_3$, water and HCl alone digest egg white).
3 Incubate the tubes in a warm place (about 35 °C) for 24 hours and then look at the cubes.

Results:

Not digested:
in tubes A$_1$, A$_2$, B$_2$, C$_2$
Sharp edges

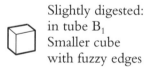

Slightly digested:
in tube B$_1$
Smaller cube
with fuzzy edges

Totally digested:
in tube C$_1$
Cube absent

Conclusion: pepsin requires acid conditions to digest cooked albumen.

7.3 Mammal alimentary canal

The normal passage of food is illustrated in Fig. 7.5.

Abnormal passage of food:

1 **Vomiting:** strong contraction of stomach fountains the food, containing toxins, too much salt, etc., out of mouth.

2 **Diarrhoea:** irritation of villi causes too much mucus and intestinal juice secretion. Sweeps out harmful microorganisms, e.g. cholera in liquid faeces.

The resulting dehydration of the body can kill, especially the very young or old.
Oral rehydration therapy involves dissolving the right amount of salts and glucose in the right volume of water and drinking it. Drinking water alone, in quantity, can kill.

3 **Constipation:** waste can be solidified too much by colon: hard faeces can cause bleeding. Roughage (fibre) in diet helps prevent this.

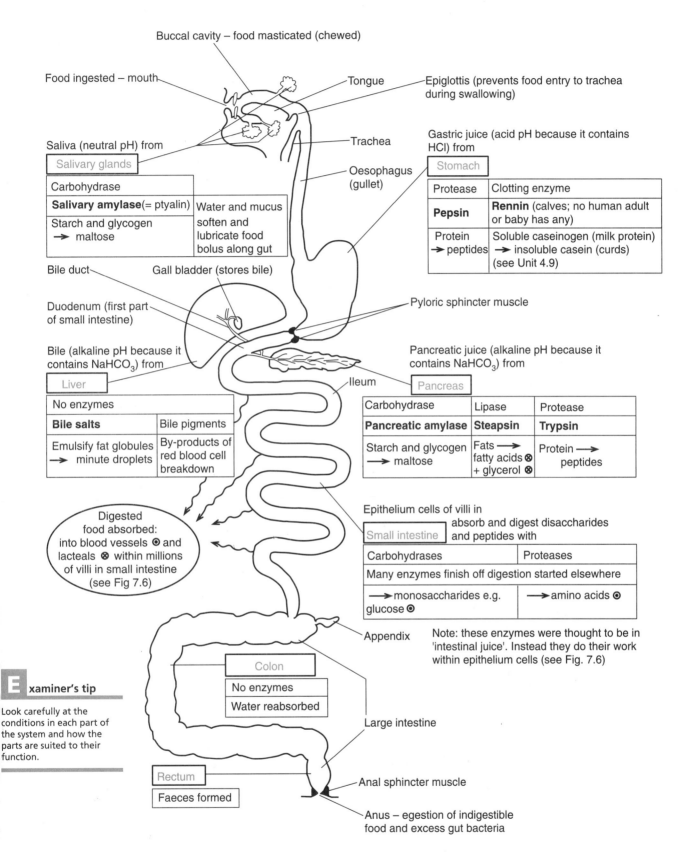

Fig. 7.5 Treatment of food from mouth to anus in mammals (based on Man)

7.4 Absorption of food at a villus and peristalsis

Millions of villi lining the small intestine provide a large surface area for absorption into blood and lymph.

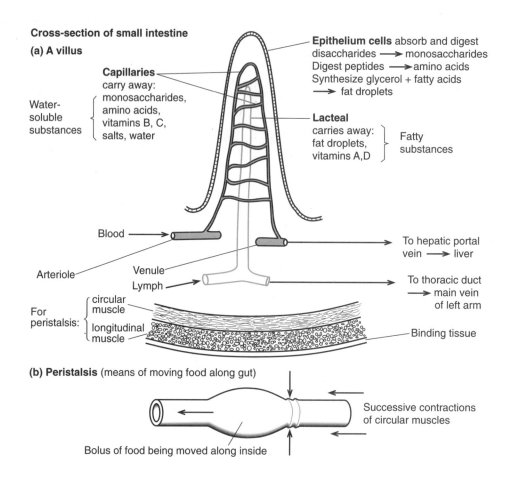

Fig. 7.6 (a) Enlarged longitudinal section of a villus; (b) Peristalsis

7.5 Storage of food

1. Monosaccharides, e.g. glucose: turned into glycogen for storage in liver and muscles; excess converted to fats stored under skin.
2. Fatty substances: stored in liver (including vitamins A, D) and under skin.
3. Amino acids: used immediately in growth and repair. *Not* stored; excess deaminated in liver (see Unit 7.6).

7.6 The liver

A large organ, concerned with homeostasis by metabolizing food and poisons and removing unwanted cells. Stores foods and blood. Receives blood from two sources (Fig. 7.7); discharges bile.

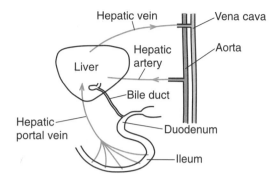

Fig. 7.7 The liver and its blood supply

- Stores *glucose* as glycogen, turning it back to glucose when needed. This is under the control of three hormones which keep the *blood level* of glucose constant (see Unit 13.10).
- Deaminates *excess amino acids* to give two parts:
  - (*a*) nitrogen-containing part (amine) becomes urea – excreted by kidneys;
  - (*b*) remainder (the acid) can be respired to give energy.
- Stores *iron* from worn-out red blood cells, which it breaks down, excreting *bile pigments* in the process.
- Makes *poisons* harmless, e.g. ethanol drunk or toxins from gut bacteria.
- Makes *bile salts* which emulsify fats in the intestine.

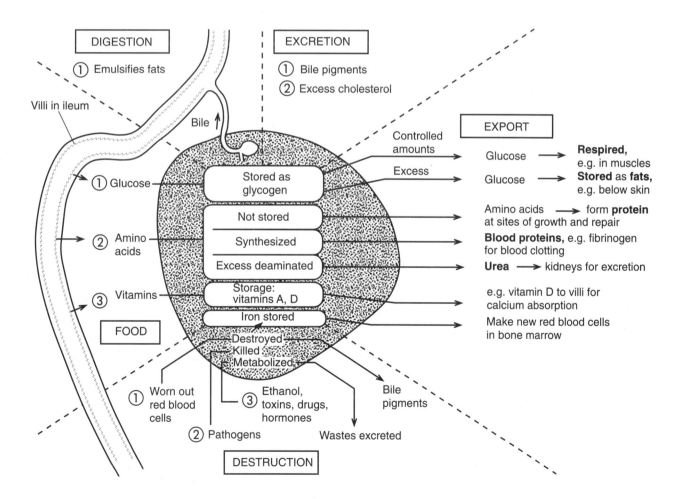

Fig. 7.8 The liver's five roles

7.7 Mammal teeth

Mammals are the only vertebrate group with *differentiated* teeth (four types with special uses):

1. **I**ncisors – for biting off food
2. **C**anines – for stabbing, holding prey
3. **Prem**olars – for grinding
4. **M**olars – for grinding

First set of teeth are shed ('milk teeth'): 20, made up of 8 **I**, 4 **C**, 8 **Pm** in Man.
Adult set includes 'wisdoms' (back molars): 32, made up of 20 larger replacements and 12 **M**.
Structure of teeth: layers of modified bone nourished from pulp cavity and shaped according to function (Fig. 7.9).

Examiner's tip

Remember to relate the shape of the tooth to its function.

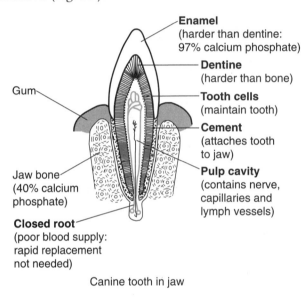

Canine tooth in jaw

Fig. 7.9 Vertical section through a tooth

7.8 Dental health

1 Growing healthy teeth need:

- food rich in *calcium* (Unit 5.4) and *vitamin D* to help in its absorption (Unit 5.6);
- *fluoride* from fluoridated water or toothpaste to harden enamel.

2 Maintaining healthy teeth requires controlling the bacteria around teeth by *dental hygiene*. There are two main dental diseases:

- *Caries* (holes in teeth) results from bacteria turning sugars into acids. Acids dissolve enamel, allowing bacteria to rot dentine.
- *Periodontal disease* (teeth fall out) results from bacteria entering space between tooth and unhealthy gums. They rot fibres holding teeth in socket.

Dental Hygiene

- *Rinse mouth with water* to remove sugars, after meals (or sweets).
- *Brush teeth* with fluoride toothpaste, especially before sleep, to remove food particles and bacteria. These form 'plaque' – a coating stuck to teeth – if left. Disclosing tablets stain it red.
- *Massage gums* by eating crisp foods and as part of tooth-brushing to keep them healthy. This prevents exposure of neck and root of tooth to bacteria.
- *Orthodontic treatment* improves hygiene by uncrowding teeth, making them easier to keep clean.

Summary

1 Animals ingest, digest and absorb food, egesting what is indigestible.
2 Feeding is followed by digestion inside a gut.
3 Digestion is the breaking down of food to molecules small enough to be absorbed through the gut wall.
4 Enzymes catalyse these breakdowns. They are affected by temperature and pH in their work.
5 Carbohydrases turn starch into simple sugars, lipases turn fats and oils into glycerol and fatty acids, and proteases turn protein into amino acids.
6 Teeth are specialized pieces of bone designed to break food up, so as to give a larger surface area for enzymes to act upon.
7 Digested food is absorbed via villi in the small intestine and most of it passes to the liver.
8 The liver processes food, directing it to where it is needed, via the blood.
9 The liver stores excess carbohydrate as glycogen, helps emulsify fats in the intestine by means of bile, and takes a hand in producing urea, bile pigments and cholesterol for excretion.
10 Foods that cannot be digested, such as cellulose (fibre), and excess bacteria are egested through the anus after reabsorption of much water in the colon.

Quick test 7

1 After food has been ingested by a human what processes, in sequence, then take place?
2 What do bile salts do, and where?
3 Name three factors which affect the rate at which enzymes break down food.
4 What products of digestion are absorbed by the small intestine and the large intestine?
5 What problems for the body do excessive vomiting and diarrhoea cause?
6 How does fibre help peristalsis?
7 Give three functions of the liver.
8 Describe the three shapes of teeth in Man and explain the function of each type of tooth.
9 What is needed in the mouth cavity to cause tooth decay?
10 Why do herbivores have a lot of large molar teeth?

Chapter 8

Water uptake and loss and food transport in plants

8.1 Importance of water

Water makes up two-thirds or more of living active cells.
Water covers two-thirds of the globe – a very important habitat for organisms.

- **It is a solvent:**
  - (*a*) all *reactions* of metabolism occur in solution.
  - (*b*) foods, hormones, etc. are *transported* in solution (in blood, sap).

- **It is a reactant:**
  - (*a*) with CO_2 during *photosynthesis*.
  - (*b*) in *hydrolysis* reactions, e.g. digestion.

- **It is a coolant:**
  - (*a*) *absorbs a lot of heat* without much change in temperature, thus keeping habitats like the sea relatively stable in temperature.
  - (*b*) *removes a lot of heat* when evaporated, keeping bodies cool, e.g. in sweating, transpiration.

- **It provides support:**
  - (*a*) aquatic organisms need less strong skeletons than land organisms because water's '*buoyancy effect*' (*Archimedes force*) makes them 'lighter'.
  - (*b*) turgor pressure in plant cells supports leaves and herbaceous plant stems; without it they wilt.

- **It is a lubricant:**
  E.g. synovial fluid in joints (see Unit 14.7); mucus in guts.

Examiner's tip

Notice how very important water is to life.

8.2 Diffusion

Substances move into cells by:

1 **Diffusion** (gases and liquids)   2 **Active transport**

xaminer's tip

efinitions of diffusion,
mosis and active transport
e often asked: understand
eir importance in life.

Diffusion is a random movement of gases or substances in solution from where they are more concentrated (A) to where they are less concentrated (B). The difference in concentration between A and B is called the **concentration gradient** (Fig. 8.1).

The rate of diffusion increases:
(*a*) the greater the difference in concentration
(*b*) the warmer the temperature

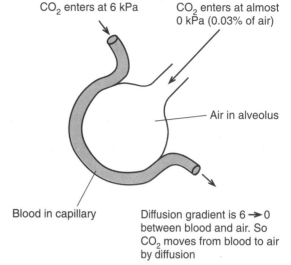

Fig. 8.1 Diffusion of carbon dioxide (CO_2) in the alveolus of a lung

When diffusion plays a large part in a biological process, the organs concerned, e.g. leaf, lung, have a large surface area (see Unit 10.6).

8.3 Active transport

Active transport is a selective movement of molecules or ions across living cell membranes. This requires energy from respiration in the cell concerned. The molecules or ions usually move *up* a concentration gradient. For example, mineral salts in *low* concentration in soil may still be absorbed into root cells where their concentration is *higher*.

Table 8.1 Comparison of diffusion and active transport

Diffusion	Active transport
Not selective	Selective (cell absorbs only what it needs)
Substances move only down a concentration gradient	Substances move in even *against* a concentration gradient
Living membrane not essential	Living membrane essential
Cell provides no energy	Respiration provides energy for absorption

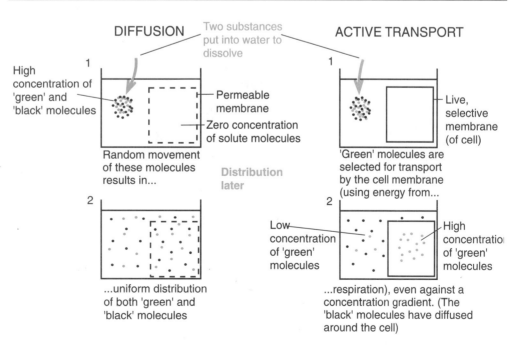

Fig. 8.2 Diffusion contrasted with active transport

8.4 Osmosis

Osmosis is the diffusion of water *only*, through a selectively permeable membrane, from where *water is in high concentration* (a weak solution) to where *water is in low concentration* (a strong solution) (Fig. 8.3).

   Requires *no* respiration (cf. active uptake of salts in roots).

   Requires *live* cell membrane for osmosis to occur in cells, but will happen with suitable nonliving membranes (e.g. Visking dialysing membrane).

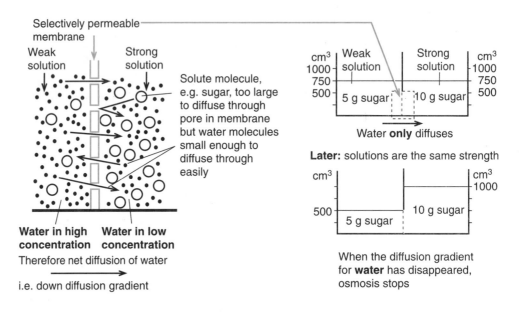

Fig. 8.3 Osmosis

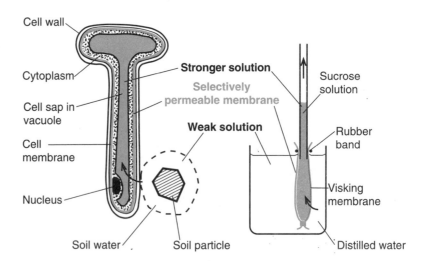

Fig. 8.4 Comparison of osmosis in a living cell (root hair) and a nonliving system

Cells prevent continued flow of water into them (which would burst them) by **osmoregulating** (see Unit 8.5 and Fig. 8.7).

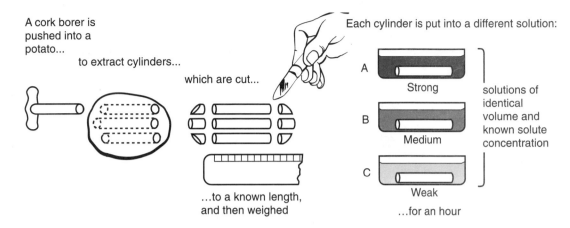

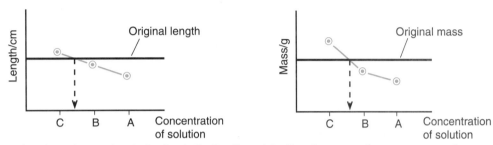

At the point where the graph cuts the line indicating the *original* length or mass the average osmotic potential of potato cells may be read off (see ↓). If this strength of solution were to be prepared, the potato cylinders should neither increase nor decrease in length or mass, i.e. no osmosis would occur

Fig. 8.5 Experiment to determine the concentration of the solution inside potato tissue

8.5 Osmosis in cells

Plant cells

Cells, in nature, fluctuate between being flaccid and fully turgid. However, plasmolysis is relatively rare (except in experiments) and will result in the cell's death if it is prolonged, e.g. when the cell suffers prolonged drying (Fig. 8.6). Such changes may be seen down a microscope when strips of rhubarb epidermis are mounted in strong, medium and weak solutions on three different slides.

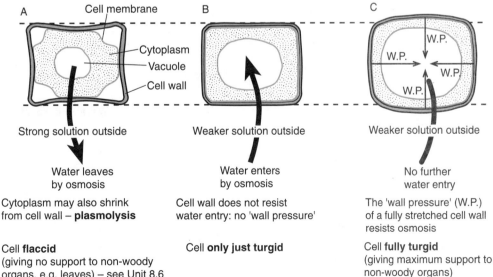

Fig. 8.6 Osmosis in plant cells

75

Animal cells

Red blood cells will burst in freshwater and shrink in strong solutions. They rely on the kidneys to keep the plasma at the right concentration (see Unit 11.2).

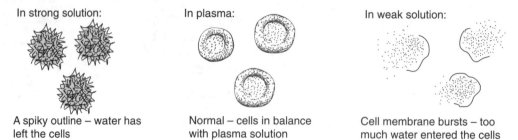

In strong solution:

A spiky outline – water has left the cells

In plasma:

Normal – cells in balance with plasma solution

In weak solution:

Cell membrane bursts – too much water entered the cells

Fig. 8.7 Osmosis in red blood cells

8.6 Water uptake and loss in flowering plants

❶ **Leaves and green stems** are waterproofed by a waxy *cuticle*, but most keep open *stomata* to get CO_2 for photosynthesis. Through stomata, **transpiration** (the loss of water vapour via the aerial parts of a plant) occurs. This creates a *suction upward* of water from below.

❷ **Old stems and roots** are waterproofed with cork (or bark). Their xylem allows passage of water. Some water loss occurs via *lenticels* (pores in bark).

❸ **Young roots** – particularly *root hair* region – absorb water by osmosis. This continues owing to suction generated by transpiration.

If soil water supply dries up, leaf cells become flaccid (see Unit 8.5) and the leaf **wilts**. Only *after* this will guard cells become flaccid, closing stomata, thus conserving water but also stopping photosynthesis (see Unit 6.5 and Fig. 8.7).

Examiner's tip

Notice how transpiration in leaves promotes osmosis in roots.

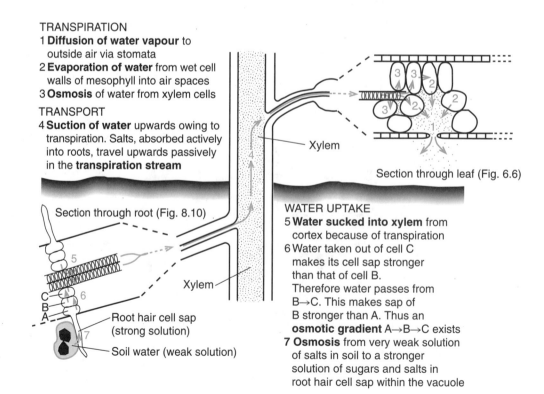

TRANSPIRATION
1 **Diffusion of water vapour** to outside air via stomata
2 **Evaporation of water** from wet cell walls of mesophyll into air spaces
3 **Osmosis** of water from xylem cells

TRANSPORT
4 **Suction of water** upwards owing to transpiration. Salts, absorbed actively into roots, travel upwards passively in the **transpiration stream**

Xylem

Section through leaf (Fig. 6.6)

Section through root (Fig. 8.10)

Xylem

C
B
A

Root hair cell sap (strong solution)

Soil water (weak solution)

WATER UPTAKE
5 **Water sucked into xylem** from cortex because of transpiration
6 Water taken out of cell C makes its cell sap stronger than that of cell B. Therefore water passes from B→C. This makes sap of B stronger than A. Thus an **osmotic gradient** A→B→C exists
7 **Osmosis** from very weak solution of salts in soil to a stronger solution of sugars and salts in root hair cell sap within the vacuole

Fig. 8.8 Water uptake, transport and loss in a flowering plant

8.7 Guard cells and stomata

Guard cells are kidney-shaped green cells found in pairs in the epidermis ('skin') of leaves and green stems. The pore between them is a **stoma** (plural: **stomata**). This appears when guard cells are turgid; disappears when they are flaccid.

Stomata normally open by day (permitting transpiration and gaseous exchange – CO_2 in, O_2 out) and shut at night.

Lack of water to plants causes wilting and the closing of stomata. Rough handling of leaves, e.g. by buffeting wind also causes stomata to close.

Determining whether conditions around the leaf affect the opening and closing of stomata:

A film of nail varnish or stencil-correcting fluid painted onto a non-hairy leaf can be peeled off with forceps when dry (30 sec). Under the microscope the dried film bears impressions of stomata. The number open can be recorded, e.g. '5/20' for the 20 stomata observed.

Films from the *same* plant leaf after being in different conditions (e.g. of light, dark, CO_2, wind and temperature) can be compared. One condition should be changed at a time.

Different species of plant can behave differently.

8.8 Transpiration

Transpiration is the loss of water vapour through the aerial parts of a plant. It occurs
(i)   mainly through open stomata
(ii)   through waxy cuticle (a small amount)
Functions:
(i)   provides a means of transporting salts upward in xylem
(ii)   cools the leaf heated by the sun, by evaporation (cf. sweating).

Factors raising transpiration rate (opposite conditions lower the rate)

❶ **High temperature** – provides more energy to evaporate water.

❷ **Low humidity** – greater diffusion gradient between air inside leaf spaces and the drier air outside.

❸ **Sunlight** – causes stomata to open, usually.

❹ **Wind** – removes water molecules as fast as they arrive outside stomata, thereby maintaining high diffusion rate. Water vapour is also 'pumped out' due to bending and unbending of leaf. (Severe buffeting by wind actually closes stomata, reducing transpiration.)

Measurement of transpiration rate
(Temperature, humidity and wind must be recorded.)

❶ **Weighing** – a leaf, or cut shoot, in a test-tube of water covered by oil; or a whole pot plant, the pot and soil sealed off in a polythene bag.

❷ **Cobalt chloride** – blue when anhydrous (dry), turns pink when hydrated (moist). Thus dry blue cobalt chloride paper, taped to upper and lower leaf surfaces, green stems and bark-covered stems turns pink with moisture of transpiration. Timing how long it takes compares rates.

E **xaminer's tip**

These factors all speed up evaporation - which is what transpiration is based upon. Know them.

③ **Potometer** – measures water uptake (not loss) of a cut shoot (a little of the water is used in photosynthesis). Change *one* condition at a time to determine which factor has greatest effect.

Note: light and dark affect opening and closing of stomata. Light may also have a heating effect.

Allow time for plant to adjust to new conditions before taking new measurement of rate.

Never allow air to get into cut end of shoot (air bubbles block the xylem) – cut shoot under water, and keep the cut wet (Fig. 8.9).

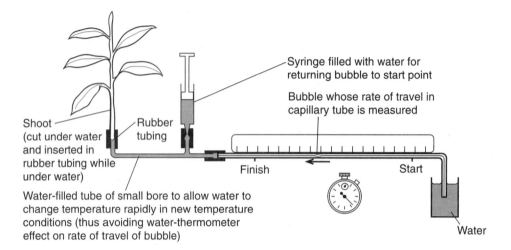

Fig. 8.9 A potometer in action

Evidence for pathway of water in a stem

If cross-sections of a stem are taken 30 minutes after putting a leafy shoot in red ink, only the xylem is stained red (Fig. 8.10). The xylem of a stem in water, used as a control, does not become red.

8.9 Transport of organic food

Flows through **phloem** sieve tube cells in bark (see Fig. 8.11). Flow rate is affected by temperature, available oxygen, poisons – this suggests a mechanism involving *living* cells. Mechanism not fully understood.

Flows both *upwards and downwards*. Photosynthesized sugars are transported as sucrose (see Unit 5.5) from leaves *up* to stem tips (for growth); to fruits and seeds (for storage as starch); *down* to root tips (for growth); and to or from storage organs, e.g. tubers (see Unit 15.2).

Evidence for pathway of organic food

- **Ring barking:** sugars accumulate where bark ends (due to cutting).

- **Tracers:** radioactive $^{14}CO_2$ supplied to a photosynthesizing leaf becomes part of sucrose (or other organic molecules). Cross-sections of stems below such leaves, when placed next to photographic film (for a week in a refrigerator), will become exposed only where there is phloem (see Fig. 8.10). Control film remains unexposed. This shows that radioactive sucrose is transported in phloem.

- **Systemic insecticides** when sprayed onto leaves are absorbed by them and pass to the phloem. Insects, e.g. aphids, sucking out the sugary sap, are thus poisoned.

8.10 Tissues in the stem and root

Fig. 8.10 Cross-sections of young stem and root of a flowering plant

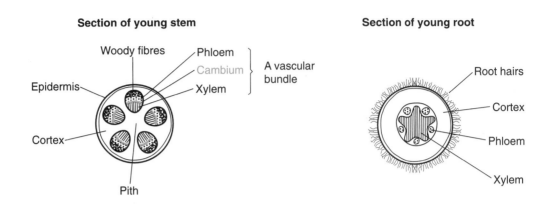

Epidermis: waterproof outer 'skin' of waxed non-green cells – and some guard cells (see leaf: Fig. 6.6).

Root hairs: water-absorbing cells having a large surface area (see Fig. 8.4).

Cortex and pith: large cells capable of storing food, e.g. starch
Cambium: cells that can divide to cause growth in diameter
Woody fibres: give strength in the wind
Xylem vessels (also woody): (*a*) give strength
(*b*) transport water and mineral salts *upward*
Phloem sieve tubes: transport sugars and amino acids *up and down*
(These cells/tissues are common to both stem and root)

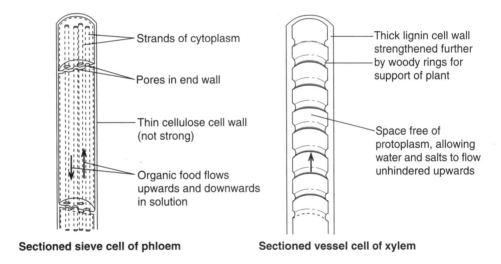

Fig. 8.11 The structure of cells conducting food in xylem and phloem

Summary

1 Life as we know it could not exist without water – as a solvent, reactant, coolant, support-giver and lubricant.

2 Substances move into and out of cells by diffusion or by active transport.

3 Diffusion is a slow, random process, occurring along a concentration gradient.

4   Diffusion of water across a selectively permeable membrane is called osmosis.

5   Organisms have to guard against osmosis by a variety of means to avoid bursting their cells, but also use it to their advantage, losing excess water by evaporation and urination.

6   Transpiration, the evaporation of water from the aerial parts of plants is useful because it cools the plant and is ultimately responsible for the uptake of water through the roots.

7   The transpiration stream provides an upward transport flow of mineral salts in the xylem.

8   The phloem transports manufactured food, e.g. sucrose, both up and down the plant, using methods that involve metabolism.

9   Active transport is the absorption or secretion of substances from cells using energy from respiration, often against a concentration gradient.

Quick test 8

1   Give three reasons why water is important to organisms.

2   Define diffusion.

3   Give three features of active transport that contrast with diffusion.

4   What part of a root hair cell (a) contains a 'strong' solution   (b) is selectively permeable?

5   What is a turgid cell?

6   Where does water enter and leave a plant during transpiration?

7   What factors increase the rate of transpiration?

8   What cells transport sugars throughout the plant?

9   What makes xylem vessels unusual as cells?

10   What stops our body cells from bursting when we have drunk a lot?

Chapter 9
Blood and lymphatic systems

9.1 Functions of blood systems

The need for blood pumped to cells by a heart

Animals are more active than plants and diffusion would be too slow to supply cells with their needs and remove their wastes. A more *rapid transport system* is necessary to prevent them from dying.

Functions of blood systems

1. Supply **foods** – sugars, fats, amino acids, vitamins, salts, water.
2. Supply **oxygen** – (exception: insects – oxygen direct to cells at tracheoles).
3. Supply **hormones** – chemical 'messages' controlling metabolism and development (see Unit 13.9).
4. Supply **white blood cells** for defence against invading organisms.
5. Supply **clotting materials** – to stop loss of blood at wounds.
6. Remove **wastes** – CO_2 and nitrogenous wastes, e.g. urea.
7. Carry **heat** – either away from cells, e.g. muscle, to cool them, or to cells needing to be warmed up, e.g. during 'sunning' of lizards.

9.2 Mammal blood and other body fluids

Blood consists of:

(*a*) **plasma**, a straw-coloured liquid (90% water, 10% dissolved substances);
(*b*) **cells**, a variety of kinds (see Table 9.1).

Exact composition of blood depends on location in the body (see Unit 9.6) and on health. Human body has 5–6 litres of blood, about 10% of body weight, pumped through arteries, capillaries and veins (see Table 9.2). Blood does not bathe cells. At capillaries, **tissue fluid** – a colourless nutritive liquid containing O_2 – oozes out to bathe cells and carry away wastes. Tissue fluid returns mainly into the capillaries; but the excess passes into the lymph vessels to become part of **lymph**. Lymph is discharged into a vein (see Unit 9.7).

Examiner's tip

Know how plasma becomes tissue fluid and lymph (see Fig 9.7). Don't confuse these terms.

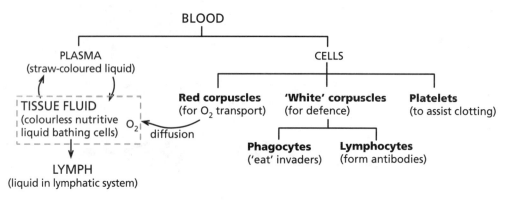

Fig. 9.1 Constituents of blood and their functions

Plasma consists of:

① **Water** – (90%) solvent for substances listed below; carrier of heat (for temperature regulation).

② **Blood proteins** – (7%) e.g. fibrinogen (for blood clotting – see Unit 23.5) and albumen (for osmosis at capillaries, Fig. 9.7).

③ **Soluble foods** – (1%) e.g. glucose, oil droplets and amino acids (from digestion).

④ **Mineral salts** – as ions, e.g. Na^+, Cl^-, Ca^{2+}, HCO_3^- (hydrogen carbonate, the main method of transporting CO_2) .

⑤ **Wastes** – e.g. CO_2, urea.

⑥ **Hormones** – in minute traces, e.g. adrenaline and insulin.

⑦ **Gases** – small quantities, e.g. of O_2, N_2.

⑧ **Antibodies** and antitoxins – proteins to combat pathogens and their poisons.

Table 9.1 Blood cells and their functions

Cell Structure		No./mm³	Formation	Destruction	Function of cells
in section	Bi-concave cell with no nucleus. Cytoplasm: mainly red haemoglobin Large surface area for absorption of O_2	5 million (more at high altitudes)	In red bone marrow, e.g. of ribs, vertebrae	In liver – by-product: bile pigments Life: 2–3 months	1 Haemoglobin (Hb) combines with O_2 to form unstable oxyhaemoglobin $(Hb.O_2)$ at lungs – Passes **oxygen to tissues** 2 O_2 detaches from Hb at capillaries, diffusing into the tissue fluid going to cells (see Unit 10.11) $Hb + O_2 \underset{tissues}{\overset{lungs}{\rightleftarrows}} Hb.O_2$
Phagocyte	Multi-lobed nucleus in granular cytoplasm; engulfs bacteria	7000 (more during infections)	In red bone marrow		Actively seek and **engulf bacteria** – even squeeze through capillary walls to reach infected tissue (see Table 9.2). Often dieloaded with killed bacteria. In boils this is seen as yellow 'pus'
Lymphocyte	Huge nucleus in little cytoplasm	2–3000 (more during infections)	In lymph nodes		React to proteins of invading organisms by making **'antibodies'**, which kill invaders and antitoxins to make their poisons (toxins) harmless (see Unit 23.6)
Platelet	Platelets are fragments of cells	¼ million	In red bone marrow		1 Stick to each other, forming a **temporary plug** in a cut blood vessel 2 Liberate an enzyme to help **clotting**; Ca^{2+} also needed (see Fig. 23.4) *Platelet plug*

Notes:

1 Haemoglobin combines 230 times more readily with carbon monoxide (CO) than O_2, forming a stable compound, **carboxyhaemoglobin** (Hb.CO), with it. Thus even at small concentrations in the air, CO (which is odourless) tends to be taken up into the blood, preventing O_2 from being carried. This can kill, e.g. someone tuning a car engine behind closed garage doors. See also *smoking* (Unit 10.12).

2 Haemophiliacs ('bleeders') continue to bleed for a long time, even from minor wounds. They bruise easily and joints may be painful from bleeds. Whereas death was premature in the past, today haemophiliacs may live less dangerously by receiving the 'clotting factor VIII' which they lack (see Unit 18.9).

3 Abnormal blood counts. Anaemia: red blood cell numbers down; exertion difficult (too little oxygen carried). Leukaemia: white blood cell numbers very markedly up; cancer of blood.

9.3 Blood vessels

Table 9.2 Blood vessels and their functions

E xaminer's tip

e very careful not to
onfuse arteries and veins.
now their definitions,
tructure and function very
ell.

Arteries	Capillaries	Veins
Carry blood *away* from heart under *high* pressure	Carry blood from artery to vein, very slowly, giving maximum time for diffusion, through a huge surface area.	Carry blood *towards* heart under *low* pressure
Carry *oxygenated* blood (except pulmonary artery)		Carry *deoxygenated* blood (except pulmonary vein)
T.S. Elastic layer, Elastic and muscle layer, Endothelium	Endothelium only / Phagocyte emerging between cells of endothelium / 10μm	T.S. L.S. (a) free flow (b) back pressure / Valve open Valve closed
(a) Heart refilling: elastic walls squeezing on blood to help it along (b) Heart pumping: 'pulse' felt as bore expands. *Thick walls* needed, but *no valves*	Tissue fluid leaking out to cells – blood pressure forcing it through (see Fig. 9.7)	No pulse: pressure is low at capillaries. *Wall thinner* than in arteries Blood returns partly by muscles of body squeezing veins – hence the need for *non-return valves*.
Bore of arteries can be altered by nerve messages to muscle, e.g. more blood to legs and less to gut during exercise.	See capillaries under the microscope in the tail of guppy fish or tadpole (head end in wet cotton wool)	Massage blood in an arm vein towards the fingers with the other thumb; valves show up as bumps (where they have closed)

Portal veins have capillaries at either end, i.e. they carry blood from one organ to another (e.g. hepatic portal vein between small intestine and liver – see Fig. 9.5).

9.4 Blood circulation

The heart consists of two pumps fused together, each having an **atrium** and a **ventricle**.
The two pumps contract simultaneously according to a heart cycle (see Fig. 9.4).
Right side pumps deoxygenated blood to the lungs for oxygenation.
Left side pumps oxygenated blood to the body, which deoxygenates it.

Thus blood passes twice through the heart before going to the body (Fig. 9.2). This maintains high blood pressure which ensures that:

(*a*) blood arrives quickly at the tissues;

(*b*) tissue fluid is squeezed out of the blood at the capillaries.

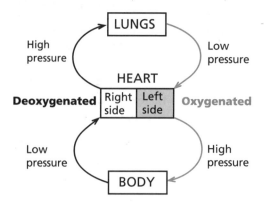

Fig. 9.2 Double circulation of blood through the heart of a mammal

9.5 The heart and heart disease

The heart lies between the two lungs inside the chest cavity.

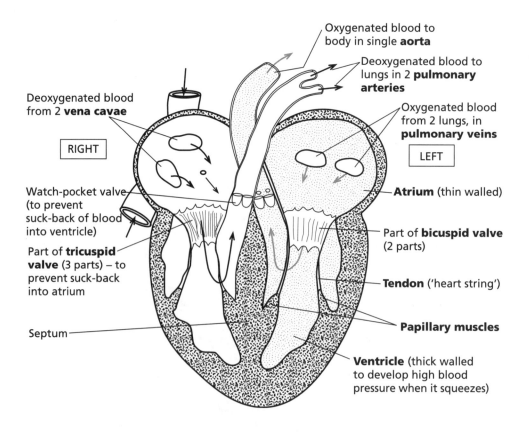

Fig. 9.3 The mammalian heart in section: structure and function

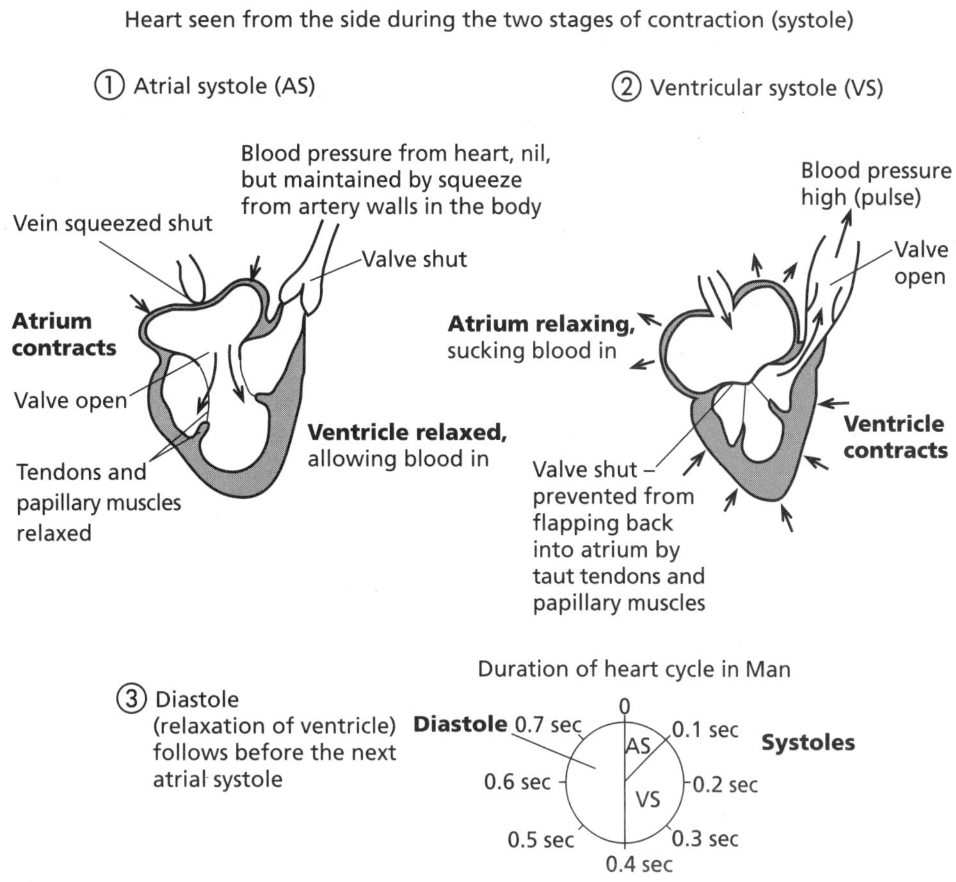

Heart seen from the side during the two stages of contraction (systole)

① Atrial systole (AS)　　　　　② Ventricular systole (VS)

Blood pressure from heart, nil,
but maintained by squeeze
from artery walls in the body

Vein squeezed shut

Valve shut

**Atrium
contracts**

Valve open

Tendons and
papillary muscles
relaxed

Ventricle relaxed,
allowing blood in

Blood pressure
high (pulse)

Valve
open

Atrium relaxing,
sucking blood in

**Ventricle
contracts**

Valve shut –
prevented from
flapping back
into atrium by
taut tendons and
papillary muscles

Duration of heart cycle in Man

③ Diastole
(relaxation of ventricle)
follows before the next
atrial systole

Diastole 0.7 sec

0.6 sec

0.5 sec

0

AS

VS

0.1 sec

0.2 sec

0.3 sec

0.4 sec

Systoles

Fig. 9.4 The heart cycle of a mammal

Heart beat

Controlled automatically by a **pacemaker**: special tissue in the atrium wall. The rhythm speeds up when

(*a*) adrenaline (hormone) is secreted (see Unit 13.9);

(*b*) nerve messages to the pacemaker arrive from the brain. A rise in blood CO_2 and lactic acid (from exercise) triggers this off.

Artificial pacemaker: a small electronic unit, attached to the chest, powered by lithium cells lasting 6–12 years, which sends minute electrical shocks to the heart muscle, causing it to contract. Used when the heart rhythm has become irregular. The best ones adjust to the needs of the body, e.g. demands of exercise, by sensing bodily changes, e.g. blood temperature and oxygen levels.

Heart disease

Two **coronary arteries** supply heart muscle with blood. They exit just above the valve at the base of the aorta. This blood returns into the right atrium. Blockage of this mini-circulation may cause death of heart muscle by starving it of nutrients and oxygen. Heart disease results from fatty material (atheroma) deposited in the coronary arteries. Smoking, excessive drinking, stress, lack of exercise, and a diet rich in saturated fats all seem to promote blockage with atheroma. This carries a high risk of heart attack – which may cause death. Warnings of this come from heart pain (angina).

Coronary artery bypass grafts (CABG) can now relieve angina and survival is 88% after 10 years. Usually the long vein at the back of the leg (saphenous vein) is removed and sections of it, without valves, are grafted to replace the sections of artery blocked by more than 50%.

9.6 Changes in blood around the circulatory system

Changes in the composition of blood

As blood passes through the capillaries of organs, it is modified. Blood leaving endocrine glands has gained hormones, while that leaving the kidneys has lost urea and water. Thus *overall* blood composition is kept constant, ensuring that the cells of the body have a constant environment (tissue fluid) to live in.

Table 9.3 Changes in blood composition in the human body

Region of body	Blood gains	Blood loses
All tissues	CO_2, nitrogenous wastes	O_2, food, hormones
Lungs	O_2	CO_2, water
Small intestine	Food: water, salts, vitamins, sugars, amino acids	
Liver	Urea and controlled quantities of glucose and fats	Glucose (for storage as glycogen), excess amino acids, worn out red cells
Kidneys		Urea, water, salts
Bones	New red cells and phagocytes	Iron (for haemoglobin), calcium and phosphate (for bone growth)
Skin	Vitamin D	Heat (by radiation and by evaporation of water in sweat), salts and urea (in sweat)
Thoracic duct	Fats, lymphocytes, lymph	

E xaminer's tip

Notice particularly the oxygen level of the pulmonary artery and vein - often asked.

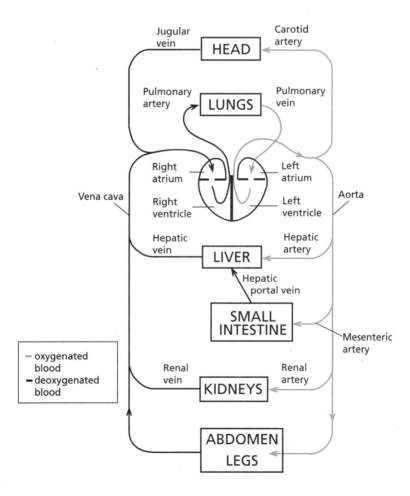

Fig. 9.5 The circulatory system of a mammal

9.7 Lymphatic system

A system of fine tubes ending blindly among the tissues, e.g. lacteals in villi of small intestine (see Unit 7.4), which join up into ever larger tubes with non-return valves. Along their length are swellings (lymph nodes). The largest tube (thoracic duct) discharges into the main vein of the left arm.

Functions:

① **Returns excess tissue fluid** to blood as lymph.

② **Adds lymphocytes** to blood (for defence).

③ **Absorbs fats** (into lacteals of villi) to discharge them to blood.

④ **Filters out bacteria** from lymph by means of phagocytes stationary within lymph nodes (Fig. 9.6).

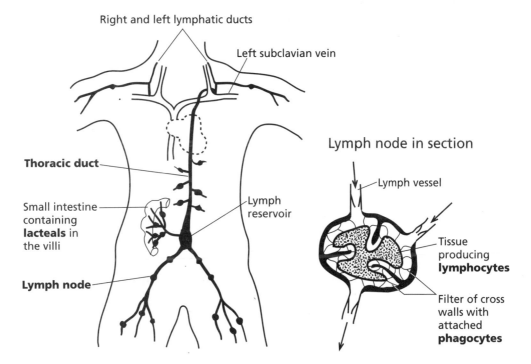

Fig. 9.6 The lymphatic system in Man

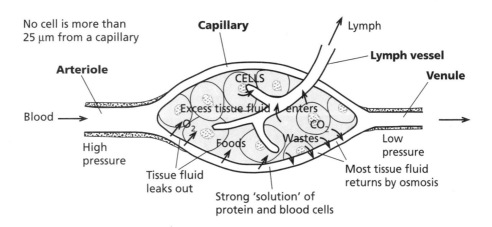

Fig. 9.7 The relationship between blood, tissue fluid, cells and lymph

Summary

1   Animals need to develop a blood system to supply their tissues rapidly enough with oxygen, food and hormones and remove from them wastes and heat from metabolism.

2   Most animals have a pumping heart and blood vessels to contain blood.

3   Mammalian blood contains red cells for carrying oxygen and white cells for defence, lying in a clear fluid called plasma.

4   Blood leaves the heart in arteries, reaches tissues in capillaries and is returned to the heart in veins.

5   Part of the plasma leaks out of the capillaries under pressure as tissue fluid, which bathes cells with nutrients and returns wastes via the capillaries and lymph vessels.

6   The heart is four chambered: the right atrium and ventricle supplying the lungs with blood, those on the left supplying the body – a double circulation pump.

7   Heart disease is a serious killer in the UK and may require bypass surgery to restore blood circulation to heart muscle, or the fitting of an artificial pacemaker when the pumping rhythm becomes faulty.

Quick test 9

1   Why do multicell animals need a blood system?

2   What part of blood is plasma?

3   What substance in blood carries oxygen?

4   Which cells in blood defend the body from infection?

5   Why are platelets important?

6   What features do veins have that arteries do not?

7   What is meant by 'your heart has a double circulation'?

8   What causes a heart attack?

9   Which is the most powerful pumping chamber in the heart?

10   What bathes cells, supplying them with food and oxygen?

Chapter 10
Respiration

10.1 Breathing, gaseous exchange and cellular respiration

Respiration is the sum of processes in organisms that leads to the release of energy from organic molecules, for use in vital functions. *All* organisms respire, plants as well as animals, forming ATP, the energy molecule that powers the chemical reactions of metabolism. Depending on the kind of organism, up to *three processes* may be involved:

1. **Breathing** (= ventilation): *movements*, in animals, that bring a source of O_2 to a surface for gaseous exchange, e.g. chest movements of mammals bring air into lungs; throat movements in fish bring water (containing dissolved O_2) to gills.

2. **Gaseous exchange:** diffusion of O_2 into the organism and of CO_2 outwards. All gaseous exchange surfaces are moist, thin and have a large surface area.

   (a) In *single-celled* organisms this exchange surface is the cell membrane.

   (b) In *multicellular animals* specialized body parts, e.g. lungs, tracheoles or gills, provide the surface for gaseous exchange. Usually gases are transported rapidly by blood between these surfaces and a second extensive surface area where gaseous exchange occurs between the blood and cells (see Fig. 10.10). Only insects pipe air directly to cells and do not use blood for this purpose.

   (c) In *multicellular plants* a network of air spaces *between* cells allows for direct gaseous exchange between cells and the air. There is no blood system.

   Thus gaseous *exchange* occurs only when organisms respire using oxygen.

3. **Cellular respiration** (= internal respiration): the chemical reactions occurring within cells that result in the release of energy to form ATP. These reactions can occur under two conditions:

   (a) anaerobically – no oxygen needed (thus **1** and **2** above are unnecessary);

   (b) aerobically – oxygen needed (thus **2** above is essential).

Note: since breathing and gaseous exchange are essentially *physical* processes occurring *outside* cells, they are often lumped together as **external respiration** to distinguish them from the *chemical* processes occurring *within* cells which are **internal respiration.**

Unfortunately the terms above are sometimes used loosely, e.g. since *Amoeba*, the earthworm and the flowering plant do not make *movements* to gain O_2, strictly speaking they do not *breathe* but they do respire.

10.2 Cellular respiration (aerobic and anaerobic)

Glucose is the main substance respired (other foods can be turned into glucose). The results of respiration are different under anaerobic and aerobic conditions:

1 Aerobic
In plants and animals:

$$\text{glucose} + \text{oxygen} \xrightarrow[\text{and in mitochondria}]{\text{enzymes in cytoplasm}} \text{carbon dioxide} + \text{water} + \textbf{a lot of energy}$$
$$C_6H_{12}O_6 \quad 6O_2 \qquad\qquad\qquad\qquad 6CO_2 \qquad 6H_2O \quad (2890 \text{ kJ/mole})$$

E **xaminer's tip**

All these three equations, at
least in words, are
frequently asked.

2 Anaerobic
(a) in plants:

$$\text{glucose} \xrightarrow[\text{matrix}]{\text{enzymes in cytoplasmic}} \text{ethanol} + \text{carbon dioxide} + \textbf{a little energy}$$
$$C_6H_{12}O_6 \qquad\qquad\qquad\qquad 2C_2H_5OH \qquad 2CO_2 \qquad (210 \text{ kJ/mole})$$

(b) in animals:

$$\text{glucose} \xrightarrow[\text{matrix}]{\text{enzymes in cytoplasmic}} \text{lactic acid} + \textbf{a little energy}$$
$$C_6H_{12}O_6 \qquad\qquad\qquad\qquad 2C_3H_6O_3$$

Table 10.1 Comparison of the two stages in respiration

	Anaerobic	Aerobic
Oxygen requirement	Nil	Essential
Useful energy from each glucose molecule respired	2 ATP	38 ATP
Chemical products	Organic, i.e. still energy-rich, e.g. lactic acid, ethanol	Inorganic: CO_2 and H_2O, i.e. no energy left
Takes place in	Cytoplasmic matrix (Unit 1.3)	Mitochondria (Unit 1.3)

Note: Aerobic and anaerobic respiration are *not* alternatives. Anaerobic reactions are the *first few stages* in a much longer set of reactions made possible under aerobic conditions (Fig. 10.1). Since aerobic respiration has the great advantage over anaerobic of providing about twenty times more energy, not surprisingly most organisms respire aerobically. Only certain bacteria cannot. However, some organisms are forced to respire anaerobically in their environment, e.g. tapeworms, or yeast in brewing operations. See Fig. 10.1 for a summary of respiration.

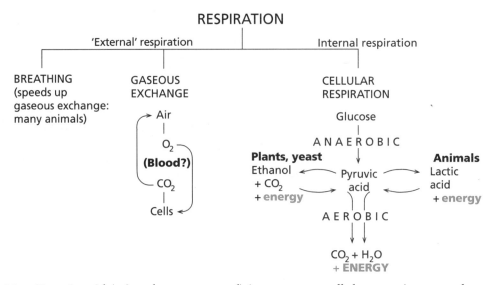

Fig. 10.1 Respiration: breathing, gaseous exchange and cellular respiration

Note: Pyruvic acid (a 3-carbon compound) is common to all three respiratory pathways

10.3 Anaerobic respiration

Examples of anaerobic respiration in aerobic organisms

1 Man

(a) At rest, most of the pyruvic acid the cells produce is oxidized to CO_2 and H_2O. The blood contains very little lactic acid.

(b) During exercise, blood samples show that the lactic acid level rises at least ten-fold, indicating that despite increased breathing and heart rates, oxygen supply to tissues is inadequate. In this relatively anaerobic state Man is in **'oxygen debt'**.

(c) After exercise this debt is 'paid off' by continued rapid aerobic respiration. One-fifth of the lactic acid is respired to CO_2 and H_2O. This provides energy to turn the other four-fifths of the lactic acid back into glycogen (stored in liver and muscles).

How soon a person stops panting after exercise ('recovery time') is a measure of their **fitness**. During training, miles of extra capillaries grow, so increasing the oxygen supply to muscles. This increases muscle power, and reduces recovery time.

2 Yeast

(a) If aerated, the colony grows very rapidly in nourishing sugared water until all the glucose disappears as CO_2 and H_2O (no use to brewers!).

(b) Without air, in similar conditions, the colony grows more slowly, eventually killing itself in the ethanol it produces. This is the basis for *making wine and beer*. The ethanol can be distilled off (as in making *spirits*, e.g. whisky). This will burn, showing it is energy rich.

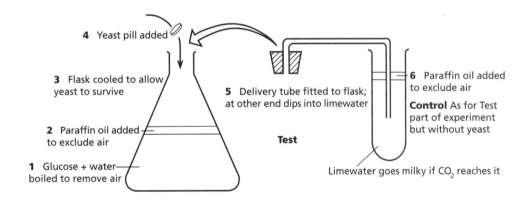

Fig. 10.2 Experiment to determine whether yeast will respire glucose anaerobically

3 Germinating peas

Half a batch of germinating peas is killed by boiling. Live and dead peas are washed in thymol solution to kill bacteria (which would produce CO_2). Both batches are put in boiling tubes in anaerobic conditions (Fig. 10.3). Two days later the live peas have produced gas in an anaerobic environment.

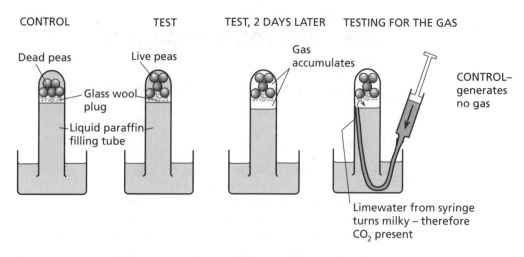

Fig. 10.3 Demonstration that germinating peas respire anaerobically

10.4 Aerobic respiration

Three lines of evidence that organisms are respiring aerobically

1. **CO$_2$ evolved** (see Fig. 10.6).
2. **O$_2$ absorbed** (see Fig. 10.4).
3. **Heat** evolved. The energy in glucose is not totally converted into useful energy (ATP) during respiration. Some energy (around 60%) is wasted as heat (see Fig. 10.5). In the experiment shown in Fig. 10.5 both the dead peas (killed by boiling and then cooled for half an hour) and the live ones had been washed in thymol solution to exclude the possibility that bacterial respiration could be causing a rise in temperature. (An animal, e.g. locust, could be substituted for peas with similar, quicker results.)

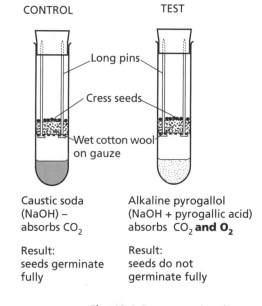

Fig. 10.4 Demonstration that seeds need oxygen to germinate

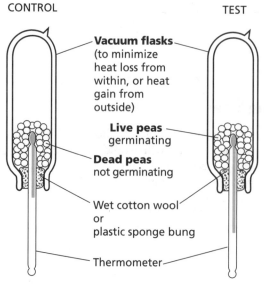

Fig. 10.5 Demonstration that germinating peas generate heat

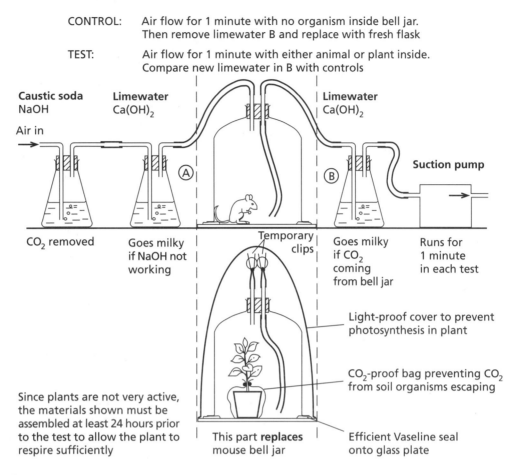

CONTROL: Air flow for 1 minute with no organism inside bell jar.
            Then remove limewater B and replace with fresh flask

TEST: Air flow for 1 minute with either animal or plant inside.
            Compare new limewater in B with controls

Caustic soda
NaOH

Limewater
Ca(OH)₂

Limewater
Ca(OH)₂

Air in

Ⓐ

Ⓑ

Suction pump

CO_2 removed

Goes milky
if NaOH not
working

Temporary
clips

Goes milky
if CO_2
coming
from bell jar

Runs for
1 minute
in each test

Light-proof cover to prevent
photosynthesis in plant

CO_2-proof bag preventing CO_2
from soil organisms escaping

Since plants are not very active,
the materials shown must be
assembled at least 24 hours prior
to the test to allow the plant to
respire sufficiently

This part **replaces**
mouse bell jar

Efficient Vaseline seal
onto glass plate

Fig. 10.6 Experiments to determine whether a mammal and a flowering plant produce CO_2

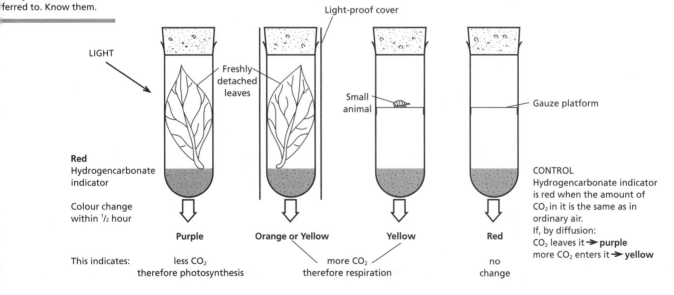

Light-proof cover

LIGHT

Freshly
detached
leaves

Small
animal

Gauze platform

Red
Hydrogencarbonate
indicator

Colour change
within ¹/₂ hour

CONTROL
Hydrogencarbonate indicator
is red when the amount of
CO_2 in it is the same as in
ordinary air.
If, by diffusion:
CO_2 leaves it ➤ **purple**
more CO_2 enters it ➤ **yellow**

Purple   **Orange or Yellow**   **Yellow**   **Red**

This indicates: less CO_2 more CO_2 no
                   therefore photosynthesis   therefore respiration   change

Fig. 10.7 Demonstration that animals and leaves respire, using an indicator method

10.5 Rate of respiration

The rate of gaseous exchange can be used to find out the **rate of respiration**
(Fig. 10.8).

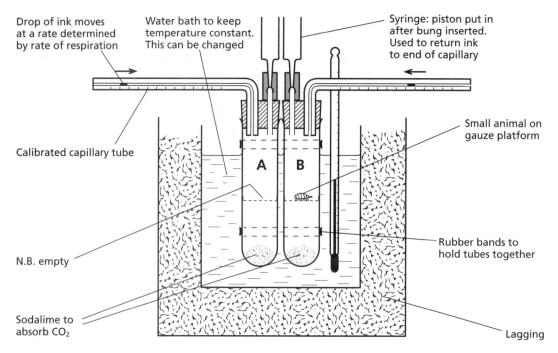

Fig. 10.8 Experiment to find out the rate of respiration, using a respirometer

Tube A will reach the temperature of the water in a few minutes. Insert its syringe plunger. Add an ink drop to the end of the capillary tube. No volume change (and therefore no movement of ink drop) is expected once the soda lime has absorbed the CO_2 in the air, since there is no organism respiring in it. Cooling or warming the surrounding water will, however, move the bubble. The distance the bubble moves in A must be subtracted from the distance moved in B.

Tube B is treated exactly as A is and at the same time. In B, however, the organisms take in O_2 and give out CO_2. Since the CO_2 is absorbed by soda lime, the volume of air in the tube becomes reduced. This causes more movement of the bubble, i.e. in addition to the movement, noted in B, owing to temperature change.

The respirometer can be used in water of different temperatures. The distance moved – in say 5 minutes – by the two ink drops is noted at each temperature.

10.6 Gaseous exchange

E xaminer's tip

The three features of all gaseous exchange surfaces are important.

All cells receive O_2 and lose CO_2 through **thin, moist membranes of sufficient surface area.** Multicellular organisms follow the same rules at their respiratory surfaces. They maintain a large surface area to volume ratio to overcome the slow process of diffusion.

1 **Cells must remain small** if CO_2 and O_2 are to diffuse across the cytoplasm fast enough to maintain life. Cell division ensures this. Thus the volume of *Amoeba*, say 0.1 mm^3, is adequately served by its cell membrane area, say 2.5 mm^2.

2 **A high rate of diffusion** can be maintained by keeping a steep diffusion gradient (see Unit 8.2). This happens by
   (a) *breathing* (continually changing the air supply);
   (b) *blood flow* (e.g. continually removing the O_2 absorbed into capillaries).

3 **The rate of supply** of O_2 and removal of CO_2 can be increased during exercise, e.g. in Man the breathing rate goes up four-fold, the volume inhaled per breath seven-fold, the heart rate doubles and the volume of blood pumped doubles or trebles (athletes can do better).

4 **The surface area** for gaseous exchange must remain high:
   (a) *with air*, e.g. in Man about 700 million alveoli in his two lungs provide a total of about 80 m^2 (area of a badminton court) to service his volume of about 80 dm^3;

(b) *with tissues*, e.g. in Man about 95 000 km of capillaries provide an area of about 700 m^2 of which about 200 m^2 are in use at any one time.

10.7 Gaseous exchange in flowering plants

In flowering plants air diffuses through *stomata* (mostly on leaves; some on green stems) (see Unit 6.6) and *lenticels* (pores on cork-covered roots and stems) to *air spaces* between cells, particularly of cortex and mesophyll.

Gaseous exchange: O_2 is absorbed and CO_2 released direct from cells to air spaces during **respiration** both day and night. However, *green cells* in sunlight absorb CO_2 and release O_2 during **photosynthesis** (see Unit 6.6) at a rate far greater than the reverse process (owing to respiration). In dim light, e.g. dusk or dawn, rates of respiration and photosynthesis can be equal – the **compensation point**. The dead cells, e.g. xylem vessels (the majority in a big tree), do not respire or photosynthesize.

10.8 The respiratory pathway in Man

Air passes to alveoli via nostrils, nasal cavity, trachea, two bronchi with many branches, and millions of bronchioles (Fig. 10.9). Dust, including bacteria, is 'filtered out' on sticky *mucus* in the nasal cavity as well as in the trachea. In both of them, *cilia* of lining cells pass the dirty mucus to the throat to be swallowed into the acid bath in the stomach.

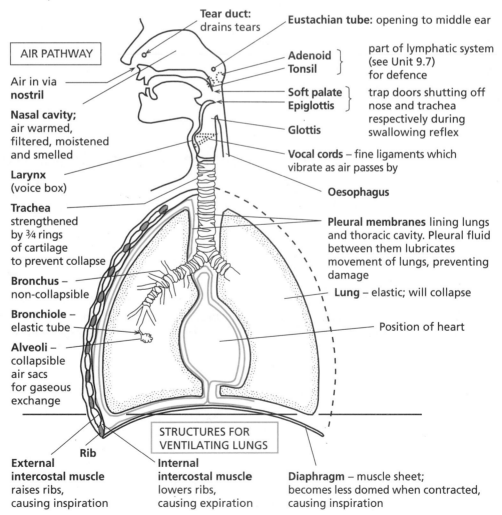

Fig. 10.9 Respiratory pathway in Man

10.9 Breathing

Air breathed

Tidal air: about 0.5 dm^3 ($\frac{1}{2}$ litre) – quiet breathing at rest.
Vital capacity: about 3.5 dm^3 – volume inhaled or expelled in forced breathing.
Residual air: 1.5 dm^3 – air that cannot be expelled at all (remains in lungs).

Table 10.2 Breathing movements

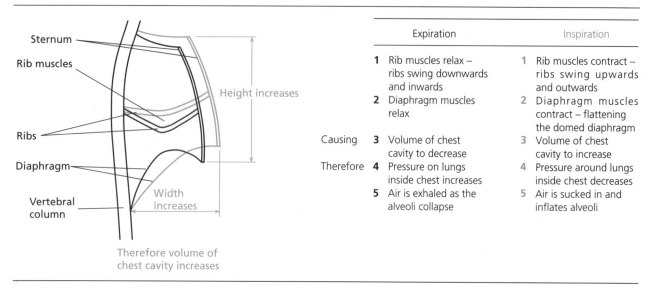

		Expiration	Inspiration
	1	Rib muscles relax – ribs swing downwards and inwards	Rib muscles contract – ribs swing upwards and outwards
	2	Diaphragm muscles relax	Diaphragm muscles contract – flattening the domed diaphragm
Causing	3	Volume of chest cavity to decrease	Volume of chest cavity to increase
Therefore	4	Pressure on lungs inside chest increases	Pressure around lungs inside chest decreases
	5	Air is exhaled as the alveoli collapse	Air is sucked in and inflates alveoli

Note: When resting, breathing out occurs mainly because lung is elastic, collapsing if allowed to, thus deflating alveoli and bronchioles. Lungs may be made functionless by introducing air between pleural membranes, e.g. medically when treating tuberculosis (TB), or accidentally in a motor crash or a stabbing.

The breathing rate is determined mainly by the CO_2-sensitive part of the brain (see Unit 13.6). A rise in CO_2 and lactic acid from exercise raises breathing rate (and heart rate) and depth of breathing.

10.10 Gas changes during breathing

Table 10.3 Approximate composition of air inhaled and exhaled (after removal of water vapour)

	Inhaled	Exhaled	Approx. change
Oxygen	21%	17%	20% decrease
Carbon dioxide	0.04%	4%	100-fold increase
Nitrogen	79%	79%	Nil

Air exhaled is also always saturated with water vapour (6%) – a variable loss of water from the body occurs, depending on how moist the inhaled air was.

10.11 Gaseous exchange in Man

- *Large surface area* at millions of alveoli in lungs.
- Alveoli are *moist* and *thin walled*, allowing rapid diffusion of O_2 and CO_2.
- *Haemoglobin* in red blood cells attracts O_2.
- Blood flow in capillary net surrounding alveoli maintains a *steep diffusion gradient* for O_2 to enter and CO_2 to leave the blood.

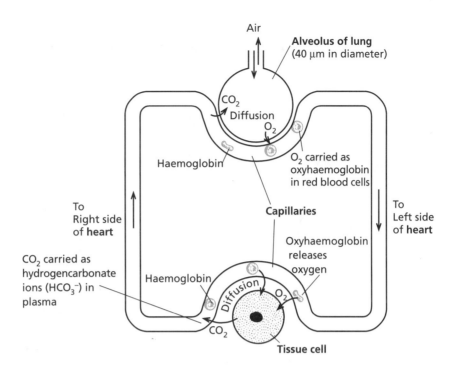

Fig. 10.10 Gaseous exchange at lungs and tissues of mammals

10.12 Smoking or health

Tobacco smoking has both short-term and long-term harmful effects (Fig. 10.11).

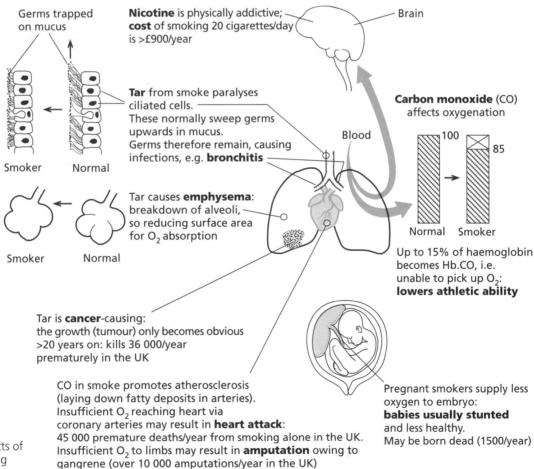

Fig. 10.11 Effects of cigarette smoking

Will-power and the use of nicotine chewing-gum or body patches are successful methods of breaking this addictive habit.

10.13 Measuring energy values of foods

To measure energy in foods they must be dried and burned. During respiration, food is neither dry nor are there any flames. But the methods below are the best we can use (Fig. 10.12).

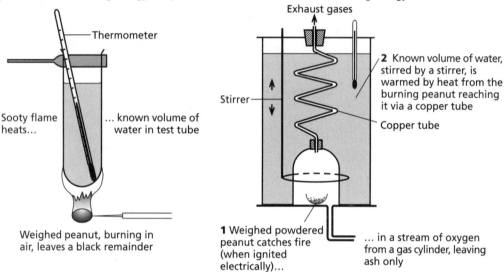

(a) A simple means of measuring energy in a peanut

— Thermometer

Sooty flame heats...

... known volume of water in test tube

Weighed peanut, burning in air, leaves a black remainder

(b) A calorimeter for measuring energy values of foods

Exhaust gases

Stirrer —

2 Known volume of water, stirred by a stirrer, is warmed by heat from the burning peanut reaching it via a copper tube

Copper tube

1 Weighed powdered peanut catches fire (when ignited electrically)...

... in a stream of oxygen from a gas cylinder, leaving ash only

Fig. 10.12 Measuring energy values of foods

In Fig. 10.12(b) there is complete burning of the peanut, and better transfer of heat to water.

$$\text{The heat energy released (in kJ)} = \frac{\text{volume of water (cm}^3) \times \text{rise in temp (°C)} \times 4.2}{1000}$$

The efficiency of transforming chemical energy of fuels and foods into mechanical energy (movement) can be judged from Table 10.4:

Table 10.4

	Efficiency of engines (%)			Efficiency (%)
	Steam	Petrol 4 stroke	Diesel	Respiration
Theoretical	30	58	65	40
Actual (approx.)	10	28	36	22

The wasted energy is lost as heat, in friction, etc.

Summary

1 Respiration supplies energy for vital functions of organisms of every kind.

2 Within the cytoplasm of cells, organic molecules are initially crudely broken up by enzymes to release a little energy by anaerobic means (not requiring oxygen).

3 The crude bits of molecules are then broken up into carbon dioxide and water to release much greater amounts of energy during an aerobic process (requiring oxygen) in the mitochondria.

4   Around 60% of the energy released in cellular respiration is wasted as heat but by controlling their heat loss, mammals and birds have a constant, warm body temperature.

5   The majority of organisms use aerobic respiration for their energy needs, obtaining oxygen and releasing carbon dioxide at wet gaseous exchange structures of large surface area, e.g. leaves and lungs.

6   To change the air at the gaseous exchange surface, many animals make breathing movements.

7   To make the pick-up of oxygen by flowing blood more efficient, mammals use red blood cells containing highly absorptive haemoglobin.

8   Smoking in particular makes gaseous exchange less efficient by causing lung diseases and diminishing the ability of haemoglobin to take up oxygen.

9   Energy values of foods may be calculated by burning small amounts in oxygen inside a 'bomb calorimeter' and measuring the temperature rise of water surrounding the burning food.

Quick test 10

1   What is the purpose of respiration?

2   Write the word equation for aerobic respiration.

3   What does 'anaerobic' mean?

4   Name the chemical products of anaerobic respiration (a) in Man   (b) in yeast.

5   Under what conditions does Man incur an 'oxygen debt' and how is it paid off?

6   If a leaf is placed in the dark inside a sealed boiling tube containing some red bicarbonate indicator solution, what colour is the solution likely to change to?

7   What do gaseous exchange surfaces, (e.g. lungs) have in common?

8   What causes lungs to inflate?

9   What effects does smoking have on respiration?

10   The energy from respiration is transferred to an 'energy molecule'. What is it?

Chapter 11
Excretion, temperature regulation and homeostasis

11.1 Wastes and their excretion

Excretion is the removal of waste products of metabolism. Wastes are often toxic, particularly if they accumulate. Examples of excretion:

- In **animals:**
  (i) CO_2 and water (from respiration);
  (ii) urea (from protein metabolism).

- In **green plants:**
  (i) O_2 (from photosynthesis);
  (ii) shedding leaves or bark (contain various wastes).

- In **all organisms:**
     Heat energy (from metabolism, especially respiration, see Unit 11.6). An important waste only in animals, when they move around. Loss of water unfortunately accompanies most forms of excretion.

Mammalian excretory organs

1. **Lungs:** excrete CO_2; lose water vapour.
2. **Kidneys:** excrete urea; eliminate excess water and salts.
3. **Liver:** excretes bile pigments (see Fig. 7.8).
4. **Skin:** excretes some urea; loses water and salts (in sweat).

11.2 Mammal urinary system

Two **kidneys** (see Fig. 11.1) at back of abdominal cavity:

- **excrete** waste **nitrogen** (from excess protein in diet) as urea;
- **eliminate** excess **salts** (e.g. NaCl in very salty food);
- **osmoregulate** to maintain **water** content of blood.

Blood pathway (see Fig. 11.1 Ⓑ)

Blood containing urea (made in the liver) passes into kidney from aorta via renal artery to about one million **glomeruli** (knots of capillaries); thence via further capillary network to renal vein and posterior vena cava. Blood is filtered at the glomeruli.

The filtrate produced is modified into urine as it passes through **nephrons** (filtration units) (see Fig. 11.2).

Urine pathway (see Fig. 11.1 Ⓐ)

Urine formed by kidneys is passed by peristalsis along two **ureters** to the bladder (storage); thence via **urethra** to outside (urination).

Urine in Man is a 2–4% solution of urea, some salts, yellow colouring (bile pigments accidentally absorbed in intestine), poisons, drugs and hormones (variously modified). Exact composition varies according to diet, activity and health. It is dilute if excess water is drunk; is concentrated after exercise. Normally about 1.5 dm^3 of urine is lost daily.

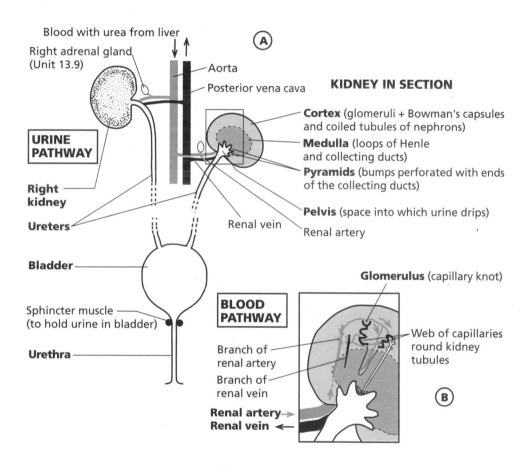

Fig. 11.1 The mammal urinary system: Ⓐ urine pathway from kidney; Ⓑ blood pathway in the kidney

11.3 The nephron

A nephron (see Fig. 11.2) is a kidney unit receiving tissue fluid and modifying it into urine. Tissue fluid (a filtrate of blood lacking cells and proteins) is forced out from the glomerulus (because of blood pressure) into the cavity of a **Bowman's capsule**. As filtrate passes along the tubules, all food and most other useful substances are reabsorbed from the tissue fluid, leaving urine (see Fig. 11.3).

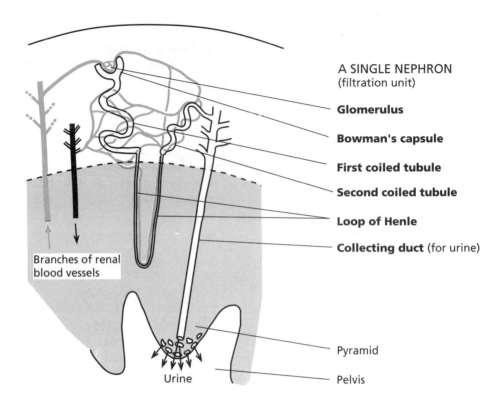

Fig. 11.2 A single nephron of a kidney

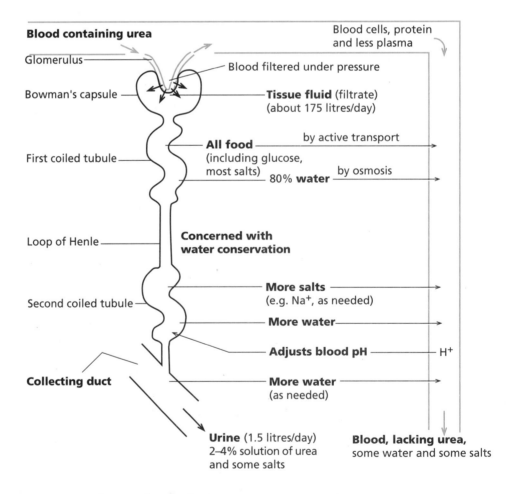

Fig. 11.3 How nephrons make urine in Man

11.4 Water conservation

The **loop of Henle** makes the tissue fluid surrounding it salty (by secreting salt from the fluid it receives). This salty solution causes water to pass out of the **collecting duct** by osmosis (but *only* if the hormone ADH, which makes the duct's walls water-permeable, is secreted). ADH is only secreted if water needs to be conserved, e.g. owing to sweating. If *excess* water is drunk, it passes out in the urine since it is not reabsorbed by the collecting duct owing to lack of ADH secretion (see Unit 13.9).

The whole body must balance water gain and loss (see Fig. 11.4).

The jerboa (desert rat) conserves its water by all possible means:

① Makes *very concentrated urine* owing to long loops of Henle and high levels of ADH.

② *Does not sweat* – no sweat glands.

③ *Evaporates little water* from its lungs – remains in a humid burrow by day.

④ Makes very *dry faeces*.

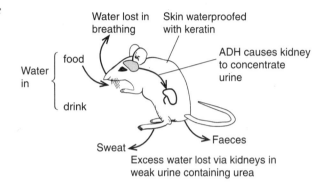

Fig. 11.4 Water balance in a mammal

The small volume of water lost is much the same as the volume it gains from respiration (see equation, Unit 10.2). Jerboas never need to drink.

11.5 Abnormal kidney function

1 Faulty excretion: sugar diabetes – glucose is passed out in urine. Lack of hormone **insulin** allows high glucose level in blood (see Unit 13.9). Consequently tissue fluid is too glucose-rich for the first coiled tubule to reabsorb it all into the blood. Therefore glucose is drained, little by little, from the body; can cause coma and death. Remedied by regular insulin injections.

2 Faulty osmoregulation: water diabetes – large quantities of dilute urine, e.g. 20 litres per day. Caused by lack of hormone ADH. Leads to dehydration of body unless large volumes of water drunk. Remedied by regular ADH ('vasopressin') nasal spraying.

3 Kidney disease: nephritis – protein appears in urine. Glomeruli are letting plasma proteins through with the tissue fluid (filtrate).

Kidneys may fail
(a) suddenly, e.g. because of low blood pressure or severe infection (so killing the cells);
(b) gradually, e.g. because of high blood pressure or an obstruction preventing urine leaving the kidney.
If only one kidney fails, the other healthy one is capable of doing the job of two.

There are three kinds of treatment for kidney failure:

1 Controlled Diet: reduced intake of protein (less urea produced); less salt and water (less urine volume); and in particular less potassium-rich foods, e.g. oranges, chocolate, mushrooms (high K^+ can stop the heart).

If this fails to help and the blood urea level rises (to five times the normal 0.3 g/dm^3) the kidneys must be either assisted by dialysis or 'replaced' by healthy ones.

2 Dialysis by 'kidney machine': blood from an artery in the arm is passed through 10 m of dialysis ('Visking') tubing bathed in a special solution. This solution is similar to blood plasma but lacks protein and urea (see Unit 9.2). The patient's urea and other wastes diffuse from the blood in the tubing into the bathing solution. The 'cleaned' blood returns to a vein in the arm. Fresh solution is used on every occasion.

It costs about £3000 per patient per year to give the necessary 12–18 hours of dialysis per week. The machines cost about £10,000.

A much simpler method of dialysis is 'CAPD' (body cavity dialysis). It allows the patient to remain active whilst dialysing (i.e. not attached to a machine.) A litre bag of glucose solution is drained into the body cavity. Wastes diffuse into the solution through the blood vessels of the gut. After some hours the solution is drained back into the bag and discarded.

3 Kidney transplant: a healthy kidney (from a person only just dead or a living relative) is surgically inserted near the bladder. Certain precautions must be taken to avoid death of the transplanted kidney:

  (i) the *blood group* of the donor (giver) and recipient (receiver) of the kidney must be the same (see Unit 18.3);
 (ii) if the *tissue type* of donor and recipient are also the same, the success rate can be over 80%;
(iii) the recipient's *antibody system* (see Unit 23.6) must be suppressed by drugs for the rest of his or her life. This avoids rejection of the kidney but also risks serious illness from other, ordinary, infections. So antibiotics are often also given.

11.6 Body temperature in organisms

Skin and temperature control

The *body generates heat* by its metabolism (60% of the energy from respiration is wasted as heat), e.g. blood leaving contracting muscles or the liver is warmer than when it entered them.

At the *skin*, blood either *loses* this heat to cooler surroundings or *gains* even more if the surroundings are warmer.

Gain or loss of heat can happen in four main ways (Fig. 11.5);

- radiation (important in air) – Man, at rest in shade, loses most this way.
- conduction (important in water) – e.g. elephants bathing.
- convection – air circulation; speeds up radiation and conduction.
- evaporation (heat *loss* only): heat transfers to water which gains enough energy to vaporize. This happens during breathing, panting and sweating in animals; and during transpiration in plants.

Some heat is also lost in *urine* and *faeces*.

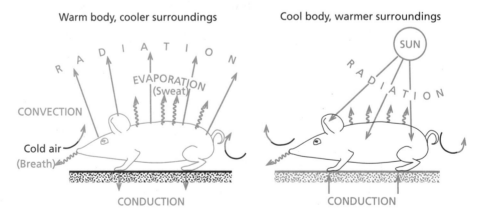

Fig. 11.5 Heat gain and loss by a mammal

Thus *most animals* (and all plants) have **body temperatures that fluctuate** with that of their environment. These animals are called **ectotherms** or 'cold-blooded'.

Birds and mammals have **body temperatures that remain constant** despite the fluctuating environmental temperature. They are called **endotherms** or 'warm-blooded'.

Table 11.1 Comparison of ectotherms and endotherms

	Ectotherms	Endotherms
In cold conditions	Become sluggish as they cool because their enzymes work more slowly. To avoid death by freezing may need to **hibernate**	Can remain **active** even in polar regions because their enzymes are kept working at their best (optimum) temperature. Only small mammals, e.g. dormice, marmots, need to hibernate
In hot conditions	Active, but may need to **aestivate** to avoid overheating, e.g. earthworm curls up into an inactive ball deep in soil	**Active** – cooling measures work; none aestivate. Some avoid heat by being active at night (cooler)
Main disadvantage	**Fall easy prey to endotherms** when not fully active – particularly when hibernating or aestivating	**Require a lot more food** to keep up their temperature

Temperature control in ectotherms and flowering plants

1 Ectotherms: rely on behaviour to keep a constant temperature – move to warm or cold places as the situation demands. Do not use skin or metabolic means as mammals do. However, wood–ant nests (28 °C) and honey-bee hives (35 °C) *are* maintained at the temperatures indicated.

2 Flowering plants: cannot move; they perennate if temperature becomes impossible (see Unit 15.2). If hot they *transpire* more (water evaporation) or *wilt* (reducing area of leaves gaining heat from sun) (see also Unit 8.5).

11.7 Mammal temperature control

xaminer's tip

now the physical control
ction particularly well.

Mammals have a *thermostat* in the forebrain (see Unit 13.6) which monitors blood temperature. Its information causes changes in:

1. **Behaviour:** e.g. seeking shade or getting wet if it is hot; seeking shelter and huddling into a ball if it is cold (see Fig. 11.6).

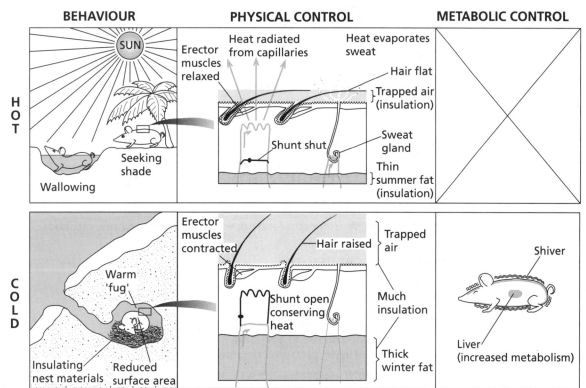

Fig. 11.6 Three ways of maintaining constant body temperature

2 **Skin (physical control):**

- **hair:** traps air – a good insulator. Amount of insulation can be varied by raising or lowering hair using erector muscles. Thicker 'coats' in winter – moulted in summer.
- **fat:** also a good insulator. Whales (in very cold water) have thick 'blubber' but camels have no fat except in hump. Mammals prepare for winter cold by laying down more fat.
- **capillaries and shunts:** skin 'flushes' with blood flowing through surface capillaries (*vasodilation*) which radiate heat when mammal is hot. Skin goes pale if cold since blood is diverted from surface capillaries (*vasoconstriction*) often by going through a 'shunt' deeper down.
- **sweat glands:** secrete sweat (salty water containing some urea). Water evaporates, removing excess heat.

3 **Metabolic control:**

- **shivering:** involuntary contractions of muscles generate heat.
- **liver:** metabolizes faster owing to increased thyroxine secretion.

4 **Shape:** a large surface area to volume ratio assists heat exchange, e.g. body stretched out to lose heat. The opposite, e.g. body curled up, conserves heat. For the same reasons, large ears of desert foxes and hares radiate heat well; small ears of arctic foxes and hares radiate less.

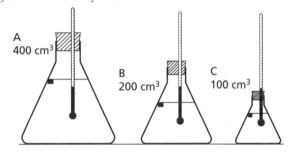

Fig. 11.7 Experiment to discover the importance of surface area to volume ratio in the cooling of water

Flasks A, B and C are filled with water at, say, 60 °C. Their temperature is read every 2 minutes and recorded. The surface area is measured by shaping and cutting graph paper to fit the outside and counting squares. Results show that C cools fastest and A slowest.

This may help explain why small mammals, e.g. shrews, need to eat so much for their size (respire a large part of their food to prevent hypothermia).

Hypothermia: body temperature falling below normal.

The elderly, through lack of skin fat or proper clothing (insulation), food or activity can die of hypothermia in cold weather.

Mountaineers and sailors, through cold wind and/or wet clothing (cooling), or lack of food can behave irrationally so endangering themselves. Unconsciousness and death may follow.

Antidotes: hot bath, hot drinks – but *not* alcohol. Sugary food.

11.8 Adaptations to extreme conditions: polar bear, camel and cactus

All three live where water and food are scarce and temperatures extreme.

Polar bear (carnivore)

1 **Small surface area** to its large volume: has small ears, curls up if cold – to retain heat.

2 **Insulation:** 8 cm blubber layer below skin, thick greasy fur which sheds water easily after swimming – to prevent hypothermia. Females build snow dens in winter to shelter their new born until summer.

3 **Locomotion:** rough horny pads on feet give traction on slippery ice, fur between pads and large feet help in snow and spread weight, streamlined body to swim powerfully for miles, run down prey easily (40 km/h).

Camel (herbivore)

1. **Temperature tolerant** allowing its body to cool below normal at night and rise slowly by day to as much as 9 °C above normal.

2. **Dehydration tolerant** allowing up to 25% water loss over a week. Can drink over 20 gallons (90 litres) of water all at once to rehydrate without harm (c.f. Man, Unit 7.3).

3. **Loses little water:** urine scanty and concentrated, little sweating.

4. **Sand tolerant:** large feet to spread load, eyelids and nostrils close tight against sandstorms.

5. **Fat** only in hump, provides energy for 10 days (and some water) when respired.

Cactus (xerophytic plant)

1. **Reduced surface area:** leaves are spines (to deter herbivores), stem photosynthesizes – reduces heat gain and water loss.

2. **Stores water** in 'succulent' stem unattractive to herbivores by taste or poisons.

3. **Reduced transpiration** (see point 1): stem stomata are few and open only in the cool of the night to allow CO_2 in, retaining water by day.

4. **Temperature tolerant** tissues – in desert it is very cool by night, very hot by day.

5. **Extensive shallow roots** – to pick up all available moisture.

11.9 Homeostasis

Examiner's tip

now the definition of
omeostasis and how the
rgans make it possible.

Homeostasis is the maintenance of a constant environment immediately around cells. For unicellular organisms this is the water they inhabit and their only means of homeostasis is to move (if they can) to a suitable area. The immediate environment of cells in a multicellular animal is the tissue fluid. In mammals the composition of this is kept very constant by a variety of organs, each of which controls particular factors in the blood (the source of tissue fluid). Mothers ensure homeostasis in their embryo via the placenta and amnion (see Unit 16.2).

Table 11.2 Organs concerned with homeostasis in Man

Organs concerned	Factors controlled in blood	Healthy blood levels in Man
Liver and islet tissue of pancreas (Unit 7.6)	Glucose	1 g/dm³
Skin, liver (Fig. 11.8)	Temperature	36.8 °C (under tongue)
Kidneys (Units 11.2–11.4)	Osmoregulation (water) pH (acidity/alkalinity) Urea (nitrogen waste)	90% pH 7.4 0.3 g/dm³
Lungs (Unit 10.10)	Carbon dioxide (carbon waste) Oxygen	550 cm³/dm³ (at rest, deoxygenated) 193 cm³/dm³ (at rest, oxygenated)

Note: blood does of course vary in composition according to where it is in the body (see Unit 9.6), but *overall* the levels of factors affecting the vital functions of cells are kept within narrow limits.

11.10 Skin functions

1. **Sensory:** sensitive nerve endings give warning of harm – pain, touch, heat or cold.

❷ **Protection:** skin acts as barrier between the internal environment of cells (tissue fluid) and the external environment (anything from climate, air or water to bacteria or predators).

Skin *resists:*

(*a*) **puncture** – (from slashes, blows or friction) by being tough and hair-padded;

(*b*) **desiccation** – (drying of body) by the waterproof protein keratin, aided by oils;

(*c*) **entry of pathogens** – (viruses, bacteria, etc.);

(*d*) **damage from ultraviolet light** – ('sunburn'; skin cancer) by suntanning, i.e. producing more pigment when in sunshine.

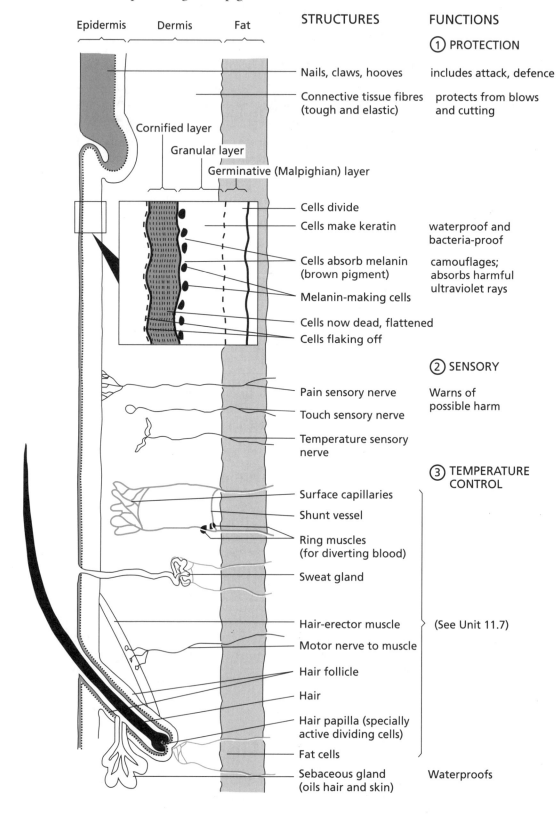

Fig. 11.8 The structure and functions of mammal skin

Skin *assists* predators and prey by providing:
(*e*) **weapons** from modified skin – (claws, hooves) for attacking or defending;
(*f*) **camouflage** – by special distribution of pigment in three ways:
  (i) *blending:* similar colour to background, e.g. khaki colour of lion.
  (ii) *countershading:* pale belly is darkened by shadow; dark back is made paler by sun. Therefore from the side the animal looks 'flat'; difficult to see, e.g. deer.
  (iii) *disruptive:* regular outline broken up by stripes or blotches to blend with light and shade among vegetation, e.g. leopard.

③ **Synthesis:** certain oils in the skin are changed to *vitamin D* (see Unit 5.6) when subjected to ultraviolet light.

④ **Excretion:** some *urea* is lost in sweat.

⑤ **Temperature control** (dealt with in Unit 11.7).

Summary

1 Wastes from metabolism and excess heat must be got rid of by excretion if an organism is to remain alive.
2 Mammals excrete urea and water via the kidneys as urine, and carbon dioxide via the lungs.
3 The unit of excretion in the kidney is the nephron, whose glomerulus sends tissue fluid into its Bowman's capsule by pressure filtration.
4 The tissue fluid is modified into urine by reabsorption of all food and much water in the tubules.
5 Kidneys that work badly may be replaced surgically by those from suitable people, or replaced functionally by passing the blood through a 'kidney machine'.
6 Exercise is the main source of excess heat in a body, but environmental conditions can affect heat gain or heat loss markedly.
7 Mammals have a range of adaptations to maintain a constant body temperature, which include behaviour, the use of hair, fat, blood capillaries and sweat glands, and shivering.
8 Certain mammals live in hot deserts and cold polar regions. They show extra adaptations and even tolerance to body temperature change and dehydration. Cacti show their own, plant, adaptations.
9 The maintenance of constant conditions around cells is called homeostasis. Temperature control and the control of water, glucose and carbon dioxide levels in the blood are all examples of homeostasis.
10 The skin is not only an organ used in temperature control; it is also a sense organ and is protective to the body.

Quick test 11

1 What wastes do you excrete?
2 Name three human excretory organs
3 What are the two major functions of kidneys?
4 What route does urine take from the kidney?
5 What is the composition of urine?
6 What is diabetes and how may it be remedied?
7 What does the hormone ADH do?
8 How does a hot mammal lose heat from its skin?
9 What is homeostasis?
10 Apart from temperature control, what other functions does the skin have?

Chapter 12
Sensitivity

12.1 Sensitivity in plants and animals

Organisms must be aware of their surroundings and respond to them, where necessary, to keep alive. Plants must seek light; animals, food. Organisms respond to various **stimuli** (detectable changes in the environment). Plants respond to light, gravity, touch (see Unit 13.14); and animals also respond to these and to temperature, chemicals in air (smells) or water (tastes) and sound. Plants use much simpler means than animals to detect and respond to stimuli (see Unit 13.1).

Table 12.1 Comparison of sensitivity and response in animals and plants

Multicellular animals	Multicellular plants
1 **Special sense cells** or organs (which usually do nothing else – e.g. eyes which only see)	No *special* sense organs, e.g. shoot tips sense light
2 **Nerves** relay messages from sensory areas	No nerves
3 **Brain** (present in most) 'computes a decision', sent to muscles	No brain
4 **Muscles** which can move the whole body towards or away from the stimulus	No muscles: cannot move the whole body

12.2 Mammal sense organs

Examiner's tip

Know what a 'stimulus' is and the six areas where stimuli are detected.

Sense organs pick up stimuli – they *sense*. But sensations are interpreted (*perceived*) by the brain, e.g. eyes may work perfectly but if the optic nerve or the visual centre of the brain is damaged, the person is blind.

Sensory cells are *transducers*, i.e. they turn the energy of a stimulus into a nerve impulse. They sense stimuli in both the external and internal environments:

External

- *Skin* – touch, heat, cold, pressure (extremes of which can cause pain) (see Unit 11.10).
- *Nose* – air-borne chemicals (smells – including the 'taste' of food).
- *Tongue* – chemicals causing perception of bitter, sweet, salt and sour tastes, *only*.
- *Ear* – sound (high frequency pressure changes); changes of body position; gravity sense.
- *Eye* – light (as light or dark, colour, and the form of objects).

Internal (often concerned with homeostasis, see Unit 11.9). Examples:

- *Thermostat* in hypothalamus of brain (see Unit 13.6).
- *Breathing centre* (CO_2-sensitive) in medulla oblongata of brain (see Unit 13.6).

12.3 The eye

❶ The outer covering of the eyeball is the tough, white **sclera**. It joins with the transparent **cornea** in front. Both are kept in shape by pressure from tissue fluid secreted from **ciliary body** capillaries (Fig. 12.1).

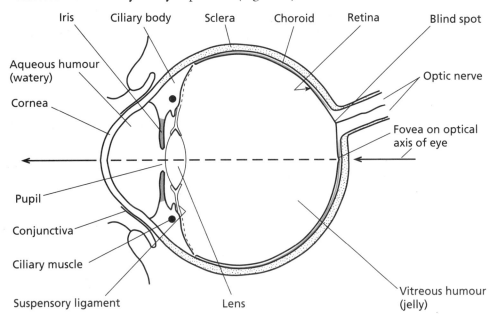

Fig. 12.1 Horizontal section through a human eye

❷ It is **protected** within a bony socket (*orbit*) and by **three reflexes:**
   (a) *weep reflex: dust and irritants* sensed by the **conjunctiva** cause an increase in tears and blinking to wash them away;
   (b) *iris reflex: strong light* on the *retina* causes a narrowing of the pupil to prevent damage to the light-sensitive cells;
   (c) *blinking reflex:* seen *objects* which may hit the head cause the eyelids to close.

❸ The **iris** is a muscular sheet bordering a hole, the **pupil**. Its size is controlled by two sets of muscle (Fig. 12.2).

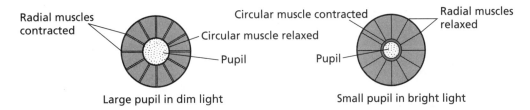

Fig. 12.2 View of the iris from within the eye

❹ The **retina** contains nerve cells linked with two kinds of **light-sensitive** cell:
   (a) *rods:* sense in black-and-white, in dim light; most are outside fovea.
   (b) *cones:* sense in colour, in brighter light; very high numbers at fovea.
   The *fovea* (called the 'yellow spot' in Man) enables objects to be seen in colour and in great detail. Image is in complete focus at this spot only. Is virtually blind in very dim light. The *blind spot* has only nerve cells (gathering into the *optic nerve*): no vision.

❺ The **choroid:**
   (a) Black pigment cells prevent internal reflection of light.
   (b) Capillaries supply the retina with tissue fluid.

E xaminer's tip

Focusing and altering the size of the pupil are often confused and not understood well.

⑥ **Focusing** (Fig. 12.3)
Cornea: responsible for most (at least 70%) of the converging of light rays.
Lens: makes the final adjustment, i.e. *accommodates*.

Far focusing: lens pulled thin by strain on suspensory ligaments exerted by sclera under pressure from tissue fluid.

Near focusing: lens collapses fat owing to its elasticity, when strain on suspensory ligaments is reduced by contraction of ciliary muscle.

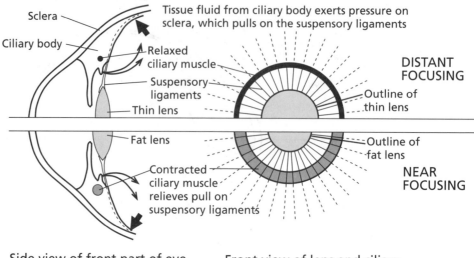

Fig. 12.3 Focusing by the eye

Side view of front part of eye

Front view of lens and ciliary muscle from within the eye

⑦ **Binocular vision:** the two different views obtained by human eyes overlap. The brain 'computes' how far away objects are.

Six muscles, attached to the sclera of each eye, swivel the eyes in their orbits to look at the same object.

Summary

1   Sensory cells change stimulus energy into nerve impulses.

2   Organisms must be sensitive to stimuli around them and from within their bodies. If they do not respond to these changes they are unlikely to survive.

3   Mammals have a range of sense organs and sensors, of which the eye and the ear are particularly important.

4   Eyes focus images via the cornea and an adjustable lens onto the retina where rod cells sense in greys and cone cells sense in colour.

5   Eyes, in pairs, contribute to the ability to judge distance.

6   Plants do not have sense organs but are nonetheless sensitive to light, gravity, chemicals and pressure.

7   Animals are sensitive to a wider range of stimuli, particularly within their bodies, to achieve control of body processes.

Quick test 12

1 What are stimuli?

2 How do sensory cells sense stimuli?

3 What organs do you use to sense chemicals?

4 Name two sensory areas of the brain concerned with homeostasis.

5 What is the most sensitive part of the retina called?

6 What muscles cause the pupil to widen?

7 What parts of the eye are concerned with focusing an image?

Quick test 12

Chapter 13
Coordination and response

13.1 Information, messages and action

1 Information from both an organism's external and its internal environments (stimuli) is received by sensory cells (see Unit 12.1). Often this has to be acted upon if the organism is to remain alive.

2 Messages of two types result from the information:

(*a*) *chemical* – hormones, transported in solution, relatively slowly (animals and plants);
(*b*) *electrical* – impulses along nerves, relatively quickly (animals only).
   This accounts for the different rates at which plants and animals react.

3 Action resulting from the message:

(*a*) in *plants* (which have no muscles or obvious glands like the liver, as animals have) is usually by:
   (i) *special growth,* e.g. tropisms, flowering, or
   (ii) *inhibiting growth,* e.g. dormancy of seed, leaf shedding;
(*b*) in *animals* action is by:
   (i) *movement* (muscles), or
   (ii) *secretion* (glands).

   Growth, although also controlled by hormones, as in plants, is a response only to the rate at which food can be built up into protoplasm.

Coordination of actions
Each response to a stimulus, unless coordinated with others, would lead to chaos. Thus feeding on bread includes muscle coordination to get the bread into the mouth (and not the ear) and to cause chewing, swallowing and peristalsis, as well as coordination of glands secreting saliva, mucus and pancreatic juice (at the right times).

13.2 Mammal nervous system

Composed of *neurones* (nerve cells). Neurones are bundled up into *nerves* in the *peripheral nervous system (PNS)*. Nerves link sensory cells and action cells (effectors) with the *central nervous system (CNS)* – the brain and spinal cord (see Figs. 13.1, 13.2).

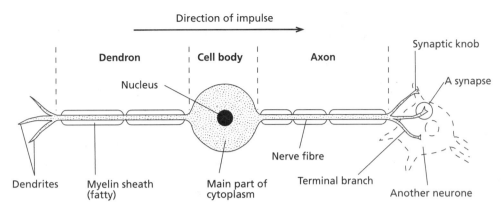

Fig. 13.1 A generalized neurone

As far as function is concerned there are *four types of neurone:*

1. **Sensory:** may connect with sensory cells, e.g. in retina of eye, or have sensory ends themselves, e.g. touch receptors in skin. Have long dendrons, short axons; carry 'messages' about the environment *to* the CNS.

2. **Relay:** always act as links between neurones, e.g. sensory neurones and either motor neurones or pyramidal neurones. This allows a large number of cross-connections, as in a telephone exchange.

3. **Motor:** usually link with relay neurones and with muscle or gland cells, to which they carry 'messages' *from* the CNS, calling for action; have short dendrons, long axons.

4. **Pyramidal:** connect with relay neurones and other pyramidal neurones which have a vast network of cell branches (up to 50 000), each a possible interconnection. This allows the 'computer' function of the brain (see Fig. 13.4).

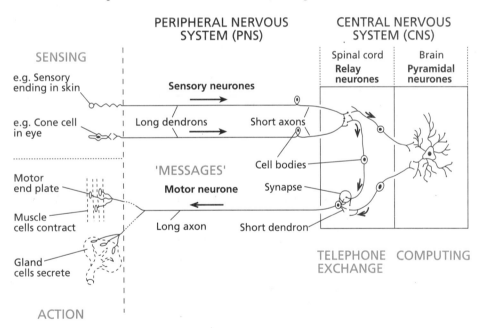

Fig. 13.2 Four different kinds of neurone and their functions in the body

13.3 Nervous impulses

An impulse ('message') is produced by the flow of Na^+ ions into a neurone and K^+ ions out. It passes along the neurone at up to 120 m/s.

Impulses *cause secretion* of a chemical substance at a *synaptic knob* which, for less than one millisecond, 'connects' two neurones electrically, allowing the impulse to pass on. The chemical is destroyed and re-created after each impulse (Fig. 13.3). Thus neurones are not physically connected to each other (as in an electrical circuit) and each neurone generates its own electricity (there is no central battery). Each synapse is effectively a connecting switch.

 xaminer's tip

Remember nervous or electrical impulses are scientifically more accurate than messages.

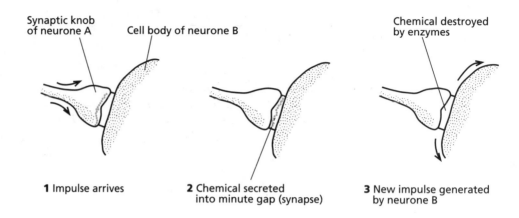

Fig. 13.3 Passing a 'message' at a synapse

1 Impulse arrives

2 Chemical secreted into minute gap (synapse)

3 New impulse generated by neurone B

13.4 Reflex action

Reflex action: an automatic rapid, *unlearned* response to a stimulus which helps the animal survive. It is a reaction to sensory information of an *urgent* nature (e.g. withdrawing hand from flame; righting oneself when overbalancing; swallowing) which could mean the difference between survival and death (see also Unit 12.3 – eye).

A maximum of *five* kinds of cell (*reflex arc*) take part in a reflex action (see Fig. 13.4, numbers ① – ⑤).

A knee-jerk reflex arc has no relay neurone.

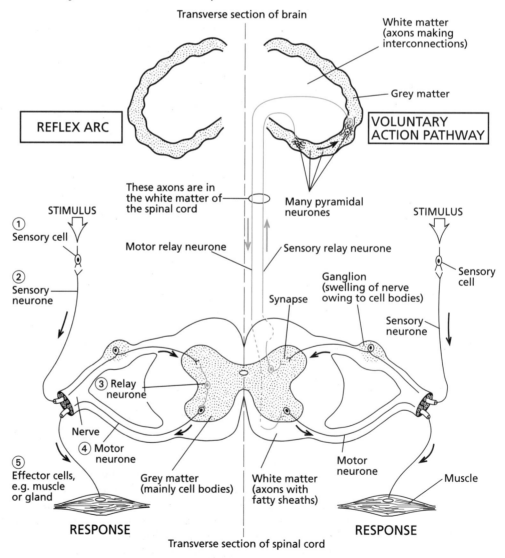

Fig. 13.4 Comparison of reflex and voluntary action pathways

13.5 Voluntary action

Voluntary action: sensory information goes to the brain before action is taken (see Fig. 13.4). All the little delays in transmission of impulses at thousands of synapses in the brain add up to make reaction time slower than in reflex actions.

Animals with small brains rely mostly on automatic reactions (instinct). Those with larger brains have more scope for working out solutions (intelligence).

13.6 The brain

Expanded front part of nerve cord; but grey matter is outside the white. In primitive vertebrates, the brain has three main parts; forebrain, midbrain and hindbrain.

In most mammals the same three parts are easily seen.

In Man, the front part (cerebrum) is so vast that it covers the midbrain and part of the hindbrain too (Fig. 13.5).

1 Forebrain

- **Olfactory lobes** (in front) – sense of smell.
- **Cerebrum** (upper part) – centre for memory, aesthetic and moral sense, hearing, vision, speech and muscular action other than in the gut and blood vessels.
- **Hypothalamus** (lower part) – receptors for control of internal environment (homeostasis), e.g. temperature, water content of blood. An outgrowth of it is the **pituitary** (the 'master' endocrine gland, see Unit 13.9).

2 Midbrain

Optic lobes (upper part) – simple auditory and visual (pupil) reflexes.

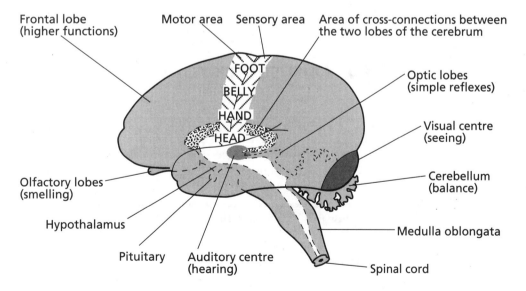

Fig. 13.5
Functional areas of the human brain. (Forebrain shown overlying midbrain and hindbrain in section)

3 Hindbrain

- **Cerebellum** (large upper outgrowth) – balance, coordination of muscle action.
- **Medulla oblongata** (brainstem, merging with spinal cord behind) – control of many vital 'automatic' actions, e.g. breathing, heart rate, constriction of arteries to direct blood to specific regions of the body, etc.

Summary of brain functions: receives all sensory information and 'processes' it (Fig. 13.6) either:
(*a*) immediately – reflex action (as in spinal cord), or
(*b*) more slowly – *storing* it as 'memory'
— using past memory to compare with the new, and *calculating*
— *coordinating* memories from other brain centres
— reaching a *'decision'*
— passing out *'orders'* via neurones and also hormones (from the pituitary).

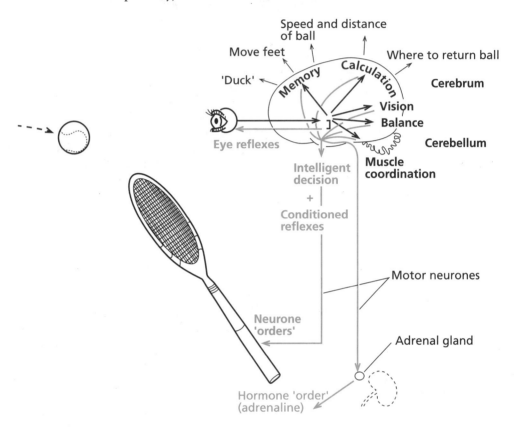

Fig. 13.6
Coordinating role of the brain in returning a tennis ball

13.7 Misuse of drugs

'Drugs' are chemicals made by humans or other organisms. Some (correctly used) assist medically, e.g. aspirin reduces pain, inflammation and temperature (see Unit 23.7). Some are 'socially acceptable drugs', e.g. caffeine, alcohol and nicotine. In Britain alcohol is used extensively but marijuana (cannabis) smoking is illegal; the exact opposite applies in some Middle Eastern Muslim countries.

Misused drugs (medicines or not) usually affect the nervous system, especially the brain, probably by affecting the way neurones transmit impulses (see Unit 13.3).

Features of the 'drug scene'

● All 'drugs' *affect the mind*, distorting judgement or sensations – which is their attraction. They probably affect the way neurones transmit impulses at synapses (see Fig. 13.3).
● They may cause *dependence*, i.e. addiction, if used regularly:
  (*a*) *psychological* dependence – addict *thinks* he needs the drug but the habit can be broken with no ill effects.
  (*b*) *physical* dependence – addict *needs* the drug. Breaking the habit results in illness (withdrawal symptoms), often severe.

- Regular drug use results in *tolerance*: the body needs ever greater amounts to achieve the same effect. This becomes very expensive and addicts may resort to crime to obtain money.
- *Addiction* imprisons the mind. Taking the drug becomes an obsession in the worst cases, excluding any possibility of a useful life. Addicts often turn to crime to pay for the habit and behave antisocially.
- *Embryos* of pregnant drug users are forced to share the drugs of their mothers through the placenta.
- Injecting drugs directly into veins carries the risk of AIDS and hepatitis when syringes are shared.

Motives for drug taking

- *Social pressure*, particularly at parties: 'I don't want to be called chicken'. 'Friends', not drug pushers, are your worst enemy.
- *Being daring:* 'I'm not afraid of these so-called dangerous things', and 'I will not get hooked'. With all the evidence around you, why test your courage in *this* way?
- *Escape:* 'I want to forget my problems'. The problems are still there when you recover – drugs do not solve them. Talk about problems with friends; then take positive action to solve them, if necessary with help.
- *Creativity:* 'Some poets and writers were addicts and did their best work under the influence'. For every famous drug-taker there are many thousands who are failures.

Table 13.1 Types of 'drug' and their general effects.

Examiner's tip

Remember to talk about biological facts rather than your opinions.

Type of drug	Example	Reasons people misuse the drug	Possible harmful effects (often linked with long-term use)
Narcotics	Heroin (injected) Methadone (drunk)	Feeling of well being (euphoria)	Overdoses fatal; physical dependency; blood vessels damaged by needles; risk of hepatitis and AIDS
Stimulants	Cocaine Amphetamine Ecstasy (also has hallucinogenic effects)	Feeling of exhilaration, increased energy, power, reduced need for sleep and food	High blood pressure; anorexia; paranoia (amphetamines); Ecstasy may cause brain, liver, kidney damage, even death
Depressants/ hypnotics/ tranquillizers	Barbiturates Valium	High dose to cause euphoria, like being drunk	Physical and psychological dependency; withdrawal may cause overactivity of depressed body systems, occasionally fits, even death
Hallucinogens	LSD Cannabis (Ecstasy)	To change perception, e.g. visual and sound distortion; slows reaction times	Flashbacks; death whilst under the influence, e.g. 'trying to fly'
Solvents	Glue Butane gas Aerosols Petrol Nail varnish	To become light headed and dizzy with dreamy visions	Increased risk of accidents while under the influence; death through choking on vomit; psychological dependency; brain, kidney, liver damage; irritant to lungs and skin

13.8 Alcohol – ethanol

Alcohol is a **sedative** (sleep-making) drug, *not* a stimulant.
Benefit: taken in moderation it reduces shyness, improving social contact; relieves stress.
Harm: excessive intake can lead to abusiveness, violence, illness and even death. Regular excessive intake (alcoholism) is an addiction, causing health and social problems.

① Effects on behaviour

Table 13.2 Alcohol and its short-term effects.

Units drunk	Blood level mg/100cm³	General effects	Effects on driving
2	30	Less cautious	Greater chance of accident
3	45	Judgement worse	Reaction time slower, e.g. braking
5	75–80	Not in full control	UK legal limit is 80 mg per 100 cm³ blood If exceeded (breathalyser test) loss of licence for 1 year, minimum
10	150	Slurred speech Loss of self-control	Very dangerous driver
13	200	Double vision Loss of muscle coordination	Incapable
26	400	Unconsciousness Vomit may be inhaled causing death	–

A healthy liver breaks down alcohol, reducing the level in the blood by about 10 mg/100 cm3 per hour.

② Effects on health of an alcoholic (long-term)

(a) *Liver cirrhosis:* liver shrinking due to death of cells poisoned by alcohol. Liver functions become less efficient (see Unit 6.10).
(b) *Brain damage:* fewer neurones live; cavities in brain enlarge. This is irreversible.
(c) *Heart disease:* pumping action weaker due to a neglected diet.
(d) *Babies* born to alcoholic mothers are smaller, less intelligent and disfigured (Foetal Alcoholic Syndrome, FAS) in most cases. Miscarriage is also more likely.

③ Social effects

Excessive spending on alcohol means little to spend on food and clothes for the family.

Effects of violence may have consequences beyond losing friends, e.g. hospitalization, prison, divorce.

Poor work performance may lead to loss of job.

In the UK (1992), 9% of men and 4% of women are 'problem drinkers'.

More than half the drivers involved in drunken driving accidents are under 20 years old; about 70% of all road deaths at night involve alcohol.

One in five pedestrians fatally injured on the road had excess alcohol in their blood.

13.9 Endocrine system

A variety of endocrine (ductless) glands secrete hormones. The pituitary is the 'master gland' controlling the rest (Fig. 13.7) by tropic hormones.

Hormones are organic compounds secreted by endocrine glands in minute quantities into the blood. They affect only certain specific cells (target cells). These chemical 'messages':
(a) arrive at the speed blood travels;
(b) have long-lasting effects (hours, days);
(c) control homeostasis (Unit 11.9), e.g. blood sugar level;
(d) control processes needing integrated control over a long period, e.g. growth or sexual development.

Glands and their hormones

① Pituitary: a pea-sized outgrowth of the brain which secretes:

(a) **Growth hormone:** promotes growth of muscle, bone (protein synthesis).
   Deficiency results in a dwarf; excess – a giant.
(b) **Antidiuretic hormone** (ADH or vasopressin): water conservation in kidney.
   Deficiency causes *water diabetes* (see Unit 11.5).

② Thyroid

Thyroxine: affects energy release at mitochondria (see Unit 1.3) in all cells, raising metabolic rate. Deficiency causes sluggishness, puffy skin; excess produces over-active person with 'pop-eyes'. Deficiency, in baby, causes *cretinism* – mental and physical retardation (see also Down's syndrome, Unit 23.1) – and in adults, *goitre* (swelling of the thyroid gland).

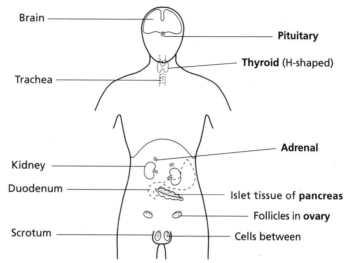

Fig. 13.7 The endocrine system in humans

③ Islet tissue of the pancreas

Insulin: causes absorption of glucose from blood into cells, e.g. by liver and muscles, to store it as *glycogen*. Deficiency causes sugar diabetes (diabetes mellitus – see Unit 11.5).

Glucagon: causes release of glucose into the blood by breakdown of glycogen (opposite to effect of insulin).

④ Adrenals

Adrenaline (the 'fight or flight hormone'): raises blood glucose level (from glycogen breakdown in liver), increases heart and breathing rates, diverts blood from guts to limb muscles. Nerves (not hormones) stimulate the adrenal, so adrenaline secretion is rapid. For control of blood glucose level see Unit 13.10.

13.10 Blood sugar level

E xaminer's tip

Compare this with other feedback control mechanisms you need to know. Try to remember the similarities.

Feedback is the means by which a hormone adjusts its own output by affecting the endocrine glands that cause its secretion (Fig. 13.9). If not self-correcting, can cause metabolic disease, e.g. diabetes (Unit 11.5).

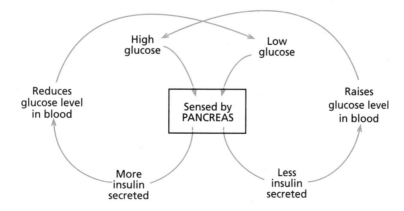

Fig. 13.8 How feedback controls blood glucose level

In addition to feedback, two hormones, glucagon and adrenaline play their part (see Fig. 13.9).

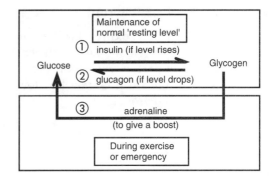

Fig. 13.9 An example of homeostasis (see Unit 11.9)

13.11 Sexual development

Ovaries and testes produce **sex hormones,** e.g. oestrogen and testosterone respectively, which promote changes in body proportions, development of gametes and hair, and changes in behaviour and voice, at *puberty* (Fig. 13.10). (For oestrous cycle, see Unit 16.3.)

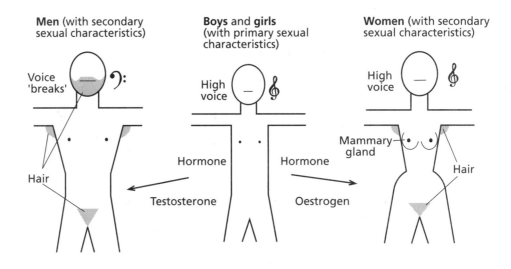

Fig. 13.10 Changes at puberty in humans

13.12 Nervous and hormonal systems compared

Both achieve coordination by *antagonistic action,* e.g. biceps/triceps control of forearm position (see Unit 14.8), and insulin/glucagon control of blood sugar (see Unit 13.10).

E xaminer's tip

When comparing, always remember to say which is hormonal and which is nervous.

Table 13.3 Comparison of nervous and endocrine systems

	Nervous system	Endocrine system
Speed of 'message'	Fast	Slow
Duration of effect	Short	Long
Reaction required	Immediate	Long-term

. Both systems are *linked to each other,* e.g. the hypothalamus (nervous) stimulates the pituitary (hormonal); nerves stimulate adrenal; adrenaline stimulates the heart, just as certain nerves do.

13.13 Taxis

Stimulus: an influence in the environment to which an organism reacts. There are two main simple responses to simple stimuli:

  1 taxis,   **2** tropism

Taxis: *movement* of an organism bodily towards or away from a stimulus. Applies to many invertebrate animals, unicells and even sperm (see Table 13.4).

Table 13.4 Examples of taxis

Stimulus (and response prefix)	Responses	
	Positive (+ = towards stimulus)	*Negative* (– = away from stimulus)
Light (photo-)	Fly, having escaped swatting, flies towards window	Woodlouse seeks darkness Fly maggots seek darkness
Water (hydro-)	Woodlouse seeks humid area	
Gravity (geo-)	Fly maggots burrow to pupate	
Chemicals (chemo-)	Blowflies are attracted to meat; so are pond flatworms (*Planaria*)	Earthworms rise from soil dosed with formalin
Contact (thigmo-)	Woodlice huddle together	

Thus woodlice can be described as negatively phototaxic and positively hydrotaxic.

13.14 Tropisms

Tropism: the *growth*-movement of a plant towards or away from a stimulus. Usually controlled by hormones (see Table 13.5).

Table 13.5 Examples of tropisms

Stimulus	Main shoot response	Main root response	Notes
Light	+ Phototropic	Neutral usually	(Lateral roots and shoots do not behave in this way)
Gravity	– Geotropic	+ Geotropic	

Key: + = positively   – = negatively

13.15 Phototropism

Phototropism: the growth of plant organs towards or away from light. By growing towards light (positive phototropism), plant shoots get the sunlight they need for photosynthesis.

    Mechanism: *auxin* (hormone) is made at shoot tips (which are sensitive). It diffuses back to region of cell elongation (Fig. 13.11) and here it affects the rate at which cells swell by osmosis (vacuolate). Under normal conditions, equal distribution of auxin gives even growth. With a one-sided stimulus, distribution becomes unequal giving unequal growth.

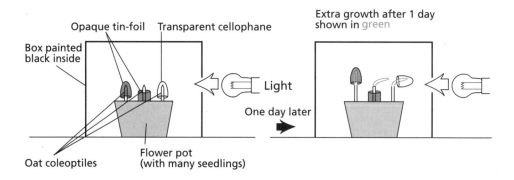

Fig. 13.11
Mechanism for the response of shoots to light from one side

Experiment to discover the region of sensitivity to light from one side in oat coleoptiles, and their response

Using *many* coleoptiles, grown in the dark, shields of three kinds are applied (Fig. 13.12). The seedlings are now given light from one side (only one seedling of each type shown):

Fig. 13.12 The response of oat coleoptiles to light from one side

It may be concluded that (*a*) the coleoptile tip is sensitive to light;
(*b*) the response is positively phototropic.

13.16 Geotropism

Geotropism: the growth of plant organs towards or away from gravity. By growing downwards (positive geotropism) plant roots usually find the water they need. Plant shoots grow upwards (negative geotropism), so finding light.

Mechanism: auxin diffuses back from the tip unequally. In the root the greater concentration on the lower side *inhibits* growth there and the root grows faster on the upper side. In the shoot the greater concentration of auxin *stimulates* growth (as it does in phototropism) (Fig. 13.13).

Shoot in dark – response to gravity

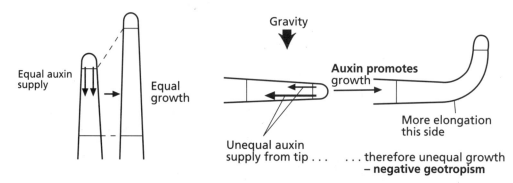

Examiner's tip

Remember there is always the same amount of auxin at the tip. The way it is distributed to the different sides causes the bendling response.

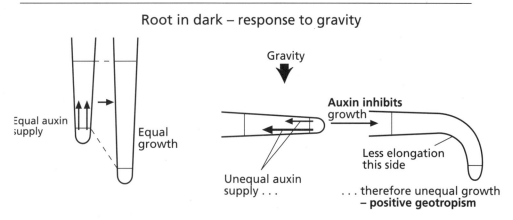

Fig. 13.13 Geotropism in roots and shoots

Experiment to test the response to gravity of bean roots

Five beans are pinned to each of two klinostats (one only shown).

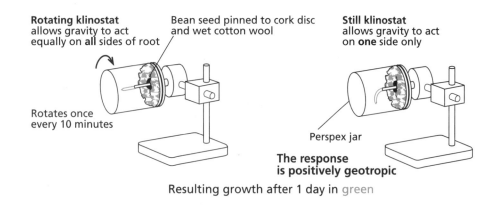

Fig. 13.14 The response of bean roots to gravity from one side

13.17 Artificial plant 'hormones'

Natural and synthetic plant growth substances can be applied to plants to affect their growth:

Auxins

● Encourage **rooting** of cuttings (see Unit 15.3). The cut end is dipped into IAA before planting.

● 2:4 D is a **selective weedkiller** when sprayed on to cereal crops and grassland. The weed species with their broad leaves and exposed growing points are more sensitive to 2:4 D and die by growing abnormally large and distorted.

● Promote fruit **formation without fertilization**. Used to produce seedless grapes and oranges.

● Delay **fruit drop** before harvest; stop stored potatoes sprouting.

Cytokinins

● Used in **tissue culture** to stimulate cell growth. Often used with auxins (see Unit 15.5).

● Used to **prolong life** of fleshy leaved plants, e.g. lettuce, cabbage; also to keep flowers fresh.

Ethene
- Speeds up fruit **ripening** (is produced naturally by ripe fruit skins).

Gibberellins
- Used to promote **flowering** in some house-plants out of season.
- Used in **malting** to break down food reserves (see Unit 4.7).

Summary

1 Information from sensors is carried to where an organism can respond to it either by chemicals (hormones) or by nerve cells (neurones).

2 Neurones pass electrical messages to other neurones across gaps called synapses, by means of chemicals which 'connect' them for milliseconds.

3 Sensory nerves carry messages from sensors to the central nervous system (which consists of spinal cord and brain).

4 Motor nerves carry messages from the central nervous system to where action can be taken – either at a muscle or a gland.

5 A simple automatic reaction to a stimulus is called a reflex action and uses a maximum of five cells, called a reflex arc.

6 Any voluntary action involves use of the brain where learning and coordination of information takes place.

7 'Drugs', including heroin, nicotine and alcohol, all affect brain function and can have serious effects, both immediately and in the long term (through addiction).

8 The endocrine system is a number of ductless glands secreting hormone messages into the blood and is controlled by the pituitary gland.

9 The nervous system is designed to send messages very quickly to precise locations.

10 The endocrine system controls long-term processes like growth, sexual development and control of blood sugar levels.

11 Hormone levels are adjusted by antagonostic effects, e.g. insulin/adrenalin or by feedback.

12 Invertebrates respond to simple stimuli by *moving* towards or away from them. This response is called a taxis.

13 Plants respond to simple stimuli by *growing* towards or away from them. This response is called a tropism.

14 Artificial plant hormones are used by Man commercially.

Quick test 13

1 Name the gap between two neurones.

2 What chemical transmits impulses across the gap?

3 What types of neurone, in sequence, make up a reflex arc?

4 What two kinds of tissue do motor neurones end in?

5 What does the cerebellum control?

6 What type of drug is LSD?

7 Name the two hormones produced by the pancreas that control the blood glucose level.

8 How does adrenaline prepare the body for fight or flight?

9 Name the hormone that causes shoot tips to grow towards light.

10 What tropistic response does a root have to gravity?

Chapter 14
Support and locomotion

14.1 Principles of support

The mass of an organism is supported by its environment (water, land or air).

Plants transmit their weight to it via *cell walls* and animals via their *skeletons* (they have no cell walls). Since most animals move, their skeletons are used both for *support and locomotion*.

The environment provides support by a 'buoyancy' effect too (Table 14.1).

Table 14.1

Water	Land and air
Great support: organism is made lighter by the mass of water it displaces (Archimedes force)	Very *little support* from air since volume of air displaced has small mass
Therefore plants and animals only need relatively *weak 'skeletons'*	Therefore *strong 'skeletons'* needed, particularly if organisms are large

14.2 Support in plants

Flowering plants use cell walls to support their weight. Cellulose cell walls are weak, woody ones strong.

- Cellulose cell walls, inflated by osmosis (see Fig. 8.6), provide most of the support in leaves and for herbaceous plants, e.g. grasses.
- Lignin cell walls (see Unit 8.10) provide woody support for trees and bushes.
- Water, through Archimedes force, supports submerged plants, e.g. *Elodea*.

14.3 Principles of movement

- **Muscle** can only *contract* (pull) – cannot push. To be lengthened again it must *(a)* relax, *(b)* be pulled back into shape by another muscle, its antagonist, e.g. biceps and triceps (see Fig. 14.8). Thus muscles work in *antagonistic pairs*.
- **Nerve impulses** are essential to make muscles *contract* (except heart). The antagonistic muscles are kept *relaxed* by impulses too (reflex inhibition).
- **Skeleton** transmits the contraction force of muscle to the environment, e.g. water, land or air, during swimming, walking and flying.

- **Load-bearing surface** in contact with the environment must get purchase on it if locomotion is to result, e.g. fish tail on water, bird wing on air, hooves on ground or claws on trees.

14.4 Mammal tissues for support and locomotion

The skeleton is mainly bone. Bone is covered at joints by cartilage. Ligaments connect bones to bones. Tendons connect muscles to bones. Each tissue has its own special properties:

1. **Bone** is both hard and flexible to some extent. *Bone cells,* arranged in cylindrical layers, secrete the mineral calcium phosphate to give hardness. Cylinders are strong. Bone cells are attached to a network of fibres which give flexibility (Fig. 14.1).

   Soak a small long-bone in 3% hydrochloric acid for three days. It comes out rubbery – the minerals have been dissolved.

   Heat a bone in a Bunsen burner flame. It becomes brittle and breaks easily – the fibres have burnt away.

2. **Cartilage** is a rubbery protein secreted by cells. It cushions the ends of bones at joints (shock absorber and smooth surface) (Fig. 14.1).

3. **Connective tissue** is of two kinds:

   (a) **Ligaments** are elastic fibres allowing 'give' at joints and between vertebrae.
   (b) **Tendons** are inelastic fibres. They ensure that muscles pull bones immediately, without having to take up 'slack'.

Examiner's tip

Questions often ask for the difference between bone and cartilage or between tendons and ligaments.

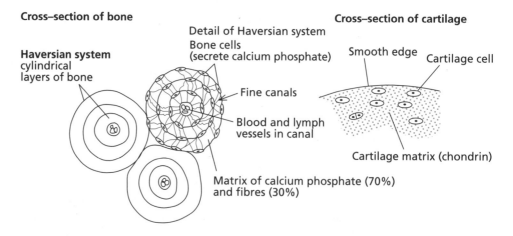

Fig. 14.1
Structure of bone and cartilage

4. **Muscle:** cells containing protein that contracts.

   (a) **Involuntary muscle,** e.g. in gut, causing peristalsis (Fig. 7.6); in iris, affecting pupil size; and arteries, affecting blood flow (Table 9.2). None is controlled by will-power.
   (b) **Voluntary muscle,** e.g. in arm. Controlled by decision.

14.5 Mammal skeleton

Skull: cranium protects brain; houses all major sense organs; jaws for chewing.
Vertebral column: protects nerve cord; acts as anchorage for four limbs via limb girdles and for ribs. Also a flexible, segmented rod from which internal organs are slung.

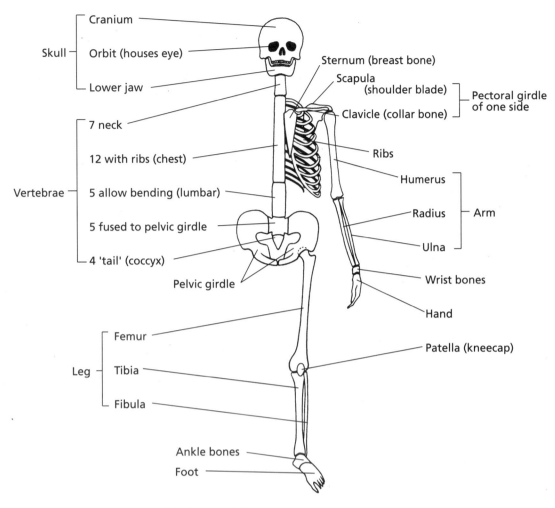

Fig. 14.2 Main parts of the human skeleton

Discs are shock absorbers between vertebrae. Their tough fibrous coat of connective tissue encloses a pulpy centre. A 'slipped disc' occurs when excessive pressure causes the disc to *bulge*, pressing on a nerve and causing pain. Most often lifting heavy objects with a bent back causes disc damage – particularly in the lumbar region (small of the back) – see Fig. 14.3

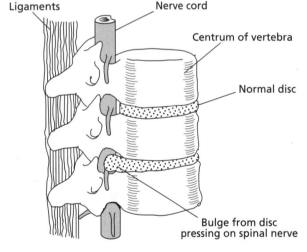

Fig. 14.3 Normal and 'slipped' intervertebral discs

14.6 Limbs and limb girdles of Man

- Arm is attached loosely to the vertebral column by the **pectoral girdle**: *scapula* has muscles to attach it to chest vertebrae; *clavicle* is linked to vertebrae via sternum and ribs (see Fig. 14.2).
- Leg is attached to the **pelvic girdle**. This strong hoop of bone is fused firmly to 5 vertebrae.

- **Limbs:** built on exactly the same plan (Fig. 14.4) – one upper bone, two lower, and same number of bones in wrist and hand as in ankle and foot.

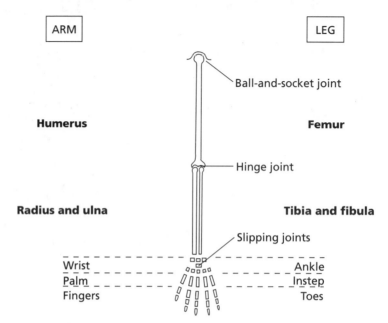

Fig. 14.4 Comparison of bones and joints of human arm and leg

First finger, i.e. thumb, is relatively free from the rest ('opposable'), allowing gripping

First toe is not 'opposable' to the rest – as thumb is in hand

14.7 Joints

Joints are where bones are linked (Fig. 14.5).

Immovable joints (sutures): wavy interlocking edges of bone, held together by connective tissue, e.g. bones of cranium.

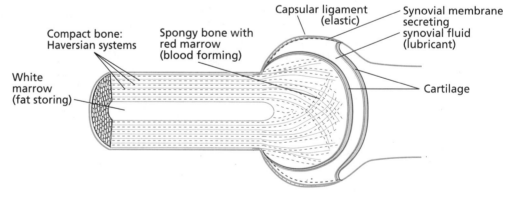

Fig. 14.5 Section through mammal synovial joint and bone

Movable joints (synovial joints): bones have cartilage ends; these move on each other, lubricated by synovial fluid secreted by a synovial membrane within a joint capsule. Types:

- *Ball-and-socket*, e.g. at shoulder, hip – rotation in *two* planes of space (see Fig. 14.4).
- *Hinge*, e.g. at elbow (see Fig. 14.6) and knee – movement in *one* plane only (like a door).
- *Slipping*, e.g. at wrist and ankle – limited rocking movement.

Examiner's tip

If you forget how different joints move - practise on your own leg or arm.

Arthritis: damaged and painful joints which swell.

(*a*) *Rheumatoid arthritis* is usually a hereditary disease. Connective tissue grows across the joint making it immovable.

(*b*) *Osteoarthritis* results from breakdown of cartilage through excessive wear and tear, damage and old age. Joints no longer move smoothly.

Artificial joints of titanium alloys (metal) and nylon may be inserted surgically to replace arthritic joints.

14.8 Movement of an arm

Bending: nerve impulses make the biceps contract, so raising the forearm. Other nerve impulses travelling to the triceps *inhibit* its contraction, so it is extended by the biceps through leverage.

Extending: nerve impulses cause contraction of the triceps. This extends the biceps, and the arm moves down.

The biceps and triceps muscles are *antagonists*. Nerve impulses stimulate one muscle while other impulses inhibit the other muscle when movement occurs.

E **xaminer's tip**

eel on your own arm to
escribe how each muscle
hanges when it contracts.

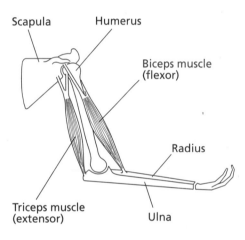

Fig. 14.8 Movement of the forearm in Man (hinge joint)

14.9 Functions of mammal skeletons

① **Support:** of body off ground; of internal organs, preventing crushing.

② **Shape:** important adaptations, e.g. Man's hand, bat's wing, porpoise's streamline and flippers.

③ **Locomotion:** system of levers.

④ **Protection:** cranium protects brain; ribs protect heart and lungs.

⑤ **Breathing:** role of ribs (see Unit 10.9).

⑥ **Making blood cells:** in red bone marrow, e.g. of ribs, vertebrae (and see Fig. 14.5).

⑦ **Sound conduction:** three ossicles in middle ear.

14.10 Exercise, sport and injuries

Regular exercise, appropriate to age, keeps the whole body healthy by:
- keeping the muscles toned, tendons supple and joints working smoothly.
- maintaining healthy lungs and heart which can cope with sudden demands.
- preventing obesity, lowering risk of heart attack and high blood pressure.
- helping alertness, providing social contact

Sport can result in **injuries**. These may result from:
1 lack of training – body not prepared for strains, e.g. pulled muscles;
2 sudden excessive stress, e.g. fractured bones, knee joint damage;
3 over-use – injuries never given time to heal properly;
4 self-inflicted causes.

① Lack of training

(a) *Stamina lacking:* The body is most vulnerable when tired. Most rugby injuries occur early in the season and in the last quarter hour of matches.

(b) *Strength lacking: both* antagonistic muscles must be built up and on both sides of the body to avoid self-injury.

(c) *Flexibility lacking:* 'warming up' must include stretching, to prepare tendons and ligaments for stress. Vital in sprinters.

(d) *Skill lacking:* poor positioning and timing can result in collision or other sudden stress.

② Sudden stress

(a) *Fractures:* bones may be cracked or broken across. The bone must be immobilized, e.g. by splints, in the right position by experts. This allows:
  (i) broken ends to be joined by connective tissue fibres;
  (ii) bone cells to attach to fibres and secrete bone minerals;
  (iii) reabsorption of any extra bone over some months.

(b) *Dislocation:* a bone displaced from its joint, straining or tearing ligaments. Best treated immediately by an expert, pulling the bone into its rightful place.

(c) *Knee joint injury,* e.g. in football or squash (Fig. 14.7). A damaged joint may swell with the extra fluid secreted into the synovial space (see also Unit 14.7, arthritis). This may have to be drained by syringe, but natural reabsorption and repair takes a few days.

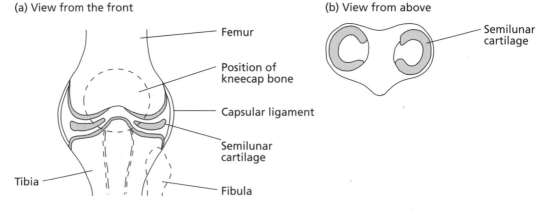

(a) View from the front

(b) View from above

Femur

Position of kneecap bone

Capsular ligament

Semilunar cartilage

Tibia

Fibula

Semilunar cartilage

Fig. 14.7 Diagram of a knee joint (severe twisting of this hinge joint may lead to splitting of the semilunar cartilages – which then have to be removed surgically)

③ Over use

Damage due to severe competition must be given time to heal *fully*. Rest is needed to avoid 'staleness' and a drop in performance that may lead to obvious injury.

④ Self-inflicted causes

(a) Contact sports, e.g. rugby, need organization on a weight basis (and not age basis) at junior level.

(b) Anabolic steroids, while improving performance by building up muscles, have serious consequences. These include increases in atherosclerosis (see Unit 10.12) and blood pressure, damage to the liver and male sterility – when used long-term.

Summary

1 Aquatic organisms are supported well by water and only need weak 'skeletons'.

2 Air and land provide little support, so strong 'skeletons' are needed to prevent the organism collapsing into a heap of cells.

3 The 'skeleton' of a plant is provided by cell walls, turgor pressure and lignin (wood) in the xylem.

4 The skeleton of mammals is made of bone and cartilage connected together by ligaments.

5 Muscles are connected to bones by tendons.

6 Muscles are only able to contract (shorten) and so are always found in antagonistic pairs. One muscle bends the limb and the other extends it.

7 Bones move upon one another at lubricated and cushioned ends called synovial joints.

8 The functions of mammalian skeletons include support of organs, protection and movement.

9 Sports injuries occur when undue stress is applied to bone, cartilage, ligaments and tendons. Many can be prevented by proper training, precautions and sensible rules for each sport.

10 As an alternative to the endoskeleton of mammals, arthropods use an exoskeleton of chitin and earthworms a fluid skeleton (more appropriate to burrowing).

Quick test 14

1 What is the skeleton used for in locomotion?

2 Why do muscles occur in pairs?

3 What is the difference between ligaments and tendons?

4 Give an example of a ball and socket joint. How is its movement different from a hinge joint?

5 How does a land plant support itself and keep its shape?

6 What type of muscle is found in the gut?

7 What do the three ossicle bones do?

8 What are the symptoms of arthritis?

Chapter 15

Reproduction: mainly plants

15.1 Asexual and sexual reproduction compared

No individual organism is immortal; reproduction avoids extinction. Most organisms reproduce sexually, many asexually as well.

Table 15.1 Comparison of asexual and sexual reproduction

	Asexual	Sexual
Parents	One	Two (unless parent is hermaphrodite, i.e. both sexes in same individual, e.g. flower)
Method	Mitosis forms either: (a) reproductive bodies, e.g. spores, tubers, or (b) replicas of adult by outgrowth, e.g. runners	Meiosis forms gametes (sperm and ova) which fuse to form zygotes (at fertilization) Zygote grows by mitosis into new organism
Offspring	Genetically identical to parent	Not identical – half its genes are maternal (mother's), half paternal (father's)
Advantage	Maintains a good strain exactly	Produces new varieties which, if 'better', favour survival and in the long-term their evolution (see Unit 19.3)
Disadvantage	Species liable to be wiped out, e.g. by disease, if not resistant to it	Excellent individuals, e.g. prize milk cow, cannot give identical offspring
Other points	Only one arrival needed to colonize a new area Often more rapid than sexual methods Always increases population	Both sexes needed Not rapid Need not increase population (two parents may produce only one offspring, then die)
Occurrence	Very common among plants and protists, e.g. *Amoeba*	Almost all plants and animals

15.2 Asexual methods of reproduction

All the offspring from one asexually reproducing parent are known as a **clone** (a genetically identical population). This is because mitosis alone has produced them (see Units 1.5 and 18.13).

Examples:

1. **Binary fission,** e.g. bacteria (see Unit 3.2).

2. **Spores,** e.g. fungi (see Unit 3.5), mosses (see Unit 2.5).

3. **Budding,** e.g. yeast (Unit 3.5).

4. **Identical twinning,** e.g. in humans, a single zygote may develop into two babies.

5. **Vegetative propagation** by outgrowths of new plantlets usually from *stems* (Fig. 15.1) but sometimes from *leaves*, e.g. *Bryophyllum*. Many of these methods of asexual reproduction also achieve **perennation** (survival over winter in a dormant state).

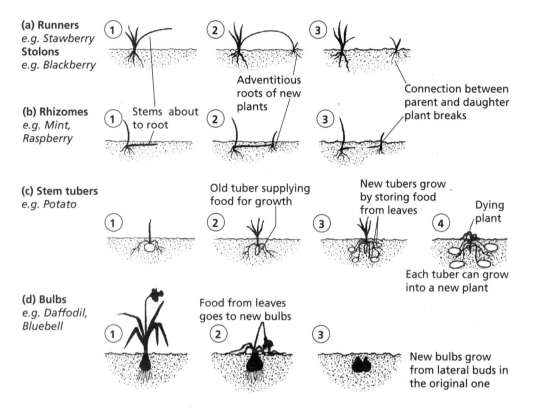

Fig. 15.1 Methods of asexual reproduction (and perennation) in flowering plants

Note: all the plants named also reproduce sexually (by flowers) at the end of the growing season.

Potato tuber: an underground *stem*-tip swollen with food (especially starch) received from the parent plant (which dies down in autumn). Each tuber is a potential new plant (thus *asexual reproduction*) and allows *perennation*. New shoots and adventitious roots arise from 'eyes' (Fig. 15.2) in spring.

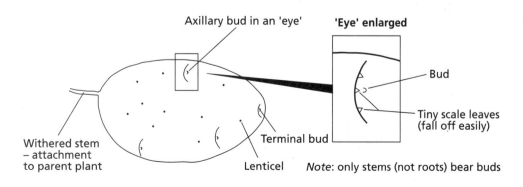

Fig. 15.2 A potato tuber

15.3 Cuttings

Artificial methods of asexual reproduction are used by Man to
(a) maintain good varieties of house-plants and some crop plants;
(b) rapidly multiply new varieties which arise by mutation (see Unit 18.16);
(c) rapidly multiply new varieties produced by selective breeding (see Unit 19.5);
(d) maintain seedless oranges and grapes – no other way possible.

Cuttings

Lengths of stem, e.g. *Pelargonium,* or a leaf, e.g. African violet, are made to grow into complete plants. This method requires:
(a) *sufficiently large piece:* enough food reserves to form the missing roots;
(b) *sand/peat mix for rooting:* enough air for respiration where roots are forming, enough water to supply needs;
(c) *removal of most leaves:* to reduce transpiration (plant would dry out);
(d) *rooting hormone:* applied to cut end, starts cells dividing to form roots.

15.4 Grafting

This is the insertion of a shoot or bud onto a related plant (Fig. 15.3a and b). The two grow into one plant which has the advantages of:
(a) the *vigour* of a specially chosen root – the **stock**;
(b) the *quality* of the product (flowers or fruit) on the grafted shoot – the **scion**.

Grafting requires:
- that cambia (see Unit 8.10) of stock and scion must meet (to grow together);
- firm binding at junction (to prevent joining tissue tearing);
- autumn grafting (to minimize death from excessive transpiration);
- waterproofing the cuts with tape or wax (minimizes infection and desiccation);
- compatible species (lemon will not graft onto an apple).

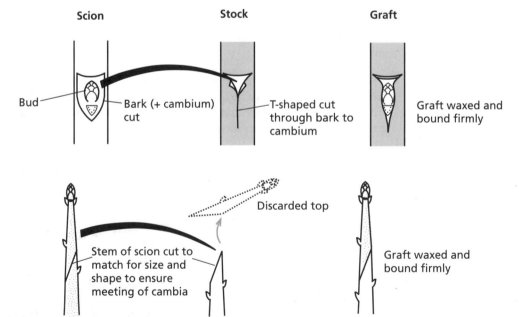

Fig. 15.3(a) Bud grafting

Fig. 15.3(b) Stem grafting

Note: Neither stock nor scion are altered *genetically* by grafting. Thus in a garden rose 'Masquerade', large beautiful roses form on the scion, but only small wild briar roses can form on 'suckers' (stems) sprouting from the stock. The 'Masquerade' genes do not affect briar genes – or vice versa.

Grafting is used extensively in producing grapes, apples, pears, citrus fruit and roses. 'Family' apple trees have a number of different varieties of apple growing on the same trunk, from separate grafts.

15.5 Tissue culture

Tissue culture is a faster way of producing plants genetically identical to their parent (clones) than taking cuttings. Small amounts of parent plant tissue, e.g. pith, are grown on agar into plantlets as illustrated in Fig. 15.4.

Method:

1. Tissue, e.g. pith, is scraped out of the parent plant. It is spread on sterile agar containing nutrients (sucrose, mineral salts, vitamins) and auxin in a petri dish.

2. After some weeks each group of cells has divided into a formless mass of many thousands of similar cells – a **callus**.

3. The callus is now made to grow roots, stem and leaves by a special mix of hormones in agar containing nutrients.

4. The resulting small plants can be planted out (Fig. 15.4).

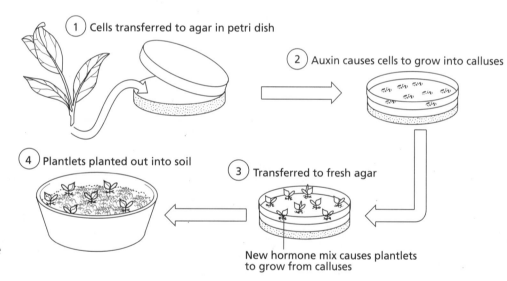

Fig. 15.4 Plant tissue culture to form a clone of new plants

One commercial application of this process is production of oil palms in Malaysia. Its advantage is that the offspring, because they are genetically identical, have all the desirable characteristics of the parent and are not as variable as plants grown from seed (see Unit 15.1).

15.6 Cloning mammals

This is more difficult than in plants but it has been used in cows.

Nuclear transplanting involves removing the nucleus of a fertilized egg and inserting a nucleus from a ball of cells (blastula) formed in a female with desirable characteristics instead (see Fig. 15.5). All eggs treated in this way are grown to blastula stage in a nutritive solution and then inserted into a foster mother's uterus which is ready for implantation because she has been treated with hormones.

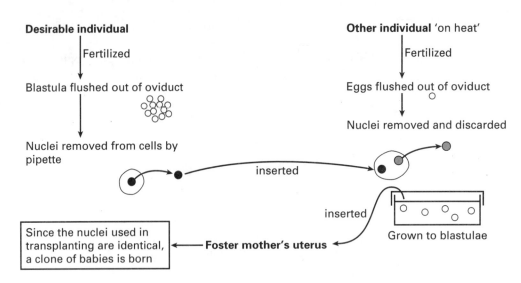

Fig. 15.5 Nuclear transplantation

Embryo division involves dividing blastula into a number of clusters of cells. This is equivalent to what happens naturally when identical twins or triplets are formed. The clusters are grown into blastulae which are then inserted into the uterus of a foster mother brought 'on heat' by injected hormones.

15.7 Flowers

A flower is the organ of sexual reproduction in flowering plants (Fig. 15.6). It is usually bisexual (hermaphrodite) but sometimes unisexual, e.g. holly.

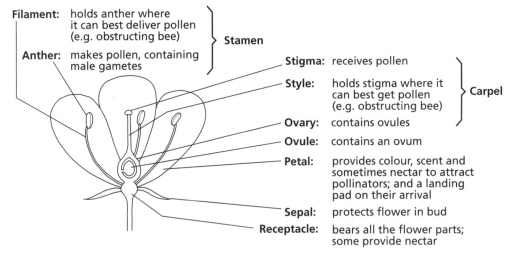

Fig. 15.6 Structure and functions of the parts of a generalized insect-pollinated flower

A flower consists of an expanded stem-tip, the **receptacle,** on which is borne four rings of modified leaves:

    (i) *sepals* – almost leaf-like but protective

    (ii) *petals* – often coloured and attractive

    (iii) *stamens* – male parts

    (iv) *carpels* – female parts

There are **two main stages in sexual reproduction:**

1 Pollination: transfer of pollen from stamens to stigmas.

2 Fertilization: fusion of male gamete with female gamete inside the ovule. This results from the growth of pollen tubes from the pollen on the stigmas to the ovules.

15.8 Self- and cross-pollination

Self-pollination: transfer of pollen from any stamen to any stigma on the *same plant* (not necessarily the same flower). Results in fewer varieties of offspring than cross-pollination. Frequent in cereal crops, grasses.

Cross-pollination: transfer of pollen of one plant to the stigmas of *another plant of the same species.* Thus rose pollen landing on an apple stigma will *not* germinate there. Results in a great variety of offspring. Since variety assists survival, many plants have means of improving the chances of cross-pollination (Fig. 15.7).

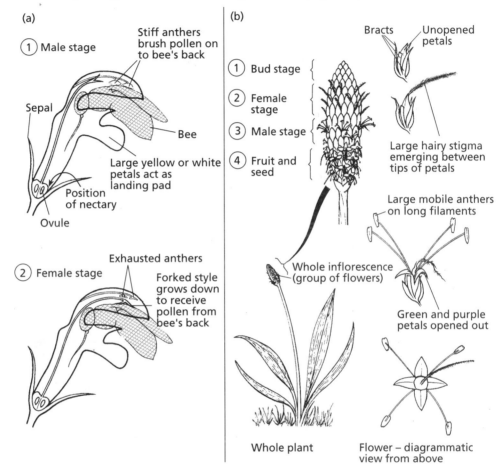

Fig. 15.7 (a) Features of an insect-pollinated flower illustrated by the deadnettle (seen in section) (b) Features of a wind-pollinated flower illustrated by the narrow-leaved plantain

15.9 Wind and insect pollination

Table 15.2 Comparison of flowers adapted for wind or insect pollination

	Wind pollination	Insect pollination
1 Petals	**Not attractive:** usually green, unscented; no nectar **Small:** leaving stamens and carpels exposed	**Attractive:** coloured, scented, often with nectaries **Large:** protect stamens and carpels inside
2 Stamens	Long filaments and large mobile anthers **exposed to wind**	Stiff filaments and anthers **obstruct visiting insects**
3 Pollen	**Large quantities** (enormous chances against it all reaching stigmas). Small, dry, light (easily wind-borne)	**Small quantities** (more certain 'delivery service'). Rougher, sometimes sticky (to catch on insect 'hairs')

Table 15.2 *(continued)*

	Wind pollination	Insect pollination
4 Stigmas	**Large, exposed** to wind (to catch passing pollen)	**Small, unexposed,** sticky with stiff style (to obstruct insects)
Examples	Plantain, grasses, hazel, oak	Buttercup, deadnettle, horse-chestnut, cherry

Note: certain flowers, which appear to be suited for insect pollination, in fact use other methods. For example:

(*a*) *peas and French beans* **self-pollinate** when still in the bud stage;

(*b*) *dandelions* develop seed from ovules without fertilization, i.e. **asexually**.

15.10 Fertilization and its consequences

① A pollen grain of the right kind on the stigma germinates to form a pollen tube (see Fig. 15.9).

② The pollen tube grows down the style and ovary wall to the micropyle of the ovule.

③ A male nucleus passes from the pollen tube into the ovule to fuse with the ovum (fertilization):

male nucleus + ovum → zygote cell

④ The zygote divides by mitosis (see Unit 18.10) to form the **embryo**:

zygote → plumule (shoot), radicle (root) and cotyledons (seed leaves)

⑤ The integuments (thin wrappings around the ovule) grow and harden into the **testa** (seed coat), still with its micropyle.

Thus embryo + testa = **seed** (see Unit 17.3).

⑥ The ovary wall grows into the **fruit** – which contains seed(s).

⑦ Most of the other flower parts drop off, i.e. petals, stamens, stigma and style, and often sepals too.

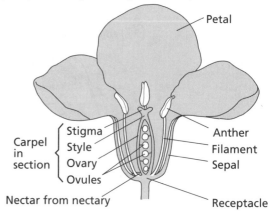

Fig. 15.8 Wallflower flower with a sectioned ovary and one petal, sepal and stamen removed

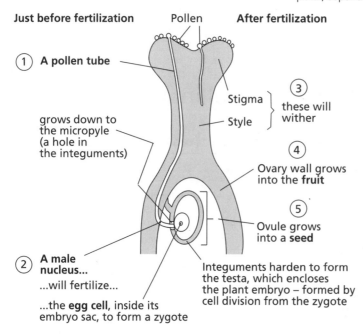

Fig. 15.9 Fertilization and its consequences in a wallflower flower

15.11 Fruits and seed dispersal

Fruits serve two main functions:

1 Protection of seed: particularly important when fruit is eaten by animals, e.g. in stone-fruits – peaches, cherries: inner part of fruit is hard.

2 Dispersal of seed (see Fig. 15.10).
(a) *Avoids overcrowding* (more likely with some methods of asexual reproduction, e.g. runners). Seedlings do not have to compete with parent for light, water and mineral salts.
(b) *Helps colonization* of new areas.

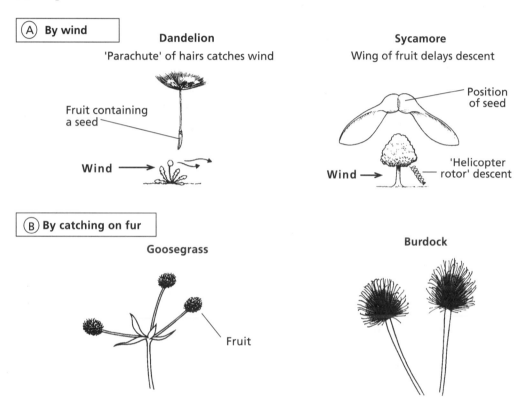

Ⓐ **By wind**

Dandelion
'Parachute' of hairs catches wind

Fruit containing a seed

Wind →

Sycamore
Wing of fruit delays descent

Position of seed

'Helicopter rotor' descent

Wind →

Ⓑ **By catching on fur**

Goosegrass

Fruit

Burdock

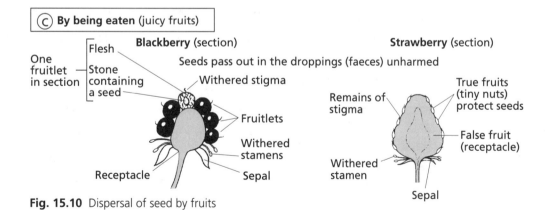

Ⓒ **By being eaten** (juicy fruits)

Blackberry (section)

One fruitlet in section
Flesh
Stone containing a seed

Seeds pass out in the droppings (faeces) unharmed

Withered stigma

Fruitlets

Withered stamens

Receptacle

Sepal

Strawberry (section)

Remains of stigma

True fruits (tiny nuts) protect seeds

False fruit (receptacle)

Withered stamen

Sepal

Fig. 15.10 Dispersal of seed by fruits

Summary

1 Asexual reproduction results from mitosis of a single organism's cells and produces identical offspring – a clone.

2 Sexual reproduction results from the meeting of a male and a female gamete at fertilization to form a zygote, which then grows into an offspring.

3 Offspring from sexual reproduction are always different.

4 Many plants reproduce naturally by asexual reproduction, e.g. from strawberry runners and potato tubers.

5 Man artificially reproduces plants by cuttings, grafting and tissue culture.

6 Man clones mammals artificially by nuclear transplantation and embryo division, putting their products into uteri of foster mothers to develop.

7 Flowers are organs of sexual reproduction and usually produce both male pollen and female ovaries.

8 Pollination (pollen reaching the stigma) precedes fertilization (a male gamete inside the pollen tube fusing with an ovum).

9 Wind pollination is chancy owing to variable wind direction, but copious pollen and feathery exposed stigmas make up for this.

10 Insect pollination is more certain and scented flowers with coloured petals and a nectar reward attract insects to the task.

11 Fertilization results in the formation of fruit (from the ovary) and seed (from the ovule).

12 Seeds are dispersed away from the parent plant by the fruit.

13 Fruits catch the wind or use animals to carry the seeds away.

Quick test 15

1 How do the offspring from asexual reproduction differ from those produced by sexual reproduction?

2 Why is rooting compound added to the base of cuttings?

3 How do the scion and stock each contribute to the resulting plant?

4 Why is auxin used in tissue culture of plants?

5 Distinguish between pollination and fertilization.

6 How is insect-carried pollen different from wind-carried pollen?

7 What happens between pollination and fertilization?

8 What do the ovary and ovule become after fertilization?

9 Give two different ways animals can disperse seeds.

10 How can cloning of mammals be achieved?

Chapter 16
Reproduction: humans

16.1 Sexual reproduction in humans

The sexual organs of man and woman are shown in Fig. 16.1.

Sequence of events in human sexual reproduction

1. Development of secondary sexual characteristics at **puberty** (12–14 years old) making reproduction possible (see Fig. 13.10).

2. **Gamete production** (Table 16.1).

E xaminer's tip

Be careful not to confuse uterus, urethra and ureter and remember the spellings.

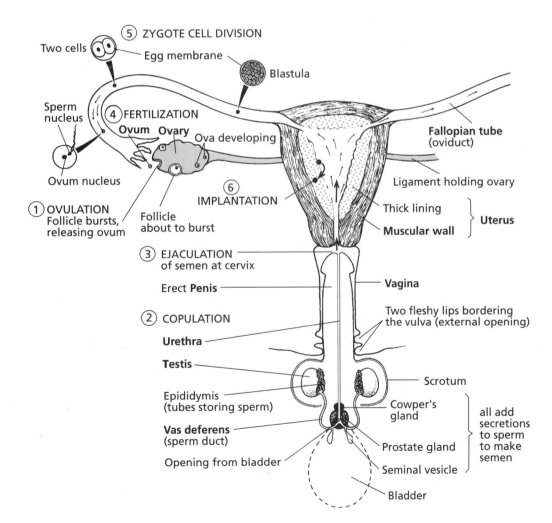

Fig. 16.1 Human male and female sex organs at copulation and the events leading to implantation

Table 16.1 Comparison of gamete production in humans

	Male	Female
Gonads	Two **testes**, kept outside the body in a sac (scrotum), produce sperm	Two **ovaries**, kept within the body cavity attached to a ligament, produce ova
Gametes	Many millions of **sperm** formed continuously throughout life after puberty (see Fig. 16.2)	Many thousands of potential **ova** formed before birth, but only about 400 will be shed between *puberty* and *menopause* (about 45 years old: end of reproductive life)
Gamete release	About **200 million** sperm are ejaculated into female by *reflex action* of the penis during copulation. They pass along sperm duct and urethra, picking up nutritive secretions from glands to form *semen*	Usually only **one** ovum is shed *automatically* per month (Unit 16.3) from an ovary. It passes into the oviduct (Fallopian tube), the only place where it can be fertilized. Once in the uterus, the ovum is lost

③ **Copulation:** the erect penis transfers sperm during ejaculation from the testes of the male to the end of the vagina (cervix) of the female.

④ **Fertilization:** any sperm that manages to swim into an oviduct containing an ovum has a chance of fertilizing it. Only one sperm enters the ovum and the two nuclei fuse, forming the zygote cell.

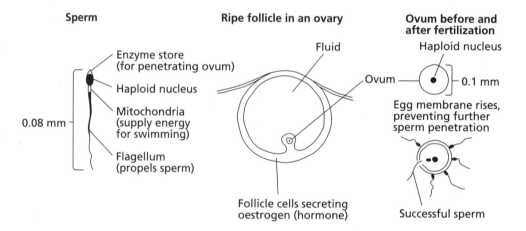

Sperm — 0.08 mm — Enzyme store (for penetrating ovum); Haploid nucleus; Mitochondria (supply energy for swimming); Flagellum (propels sperm)

Ripe follicle in an ovary — Fluid; Ovum; Follicle cells secreting oestrogen (hormone)

Ovum before and after fertilization — Haploid nucleus; 0.1 mm; Egg membrane rises, preventing further sperm penetration; Successful sperm

Fig. 16.2 Human gametes and fertilization

⑤ **Cell division:** the zygote divides into a ball of cells (blastula); passes down oviduct.

⑥ **Implantation:** the blastula sinks into the uterus lining.

⑦ **Growth:** the blastula grows into two parts – the **embryo** and its **placenta,** joined by the umbilical cord. The embryo lies within an **amnion,** a water-bag, which cushions it from damaging blows and supports it. Growth lasts 40 weeks (9 months) – the **gestation** period. Premature birth, before 7 months, can result in the embryo's death (spontaneous abortion or miscarriage).

⑧ **Birth:** the **baby** is pushed head first through a widened cervix when the uterus muscles contract. This bursts the amnion. The umbilical cord is cut by the midwife. When the baby's end of the cord dries up, it drops off leaving a scar (the navel). Babies are usually born head first.

  A baby about to be born *feet* first poses difficulties. The doctor may get it out by cutting open the abdomen and uterus (Caesarian section).

⑨ **After birth:** within 30 minutes after the birth, further contractions of the uterus expel the **placenta** (the afterbirth).

16.2 Placenta, amnion and amniocentesis

The placenta: a temporary organ grown in the uterus during gestation to supply the needs of the embryo as it grows into a fetus and then baby. These needs are:

Supply of:

(a) *food* – soluble nutrients, e.g. amino acids, glucose.
(b) *oxygen* – for respiration.

Removal of:

(a) *urea* and other wastes.
(b) *carbon dioxide.*

This exchange of substances occurs at capillaries, inside villi, at the end of the umbilical cord (Fig. 16.3). The villi lie in spaces filled with mother's blood. Mother's blood does not mix with the fetus's blood. If it did

(a) her blood pressure might burst the fetus's blood vessels;
(b) blood clumping might occur if the two blood groups were different (see Unit 18.3).

Placenta also supplies large amounts of *progesterone* to cause placenta to grow and maintain more blood vessels (see Unit 16.3).

E **xaminer's tip**

emember to explain clearly
hat passes from the
other's blood to the
tus's blood and what
asses in the opposite
rection.

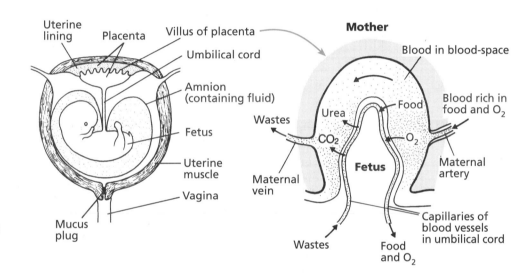

Fig. 16.3 Placenta: relationship between mother and fetus

The **amnion** supports the fetus and cushions it from blows, through its fluid. This fluid contains stray fetus cells which can be withdrawn by syringe and grown in culture. This technique, **amniocentesis**, allows doctors to see abnormal chromosome numbers that warn of Down's syndrome or other abnormalities.

16.3 Menstrual cycle

Menstrual cycle: period of approximately 28 days during which a reproductive woman alternately ovulates and menstruates (see Fig. 16.4) Cycles start during puberty (*menarche*) and continue until the *menopause*. Pregnancy will interrupt the regular cycle. Other factors that can also interfere with a normal menstrual cycle include stress, excessive physical exercise and poor diet.

Ovulation: shedding of an ovum when a follicle in the ovary bursts. Copulation within 3 days either side of the 'fertile period' could lead to fertilization, so the uterus lining (endometrium) is prepared for implantation (see Fig. 16.4).

Menstruation: shedding of most of the uterus lining 14 days after ovulation, when fertilization or implantation are unsuccessful. This occurs over 4 days with the loss of up to 500 cm^3 of blood and tissue through the vagina.

The cycle is controlled by the interaction of four hormones: follicle stimulating hormone (FSH), oestrogen, luteinising hormone (LH) and progesterone.

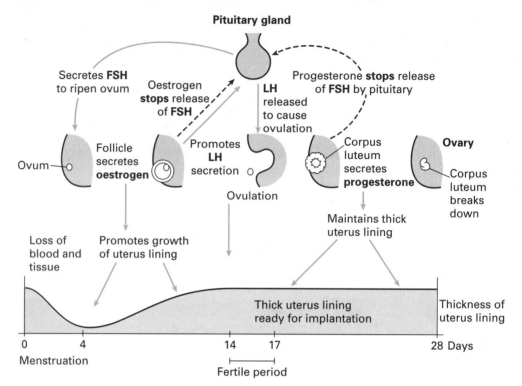

Fig. 16.4
Menstrual cycle

If fertilization and implantation do not occur the corpus luteum degenerates. This lowers the level of progesterone in the body so:

(*a*) the uterus lining breaks down causing menstruation;
(*b*) the stop on FSH secretion is removed, causing development of a new follicle. A new cycle begins.

If fertilization and implantation occur resulting in pregnancy, the corpus luteum does not degenerate. This means progesterone levels remain high so:

(*a*) the uterus lining remains intact;
(*b*) FSH inhibition remains and no further ova ripen.

After about twelve weeks the placenta takes over production of progesterone from the corpus luteum. This is a time when **miscarriage** (loss of the embryo) may occur.

16.4 Infertility and its treatment

A rising number of healthy couples (now 1 in 6) have infertility problems. Treatments for infertility raise personal and ethical problems. Table 16.2 shows some of the causes and treatments for infertility. In many cases the success rate of treatments is not high.

Table 16.2

Cause	Treatment
Ovary not ovulating (lack of FSH from pituitary)	FSH (see Unit 16.3) given to promote ovulation. This permits pregnancy in the normal way. Can lead to multiple births (due to excessive ovulation).
Blockage of oviduct (see Unit 16.1)	1. Doctors blow air up oviducts to clear them. If ineffective (scarred) then no. 2.
	2. FSH given to promote ovulation. Mature ova collected from the ovary. Husband's sperm collected and used to fertilize the eggs in the laboratory ('*in vitro*' fertilization, **IVF**). The zygote is returned to wife's uterus once it is dividing. Alternatively, the eggs and sperm are mixed *in vitro* and syringed into the oviduct beyond the blockage to allow 'natural' fertilization. Other eggs and zygotes can be kept alive, deep frozen, as a backup.

Table 16.2 (*continued*)

Cause	Treatment
Low sperm count	1. Sperm from a woman's husband is concentrated and/or injected into her oviducts (artificial insemination husband, **AIH**). Anonymous donor's sperm can be used instead (**AI**).
	2. Ova are collected from an ovary. A single sperm is injected into each ovum by microsyringe (intracellular sperm injection, **ICSI**). The zygote is returned to the woman's uterus once it is dividing.
Woman has high risk of miscarriage; has had womb removed	Surrogacy – an ovum is taken from the woman and fertilized using **IVF**. The zygote is put into the uterus of another woman at her fertile period for her to become a pregnant foster mother. (Also used in animals see Unit 15.6)

16.5 Contraception

Contraception: the prevention of fertilization and implantation.

1 Unreliable methods

(*a*) *Withdrawal:* removing penis just before ejaculation;

(*b*) *Rhythm:* not copulating during the 'fertile period' of the menstrual cycle, i.e. when an ovum is passing down the oviduct (see Fig. 16.4). Ovulation is sometimes irregular; and sperm may survive for 48 hours inside the woman. Very healthy sperm may survive inside the woman for up to 7 days. The ovum can only be successfully fertilized in the first 12 hours after ovulation.

2 Reliable methods (Fig. 16.5) include:

(*a*) *temporary* methods allowing sensible spacing of a family. This places less physical strain on the mother; and more time and finance can be given to the care and attention of each child.

(*b*) *permanent* methods, when desired family size has been reached. Removal of testes (castration) or ovaries achieves the same result but is undesirable since a person's 'nature' is changed owing to lack of sex hormones from these organs.

Examiner's tip

When answering questions try to give at least one example of each different method of contraception.

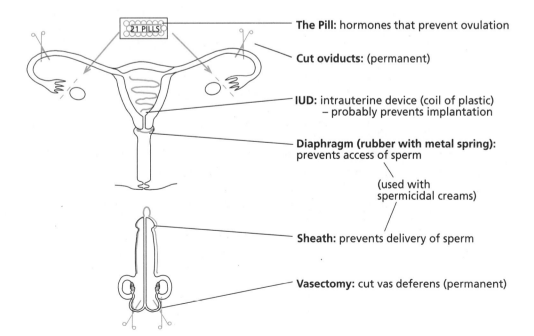

The Pill: hormones that prevent ovulation

Cut oviducts: (permanent)

IUD: intrauterine device (coil of plastic) – probably prevents implantation

Diaphragm (rubber with metal spring): prevents access of sperm

(used with spermicidal creams)

Sheath: prevents delivery of sperm

Vasectomy: cut vas deferens (permanent)

Fig. 16.5 Reliable methods of contraception

3 Recent developments

1 Hormone implant (Norplant) of synthetic progestogen in six flexible matchstick size capsules inserted under the skin in a fan formation gives protection for up to 5 years. Remembering to take 'the pill' each day is banished, and fertility is restored within 12 hours of removal of the capsules.

2 The 'morning after pill': two pills of oestrogen of high dosage must be given by a doctor within 72 hours of intercourse, and a further two within 12 hours. If it is too late for this, a coil (IUD) inserted within 5 days usually prevents implantation. These methods must only be used in an emergency and should not be used as a regular contraceptive standby.

Practice of contraception worldwide is essential if humans are to avoid destruction of their environment by pollution (see Unit 21.3), erosion and social problems. A stable or falling birth rate has been achieved in a number of industrialized nations already; developing nations lag behind in effective contraception. A notable exception is the People's Republic of China where there are severe social penalties for couples who have more than one child. The birth rate has fallen.

16.6 Sexually transmitted diseases (STD)

Sexually transmitted diseases are those passed on through copulation.
Copulation can occur in two ways:
1 *Heterosexually* (between man and woman) – the normal way, used in reproduction (see Unit 16.1). Both penis and vagina are adapted for this biologically important act.
2 *Homosexually* (between man and man). A penis is inserted into his partner's rectum. The rectum is not adapted for the sex act and tears easily, causing bleeding. This act has no biological function, so some people regard it as abnormal.

Bisexuals copulate both heterosexually and homosexually.

There are two main types of pathogen in STD:
1 Bacteria – which can be killed by antibiotics;
2 Viruses – incurable.

Bacteria

1 Syphilis: this disease occurs in three stages; by the third it is incurable.
(*a*) A painless *sore* appears at the point of contact, e.g. the penis tip or the cervix (thus the woman is often unaware of her infection) within 90 days of sexual contact. This disappears.
(*b*) Four to eight weeks later skin *rashes* may appear or patches of hair may fall out.
(*c*) After some weeks, infection reaches the *nervous system*, leading to paralysis, idiocy, blindness, etc.
    Unborn babies can be infected via the placenta; they may suffer abnormalities or be born dead.
2 Gonorrhoea: within 2 to 8 days of sexual contact a yellowish discharge of mucus may appear from penis or vagina. In both sexes there may be permanent *problems with urination;* and both may become sexually *sterile* (through blocking of the sperm ducts or the oviducts with scar tissue where there has been infection).
3 *Chlamydia:* causes inflammation of oviducts (may block them with scar tissue resulting in female infertility) and inflammation of epididymis in male.

Viruses

AIDS (**A**cquired **I**mmune **D**eficiency **S**yndrome): caused by the HIV virus. This attacks the immune system so that the body becomes defenceless against infection. Few of those infected with the virus develop AIDS immediately; the great majority are homosexual men (see below★).

AIDS symptoms can take 6 weeks to 15 years to develop – the average incubation period is 8–10 years. During this time antibodies to the virus appear in the blood: the person is well, but 'HIV-positive'.

AIDS symptoms include:
(*a*) weight loss, fever and night sweats, extreme tiredness;
(*b*) a rare kind of pneumonia;
(*c*) skin blotched purple by a rare skin cancer.
All AIDS cases die: no vaccine has been developed yet (but see Unit 18.17). The virus can also be passed on by nonsexual methods:
(*a*) the placenta and by breast feeding;
(*b*) any shared puncturing device (ear-piercing, needles for drug abuse);
(*c*) toothbrushes, razors (any chance of bleeding).
Saliva, tears, crockery and towels cannot pass the virus on.

The simplest way to avoid all STD is not to have casual sex; and have a partner who is dependably clear of STD.

★*Note:* In the UK up to December 1993, there were 21 101 HIV-positive reports. There were 8529 AIDS cases. Of the HIV-positive cases, 12 741 resulted from homosexual intercourse, 2296 from heterosexual intercourse where the other partner had been to countries where the majority of cases arise heterosexually, 1364 from blood transfusion or haemophilia factor VIII use, and 1516 from drug abuse involving injection. The number of heterosexual transmissions has risen sharply (to about 600 in each of the three years 1991–1993).
Worldwide, the majority of cases have been transmitted heterosexually.

Summary

1 Human sperm are produced in two testes; ova are produced in two ovaries.

2 Copulation (insertion of penis into vagina) and ejaculation of sperm at the cervix precede fertilization within the oviduct.

3 The zygote divides to form a ball of cells (blastula) which implants in the uterine wall.

4 The blastula grows into an embryo surrounded by salty fluid within the amnion and is sustained by the placenta.

5 The placenta provides the embryo with nutrients and oxygen and removes its wastes.

6 Eggs are shed (ovulation) monthly under the influence of hormones.

7 These hormones also affect the thickness of the uterine lining, which is shed monthly through the vagina. This is the menstrual cycle.

8 Infertility is an increasingly common complaint but can be treated by hormones or manipulation of the normal processes affecting fertilization – IVF, AI or ICSI

9 Contraception aims at preventing sperm meeting ova or preventing a blastula implanting.

10 Sexually transmitted diseases are in many cases serious if not treated early.

11 AIDS is a fatal sexually transmitted disease commonest in the UK amongst male homosexuals and injecting drug users.

12 Abnormality in embryos, e.g. Down's syndrome, can be detected by amniocentesis.

Quick test 16

1 Where in the female reproductive system does fertilization occur?

2 What is the function of each of the three parts of a sperm cell?

3 Why are hormones given to some women with fertility problems?

4 Why are there villi in the placenta?

5 Give two functions of the amnion.

6 Which hormone promotes ovulation and where is it produced?

7 What is the function of the corpus luteum if a fertilized egg is implanted?

8 How do intrauterine devices (IUDs) prevent pregnancy?

9 Which is the main hormone contained in the contraceptive pill that prevents ovulation?

10 What does it mean if a person is HIV positive?

Chapter 17
Growth

17.1 Principles of growth

Growth: irreversible increase in size or mass of an organism.
Processes involved in growth

1. Formation of **more protoplasm**, especially proteins: cell size increases.
2. Cell division by **mitosis** (see Unit 18.10): maintains small size of cells.
3. Vacuolation – in plants only; absorption of much water, swelling the cell.
4. **Differentiation** – cells become different for special purposes (Fig. 17.1).

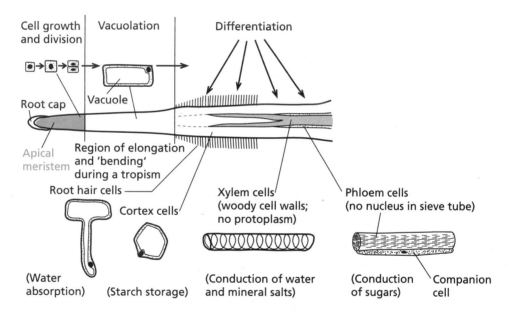

Fig. 17.1 Longitudinal section through a root showing regions of cell division (in green) and subsequent stages in growth

In a similar way, animal cells divide (but do not form vacuoles) and differentiate into cheek cells, muscle cells, neurones, blood cells, etc.

All four processes are controlled by hormones (see Unit 13.9, pituitary; Unit 13.15, auxin).

Growth involves changes of shape as well as size.

Shape

Plants and animals grow differently to suit their type of nutrition.

Green plants grow at their tips giving a branching shape with a large surface area for absorption of nutrients (necessary when anchored), and of sunlight energy.

Animals' bodies grow into a compact shape, except for their limbs (needed for food-seeking).

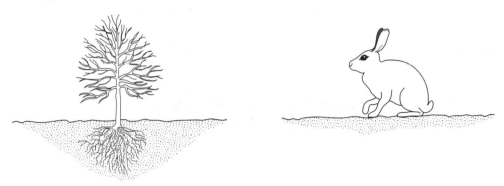

Size

Unicells have a large surface area for their tiny volume, so diffusion of materials meets most of their needs. The same applies to the individual cells of multicellular organisms.

Multicells specialize their cells, grouping them into tissues and organs. These meet the common needs of all cells more efficiently. Diffusion of food, oxygen and wastes through the body's large volume would be too slow to ensure survival (see Unit 10.6).

So special tissues are needed for
- *absorption and excretion*, e.g. in roots, guts, lungs, leaves, kidneys;
- *transport*, e.g. blood, xylem, phloem;
- *support*, e.g. bone, xylem;
- *coordination*, e.g. hormone-producing cells, neurones;
- *reproduction*, e.g. in genitals, flowers, and as gametes.

Large size gives advantages in nutrition. Tall plants can starve small ones by shading them. Large animals can use their greater power to gain more food than small ones; and to respond to predators' attacks.

Small size is useful where food is scarce, and for hiding from predators.

17.2 Factors affecting growth

Table 17.1 Some effects of genes and environment on growth

	Plants	Animals
Genes	Inherited factors: determine *size*, e.g. tall and dwarf varieties of pea plants – through growth hormones *shape*, e.g. beetroot, runner bean, gooseberry bush, poplar and oak trees *colours*, e.g. flowers *rate of growth*, e.g. pine trees grow faster than oak	Inherited factors: determine *size*, e.g. large and small dogs – through hormones (see Unit 13.9) *shape*, e.g. dachshunds and bulldogs *colouring*, e.g. tabby cats and Siamese *growth pattern* *rate of growth*, e.g. sealions grow faster than humans
Climate	*Light* is essential for nutrition (photosynthesis) and therefore growth *Increased temperature* speeds up metabolism, e.g. respiration and photosynthesis, and thus rate of growth	*Light* is necessary for making vitamin D, needed for bone growth (see Unit 5.6) *Increased temperature* speeds up growth and development of ectotherms (Unit 11.6) but not endotherms, e.g. mammals
Nutrients	*Mineral salts* of the right kinds (see Unit 5.3) and quantity, e.g. from fertilizers, promote growth *Water* and carbon dioxide essential	*Food* of the right kinds and quantity (a balanced diet) promotes growth (see Unit 5.7) *Water* essential

Gene expression is affected by:

(a) *climate*: stoats change their brown summer coats for white ('ermine') ones in the winter; black markings of dark moths reared in cool conditions are paler (brown) if reared in warm conditions.

(b) *nutrients*: both size and intelligence of humans are less when they are continually under-nourished (see Unit 5.7); genes cannot express themselves fully.

17.3 Seed structure and germination

Seeds are embryo plants enclosed by the testa (seed coat). They develop from the ovule after fertilization (see Unit 15.10). When shed they are dry (about 10% water).

The *embryo* consists of a radicle (root), a plumule (shoot) and one or more cotyledons (first seed leaves).

The *testa* bears a hilum (scar where the seed broke off the fruit) and a micropyle (pore for water entry during germination) (Fig. 17.2).

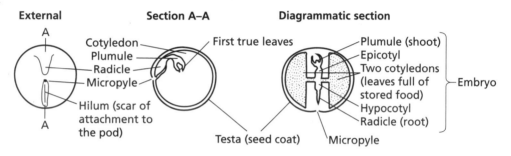

Fig. 17.2 Structure of a pea seed (beans are similar)

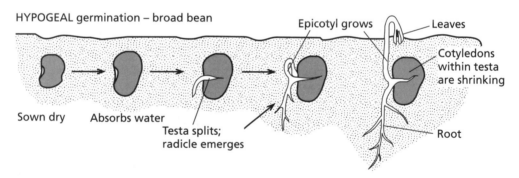

Fig. 17.3 Germination of a broad bean seed

In peas and beans the food for the seedling's growth is stored in the cotyledons. In wheat and maize the food store is the endosperm (outside the embryo) (Fig. 17.4).

When barley germinates, enzymes turn its starch into maltose. This 'malt' can be fermented by yeast to make beer (see Unit 4.7).

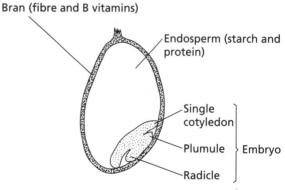

White bread is made mainly from endosperm. Wholemeal bread uses the whole grain

Fig. 17.4 A grain of wheat

17.4 Conditions necessary for germination

1 **Water:** to hydrate protoplasm, activating enzymes which digest stored food (e.g. starch to sugars).
2 **Warmth:** to enable enzymes to work.
3 **Oxygen:** for aerobic respiration to supply energy for growth.
   Some seeds require *light*, others dark, for germination; for most these do not matter.

All tubes, except C, are put in a warm place

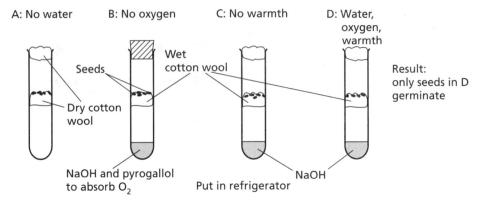

A: No water   B: No oxygen   C: No warmth   D: Water, oxygen, warmth

Seeds
Wet cotton wool
Dry cotton wool
NaOH and pyrogallol to absorb O₂
Put in refrigerator
NaOH
Result: only seeds in D germinate

Fig. 17.5 Experiment to determine the conditions necessary for seed germination

17.5 Growth measurement and its difficulties

1 **Length or height** – all organisms. A crude method: volume would be better.
2 **Live mass** – terrestrial animals. Difficult for:
   (*a*) plants: roots are broken off, or soil remains attached to them;
   (*b*) aquatic organisms (how much should one dry them before weighing?).
3 **Dry mass** – all organisms, but they have to be killed (and dried in an oven at 110 °C). Avoids errors of hydration likely in no. 2 above, e.g. Did the animal drink or urinate before it was weighed? Were the plant cells fully turgid on weighing?

   It is essential when measuring growth of organisms to
(*a*) have a large number growing (avoids results from a freak individual);
(*b*) control *all* factors affecting growth (including crowding), e.g. food, temperature, light.

Examiner's tip

There are advantages and disadvantages to each of these methods of measuring growth.

17.6 Cancer

Tumours ('growths') appear when certain cells start to divide out of control. **Benign tumours** are harmless but may need to be cut out. **Malignant tumours** (cancers) are life threatening. They must be destroyed.

Treatment: cure is easiest when the cancer is detected early, i.e. when
(*a*) the tumour is small and easily destroyed;
(*b*) cells from the original tumour have not broken away into the blood to form new tumours in other organs, damaging their function.
The cancer can be destroyed by
(*a*) surgery;
(*b*) chemicals that stop cell division (chemotherapy);
(*c*) radiation, e.g. γ-rays focused on the tumour to kill it (radiotherapy).

Cause: 80 to 90 per cent of all cancers are *environmentally* caused, e.g. Japanese emigrants to the USA soon show a lower rate of stomach cancer (very high in Japan), but higher rates of bowel and breast cancer (matching those of Western people). Lung cancer rates rise greatly with smoking. See Table 17.4.

Table 17.4 Some causes of cancer – radiation, chemicals and viruses

Cancer	Cause
Skin	Too much sunshine – ultraviolet radiation can cause cell mutations
Lung	Chemicals in tobacco smoke (90 per cent of cases are fatal)
Stomach	Diet and drink (the commonest form of cancer worldwide)
Cervical	Probably the papilloma virus, sexually transmitted (see Unit 16.6)

Prevention: health education (e.g. about diet and the risks of smoking); high safety standards in the nuclear and chemical industries; regular medical checks to increase early detection, e.g. the 'smear' test for cervical cancer and X-ray examination for breast cancer. Screening for prostate cancer (kills more men than breast cancer does women) is not provided by NHS: surgery often causes permanent problems with urination and penis erection. About a third of all cancers are preventable, another third curable.

Summary

1   Growth is an irreversible increase in the size or mass of an organism.

2   Growth involves making more protoplasm, cell division by mitosis and differentiation into specialized cells.

3   Three main factors affect growth: the genes, the climate and the food available.

4   The factors necessary for germination of seeds are water, warmth and oxygen.

5   Growth can be monitored by measuring changes in length, height, and live or dry mass.

6   Ionizing radiations, some chemicals and some viruses can cause cancer.

7   Cancer results from cells multiplying out of control.

8   Most cancers are environmentally caused; one third of these are preventable.

9   Health education and medical screening help to prevent cancer fatalities.

Quick test 17

1   Define growth.

2   What is the area of cell division called in a root?

3   What are the stages of cell growth after cell division has occurred in plants?

4   What three different types of factor affect growth?

5   Which part of the embryo emerges from the seed first?

6   What is the main food store of the seed?

7   Why is oxygen needed for germination?

8   What is the main disadvantage of using dry mass as a measurement of growth?

9   What is cancer?

Chapter 18

Genes, chromosomes and heredity

18.1 The nucleus, chromosomes and genes

The **nucleus** normally contains long threads of DNA (see Unit 1.3) which are not visible under the light microscope.

Before cell division each DNA thread coils up, with protein, into a compact 'sausage' called a **chromosome**. When stained, this is visible under the light microscope (Fig. 18.1). Chromosomes are present in **homologous pairs**, both members having the same length (and number of genes). One chromosome of the pair came from the male parent, the other from the female parent, when their gametes fused together to form a zygote (see Fig. 18.6). Sections of the DNA threads are **genes**; each controls the making of an enzyme (see Unit 1.4).

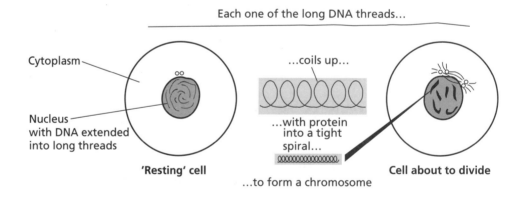

Fig. 18.1 Chromosome formation within the nucleus of a cell

18.2 Genes and characteristics

Two factors influence the characteristics of an organism: genes and environment.

① **Genes** control the making of enzymes. Each enzyme controls a particular chemical change. This small change is a part of larger changes controlled by groups of enzymes. One or more chemical changes of this sort help to determine a **characteristic**.

For example:

one gene causes sickle cell anaemia (Unit 19.2);

many genes cooperate to give curly black hair – those for making hair protein, for black colour and for curly growth.

2 **Environment** influences the way genes act (see Unit 18.15). For example, a well-fed youngster is more likely to develop into a larger adult than his starved identical twin (even though both have identical genes). The genetic make-up of an organism is called its **genotype**. The interaction of its genotype with the environment is called its **phenotype**, i.e. its observable or measurable **characteristics**.

To simplify the above, consider an unfastened pearl necklace. The pearls are genes, the necklace a chromosome. A similar necklace would be its homologous partner (Fig. 18.2). Genes at an identical position (locus) on two homologous chromosomes determine a characteristic between them.

Diagram of chromosomes	a ⸜⸜⸜⸜●⸜⸜⸜⸜⸜⸜⸜⸜⸜⸜⸜⸜⸜⸜●⸜⸜⸜ B	**Pair 1**	C^1 ⸜⸜⸜⸜●⸜⸜⸜⸜⸜ **Pair 2**
	⸜⸜⸜●⸜⸜⸜⸜⸜⸜⸜⸜⸜⸜⸜⸜●⸜⸜⸜⸜		⸜⸜⸜●⸜⸜⸜⸜⸜
	a b		C^2
Genotype	aa Homozygous	Bb Heterozygous	$C^1 C^2$ Heterozygous
Status of these genes	Recessive	B: dominant b: recessive	C^1 and C^2 are codominant
Phenotype	a	B	C^1/C^2 (both)

Fig. 18.2 Genetical terms illustrated with reference to two homologous pairs of chromosomes

Dominant genes (shown by capital letters) always express themselves as a characteristic. **Recessive genes** (shown by small letters) only express themselves when the partner is also recessive.

Thus genotype **AA** or **Aa** will be expressed as an **A** phenotype and genotype **aa** is the only way of producing the **a** phenotype (Fig. 18.3). Organisms with two identical genes at a locus (**AA** or **aa** genotypes) are said to be **homozygous**; those with alternative genes at the locus (**Aa**) are called **heterozygous**.

The alternative genes (**A** and **a**) are called **alleles**.

Gene	Phenotype	Genotype	Phenotype	Genotype
Dominant	Normal mucus secretion in lung	CC or Cc	Mental deterioration with involuntary movements, in adults (**Huntington's chorea**)	HH or Hh
Recessive	Thick secretion: liability to severe lung infections (**cystic fibrosis**)	cc		hh

Fig. 18.3 Examples of dominant and recessive disease genes in humans

N.B. 'Tongue rolling' is a characteristic now known *not* to be inherited. You can learn, by practice, to roll your tongue into a gutter shape.

18.3 Human blood groups: codominance

Codominance

Certain alleles are **codominant**: both alleles express themselves, e.g. in the determination of human blood group AB (Table 18.1).

Table 18.1 Genetics of blood groups A, B and O in humans

Gene status	Blood groups (i.e. phenotypes)	Genotypes
I^A (dominant)	A	$I^A I^A$ or $I^A I^O$
I^B (dominant)	B	$I^B I^B$ or $I^B I^O$
I^O (recessive)	O	$I^O I^O$
I^A and I^B are **codominant**	AB	$I^A I^B$

In **blood transfusion** the blood groups of both giver (donor) and the patient receiving blood should ideally be the *same*. This avoids clumping together of the donor's red blood cells inside the patient's veins. Clumping occurs if the patient's antibodies (in the plasma) react with the donor's red blood cells (bearing antigens, e.g. A or B), making their cell membranes sticky. Note: clumping is *not* clotting.

Clumps not only block capillaries; but as the cells in them burst, the released products can cause kidney failure.

Incomplete dominance is not the same as codominance: the two alleles express themselves unequally. Examples are shown in Table 18.2.

Table 18.2

Characteristic	Genotypes and their phenotypic effect		
Blood clotting time (see Unit 18.9)	$B^H B^H$: normal	$B^H B^h$: very slightly longer	$B^h B^h$ or B^h – (in male): very long (haemophilia)
Anaemia (see Unit 19.2)	$H^N H^N$: none	$H^N H^S$: very slight	$H^S H^S$: severe (sickle cell anaemia)

18.4 Mendel's experiments

Genetics (the study of heredity) was only put on a firm basis in 1865 thanks to **Gregor Mendel**, an Austrian abbot, who published his research on inheritance in peas.

His materials: *Pisum sativum*, the garden pea. This:
(a) normally *self-pollinates* (and self-fertilizes) when the flower is still unopened. To *cross-pollinate* plants, Mendel had to remove the unripe anthers of strain **A** flowers and dust their stigmas with pollen from ripe stamens of strain **B**. Interference by insects was avoided by enclosing the flowers in muslin bags.
(b) has *strongly contrasting phenotypes*, e.g. pea plants are either tall (150–180 cm) or dwarf (20–45 cm); the seeds are either round or wrinkled.

His methods: As parents (P_1, or first parental generation) he chose two contrasting 'pure lines' which 'bred true', i.e. were homozygous. These he mated by cross-pollination. The offspring (F_1, or first filial generation) were allowed to self-pollinate. This gave the F_2, or second filial generation.

Results from one such experiment:
P_1 Tall × Dwarf
F_1 All Tall

Conclusion 1: factor for Tall is dominant to factor for Dwarf.

F_2 Ratio of 3 Tall: 1 Dwarf

Conclusion 2: factor for Dwarf was not lost (as it seemed to have been in the F_1). This suggested that 'factors' were particles of hereditary material which remained unaltered as they were handed on at each generation.

We now know that 'factors' are genes, and that the material of genes is DNA in chromosomes.

Table 18.3 Summary of a Mendelian experiment using modern genetical terms

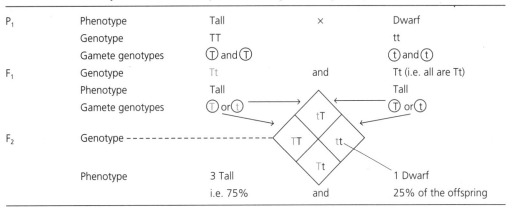

18.5 Hints on tackling genetic problems

When genetics problems are set as questions it is essential that the eight lines of terms relating to the **P₁**, **F₁**, and **F₂** on the left of Table 18.3 be set out first before the data in the question is inserted in the appropriate places. By reasoning, the rest of the 'form' you have thus created can be filled in. It is vital to remember that gametes are **haploid** (have *one* set of genes) and organisms are **diploid** (have *two* sets of genes). The diamond checkerboard giving the genotypes of offspring is called a Punnett square.

18.6 Test cross

Test cross test shows whether an organism of dominant phenotype is homozygous (TT) or heterozygous (Tt). The organism is crossed with a double recessive organism.

Table 18.4

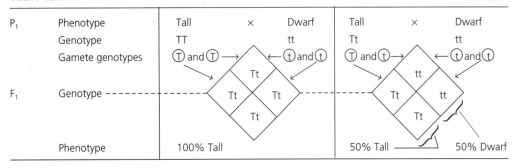

Only heterozygotes can give recessive phenotype (dwarf) offspring. Those that do not (homozygotes) can be used as 'pure line' parents in selective breeding.

18.7 Ratios of phenotypes

Tables 18.3 and 18.4 state certain ratios of offspring: 75:25 and 50:50. These are only *expected* ratios. The ratios *obtained* in a breeding experiment are rarely identical with those expected. Thus Mendel obtained 787 Tall:277 Dwarf in the **F₂** of the experiment

explained in Table 18.3, a ratio of 2.84:1. Likewise a coin tossed 1000 times is *expected* to give 500 'heads' and 500 'tails' – but rarely does so. Scientists apply a 'test of significance' to ratios obtained to see whether they are near enough to the expected ratios to be regarded as the same. For example, is 26:24 near enough to 25:25 to be regarded as 50% of each?

Note: you are not expected to know the 'test of significance'. But if you were given a ratio of, say, 505:499 offspring in a question, you must first *explain why* you assume this is a 50:50 ratio before proceeding.

Mendel used *large numbers* of organisms in his experiments to obtain ratios of offspring that were meaningful. Much modern genetical knowledge has come from breeding *Drosophila* (fruit fly) which

(*a*) is easy to culture (in small bottles on banana paste and yeast);
(*b*) produces many offspring (100 per female);
(*c*) has a short development time (10 days from egg to adult).

Investigating the genetics of slow-breeding species (e.g. cows, Man) is less easy. Experiments are lengthy and costly, and in Man's case not allowed. Information must come from herd, family or hospital records.

18.8 Sex determination in mammals

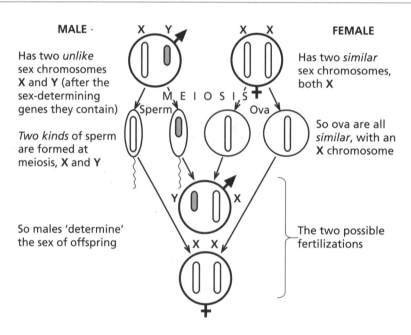

Fig. 18.4 Sex determination

Thus males and females are born in approximately equal numbers.

18.9 Sex linkage

Sex linkage: the appearance of certain characteristics in one sex and not the other (in mammals these appear in the male).

The **Y** chromosome, being shorter than the **X** (see Fig. 18.4), lacks a number of genes present on the longer chromosome. In a male (**XY**) therefore, these genes are present singly and not in pairs, as in the female (**XX**). All these 'single' genes come from the mother (on the **X**) and express themselves, even if recessive. Examples: red/green colour blindness and haemophilia.

About 4% of males are affected by **red/green colour blindness** (the two colours appear grey). Females can be affected too, since the condition is not lethal.

In **haemophilia** blood fails to clot, so trivial cuts and tooth extractions can be lethal through bleeding. Ordinary blows can cause internal bleeding and extensive bruising and joints may bleed after vigorous exertion. Nowadays, injections of the clotting factor that they lack (Factor VIII) can help haemophiliacs to lead near-normal lives.

Possible types H = normal, is dominant to h = haemophiliac

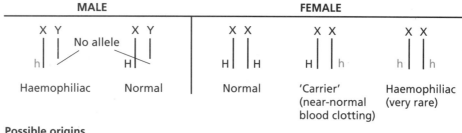

Examiner's tip

Males either have the symptoms or they don't because they only have one gene for the characteristic.

Possible origins

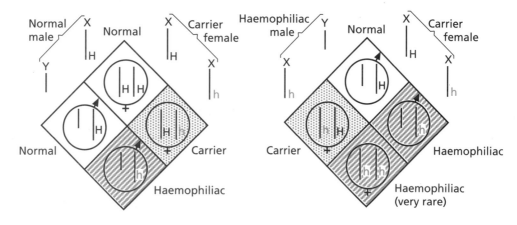

Fig. 18.5 Inheritance of haemophilia

18.10 Mitosis and meiosis in the life cycle

Examiner's tip

Misspelling mitosis or meiosis can make it difficult to know which process you mean. This can cause you to lose marks unnecessarily.

- Most organisms start from a **zygote** cell containing chromosomes in pairs, i.e. it contains a double set or **diploid** number of chromosomes ($2n$). One set comes from each parent.
- The zygote divides by **mitosis** to form new cells, also containing the $2n$ number, during **growth**.
- In a multicellular organism these cells **differentiate** (see Unit 17.1) into cells as different as neurones and phagocytes. This happens because although all the cells possess identical genes (see Unit 18.13), they use different combinations of them according to their location in the body. For example, muscle cells do not use their hair colour genes.
- Certain cells in sex organs divide by **meiosis** to become **gametes**. These contain a single set or **haploid** number of chromosomes (n).
- At **fertilization**, gametes fuse to form a zygote ($n + n \rightarrow 2n$). Meiosis thus ensures that the chromosome number does not double at each new generation (which it would if gametes were $2n$, i.e. $2n + 2n \rightarrow 4n$; $4n + 4n \rightarrow 8n$ and so on).

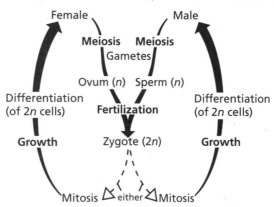

Fig. 18.6 Mitosis and meiosis in a life cycle

18.11 Mitosis

Mitosis – division of non-sexual cells, e.g. in growth, is a continuous process (see Fig. 18.7). Cells spend most of their time in interphase. During this time they are not dividing, but carrying out their normal functions, e.g. DNA is being used to produce proteins for the cell's biochemical processes (see Unit 1.5).

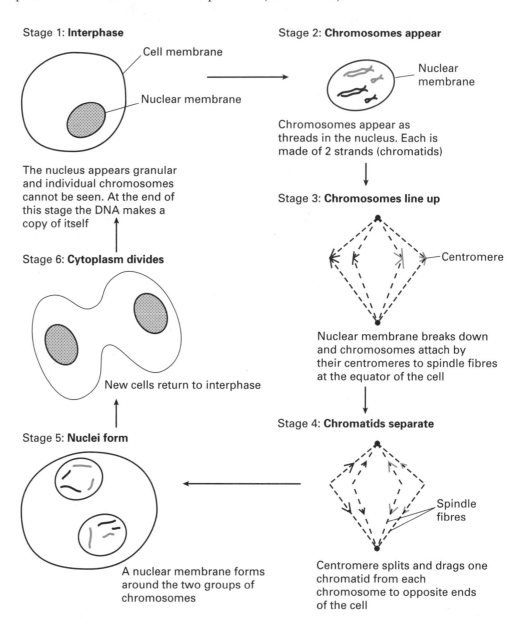

Stage 1: **Interphase**

Cell membrane

Nuclear membrane

The nucleus appears granular and individual chromosomes cannot be seen. At the end of this stage the DNA makes a copy of itself

Stage 6: **Cytoplasm divides**

New cells return to interphase

Stage 5: **Nuclei form**

A nuclear membrane forms around the two groups of chromosomes

Stage 2: **Chromosomes appear**

Nuclear membrane

Chromosomes appear as threads in the nucleus. Each is made of 2 strands (chromatids)

Stage 3: **Chromosomes line up**

Centromere

Nuclear membrane breaks down and chromosomes attach by their centromeres to spindle fibres at the equator of the cell

Stage 4: **Chromatids separate**

Spindle fibres

Centromere splits and drags one chromatid from each chromosome to opposite ends of the cell

Fig. 18.7 Mitosis

Examiner's tip

When the two strands are attached they are chromatids of the same chromosome. When they separate they are each called chromosomes.

18.12 Meiosis

Meiosis produces four cells each with half the normal chromosome number. It occurs in special cells in the sex organs to produce sex cells, i.e. gametes (eggs, sperm or pollen).

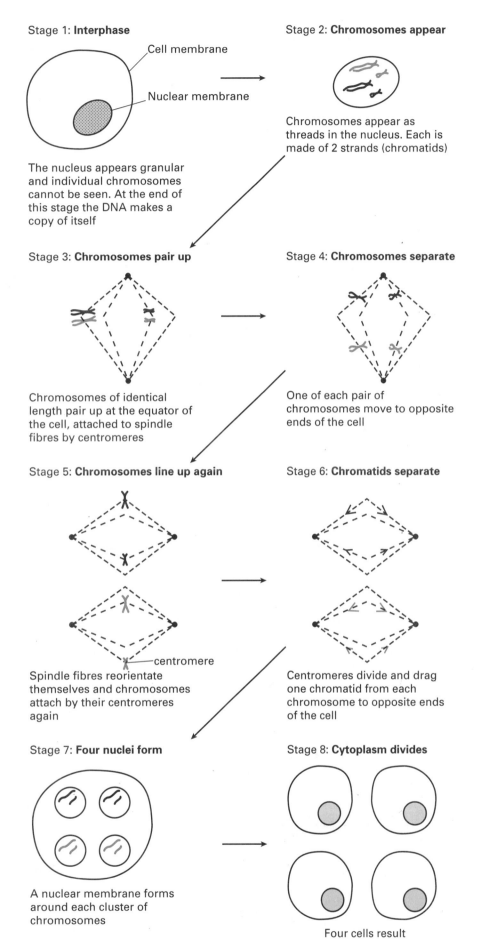

Stage 1: **Interphase**

Cell membrane

Nuclear membrane

The nucleus appears granular and individual chromosomes cannot be seen. At the end of this stage the DNA makes a copy of itself

Stage 2: **Chromosomes appear**

Chromosomes appear as threads in the nucleus. Each is made of 2 strands (chromatids)

Stage 3: **Chromosomes pair up**

Chromosomes of identical length pair up at the equator of the cell, attached to spindle fibres by centromeres

Stage 4: **Chromosomes separate**

One of each pair of chromosomes move to opposite ends of the cell

Stage 5: **Chromosomes line up again**

centromere

Spindle fibres reorientate themselves and chromosomes attach by their centromeres again

Stage 6: **Chromatids separate**

Centromeres divide and drag one chromatid from each chromosome to opposite ends of the cell

Stage 7: **Four nuclei form**

A nuclear membrane forms around each cluster of chromosomes

Stage 8: **Cytoplasm divides**

Four cells result

Fig. 18.8 Meiosis

18.13 Mitosis and meiosis compared

Table 18.5 Summary comparison of mitosis and meiosis

	Mitosis	Meiosis
Number of cell divisions	1	2
Resulting cells are	Diploid, identical	Haploid, not identical (Unit 18.14)
Purpose	Growth, replacement (e.g. of skin, blood cells) Asexual reproduction	Gamete formation
Occurrence in	Growth areas (Unit 17.1) Replacement tissues, e.g. skin, bone marrow Where runners, tubers form	Gonads, e.g. testes, ovaries; anthers, ovules (Units 15.7, 16.1)

Occasionally cells dividing by mitosis can produce different offspring, but only by mutation (see Unit 18.16).

Examiner's tip

When comparing mitosis and meiosis make it clear which one you are talking about.

18.14 Meiosis shuffles genes

In addition to halving the chromosome number, meiosis shuffles genes at the stage when chromosomes 'pair up' (see Fig. 18.8 Stage 3). They can pair up:

Fig. 18.9 How meiosis shuffles genes

So when the chromosomes separate (Stage 4) the resulting nuclei would be different genetically.

In a human cell with 46 chromosomes (and not 4) this alone makes 2^{22} (over 4 million) different varieties of gamete. Both sperm and egg show this huge variety. So the number of genotypes resulting from fertilization is vast.

18.15 Variation in populations

Variety arises from

1 **Sexual reproduction:**

Male and female have *different genes*.

Meiosis shuffles their genes to make *gametes different* (Unit 18.14).

Each pair of gametes fusing at fertilization gives a different *combination* of genes from any other pair. So offspring are unique.

2 **Mutation:** inheritable changes that are 'new' (see Unit 18.16).

3 **Environmental effects**

Food supply affects size, e.g. poor soil grows small crops; malnutrition causes obesity or deficiency diseases.

Temperature affects metabolism, e.g. warmth speeds growth; affects colour, e.g. dark moths turn out paler if reared in warm conditions.

Overcrowding affects size through competition for food and water; affects behaviour, e.g. locusts will migrate.

Only variation resulting from **1** and **2** can be passed on (inherited). This can affect evolution (see Unit 19.3). Environmental effects cannot be inherited.

Environmental effects can best be demonstrated using a clone (see Unit 15.3). Cuttings of equal length from a *Tradescantia* plant, rooted in sand, can be grown in different mineral salt solutions (see Unit 6.9). Any differences in growth must be due to differences in the mineral salts present, i.e. environment, since the genes in each plant cutting are identical.

Two patterns of variation are seen in populations:

Continuous variation	Discontinuous variation
E.g. human height, intelligence, fingerprints.	*E.g.* height of pea plants; human blood groups.
1 A complete *range* of types, e.g. from giants to dwarfs in humans.	**1** Sharply *contrasting* types, e.g. tall and dwarf pea plants.
2 Phenotype controlled by (*a*) *many pairs* of alleles; (*b*) environment (may play a major part).	**2** Phenotype controlled by (*a*) a *single pair* (or a few) alleles; (*b*) environment (plays little part).

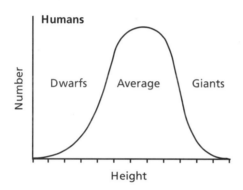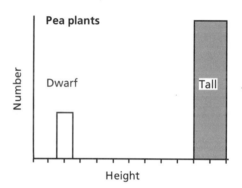

Fig. 18.10 Continuous and discontinuous variation in populations

18.16 Mutation

Mutation: an inheritable change in a cell. The nature of the DNA, or its quantity, alters.

Cause: cosmic rays, ultraviolet rays, radioactive emissions and certain chemicals, e.g. mustard gas, are mutagenic agents (cause mutations). These (and other causes) have effects on:

(*a*) **Genes:** a minute part of DNA once altered, may produce altered proteins in the cell (see Unit 1.4). These may be useless, e.g. *haemophilia* (no Factor VIII for clotting); useful, e.g. *melanism* (black pigment in peppered moths); or a bit of both, e.g. *sickle cell anaemia* (haemoglobin in red blood cells changed) – see Unit 19.2.

(*b*) **Single chromosomes:** through accidents at the separation of chromosomes in meiosis, extra chromosomes reach gametes, e.g. older mothers have a higher chance of producing Down's syndrome babies by this means. These have $2n + 1$ chromosomes, i.e. 47.

(*c*) **Whole sets of chromosomes:** meiosis may go completely wrong and produce diploid ($2n$) gametes. If these are used in fertilization then

$2n + n$ (normal gamete) $\rightarrow 3n$ (triploid chromosome number).

Many apple varieties are $3n$.

Cells with more than 2 *sets* of chromosomes (polyploids) are larger than diploid ($2n$) ones. So Man encourages and selects for these mutations to give bigger crops, e.g. wheat is $6n$.

Man also 'mutates' cells by genetic engineering (Unit 18.17).

Mutations occur constantly in populations. New strains of viruses, e.g. flu, catch human defences unprepared. New strains of bacteria, e.g. syphilis, are resistant to antibiotics. Mutant pest insects, e.g. mosquito, are surviving insecticides. Mutant rats in the UK have become Warfarin (poison) resistant.

18.17 Genetic engineering

Genetic engineering is Man's transfer of useful genes from one organism into another. Two main methods:

1 (*a*) **Bacteria** can be given selected genes using plasmids (Fig. 18.11). Inside the bacterium the genes function normally. They are reproduced when bacteria divide. The wanted products (e.g. insulin, growth hormone, vitamins or enzymes) can be extracted in large quantities from the fermenter (in which the bacteria reproduce rapidly – see Fig. 4.1).

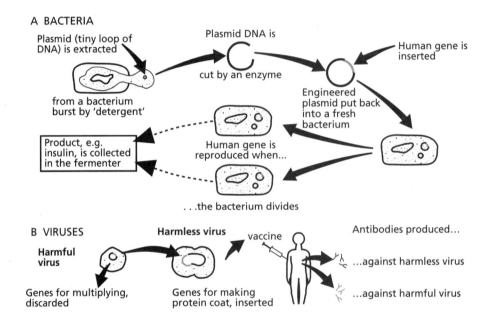

Fig. 18.11
Genetic engineering of bacteria and viruses

(*b*) **Viruses:** Genes for the protein coat of a harmful virus, e.g. AIDS, can be put into a harmless virus, e.g. cowpox. If this 'engineered' virus is used as a vaccine, the body produces antibodies against the harmful virus. Such ideas are on trial.

2 Fusing two kinds of cells together. Lymphocytes producing particular antibodies (e.g. against measles) can be fused with cancer cells (which divide rapidly). Inside fermenters, these 'engineered' cells both divide rapidly and produce antibodies in very large quantities. The antibodies can be extracted to make vaccines (see Unit 4.12).

Plant cells can also be fused – after removing the cell wall. Attempts are being made to produce a cereal plant with the ability to fix nitrogen (producing its own 'fertilizer').

18.18 Genetic fingerprinting

The DNA is extracted from cells. Selected parts are chopped by enzymes into bits large and small. These are treated to be radioactively labelled and placed on a nylon membrane. A direct current applied along the membrane separates the bits of DNA (electrophresis) into what looks like a bar code when it is laid against a photographic film (autoradiography). Each person's bar-code ('fingerprint') is unique.

Genetic fingerprinting is used in forensic science to identify blood, semen and skin samples (see Fig. 18.12). Paternity disputes can also be resolved by this method.

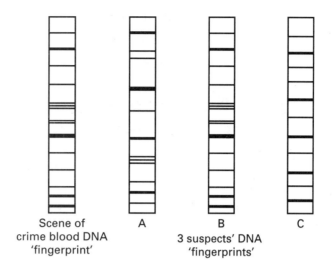

Fig. 18.12 DNA fingerprinting evidence: suspect B will be accused

Scene of crime blood DNA 'fingerprint'

A   B   C

3 suspects' DNA 'fingerprints'

Summary

1   Genes are lengths of DNA within chromosomes in the nucleus of a cell.

2   Chromosomes are found in pairs. One of the pair came from the sperm, the other from the ovum when they fused at fertilization.

3   Humans have 23 pairs of chromosomes.

4   Genes may be dominant, recessive or codominant, according to whether they express themselves or not.

5   Mendel's experiments with peas determined the basic rules of inheritance of characteristics.

6   Genotypes (genetic make-up) determine phenotypes (observable characteristics).

7   The phenotypes of offspring of a particular pair of parents can be predicted if the parental genotypes are known and a Punnett square is used.

8   Males produce sperm with either an X or a Y chromosome, while all ova have an X chromosome. An XY fertilization produces a boy and an XX fertilization a girl.

9   Certain genes are called sex-linked because they are not present on the shorter Y chromosome. The only genes of this kind in a male have come on the X chromosome from his mother.

10 Mitosis is the cell division of growth and asexual reproduction, and produces identical diploid cells.

11 Meiosis is the cell division that forms gametes, each of them different and haploid.

12 Mutation is the changing of genes or the number of chromosomes in a cell and is the raw material of evolution, since new and better phenotypes give a better chance of survival to their owners.

13 Variation in populations arises through sexual reproduction and mutation, and is inheritable.

14 Variation due to the environment, e.g. amount of food, is not inheritable.

15 Genetic engineering is the transfer of useful genes from organisms into bacteria to obtain useful products such as enzymes, vaccines and hormones. But it has its dangers too.

16 Genetic fingerprints, unique DNA profiles for each individual, can be used to identify criminals from suspects by matching up DNA samples.

Quick test 18

1 What is a chromosome made of?

2 How does a gene control the characteristics of a person, for example eye colour?

3 What is the difference between genotype and phenotype?

4 If tall is dominant to dwarf, what are the possible parental genotypes of two tall parents who have a dwarf offspring?

5 Haemophilia is a sex linked gene. Write down the five possible genotypes and phenotypes.

6 Cells can divide by mitosis or meiosis in order to reproduce organisms. Explain the purpose of each.

7 What is the main difference between the genetic control of characters showing continuous and discontinuous variation?

8 Define a mutation.

9 Which two groups of microorganisms are extensively genetically engineered?

10 What is a genetic fingerprint?

Chapter 19
Evolution

19.1 Selection of the 'best' from a variety

Organic evolution is the change in a population of a species (over a large number of generations) that results in the formation of a new species. The change is brought about by selection of only the 'best' from the variety of types present in the population.

Variety in a population arises from:

(*a*) *new combinations of genes* at fertilization (mother and father are different);

(*b*) *meiosis* (it shuffles the genes to make all gametes different – see Unit 18.14);

(*c*) *mutation* (which includes the origin of 'new genes' – see Unit 18.16);

(*d*) *environmental influences* (other than mutagenic agents), e.g. poor soil grows stunted plants.

Note: (*a*) and (*b*) are *rearrangements* of existing genes; (*c*) is the creating of *new* genes; but (*d*) does not change genetic material at all.

Natural selection occurs when the *environment* permits only those best adapted to it to survive. The survivors are the 'fittest and best' for the particular conditions of the environment at that time (Fig. 19.1). If the conditions change, new kinds of survivors appear since the previous survivors may no longer be the fittest (see Unit 19.2A and C).

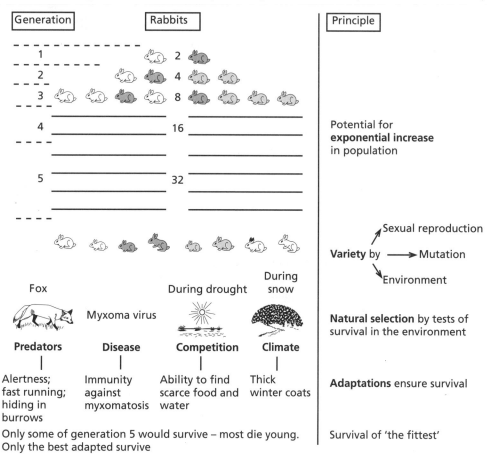

Fig. 19.1
Natural selection results in survival of the fittest

An **adaptation** is a solution to a biological problem (see Unit 11.8). Adaptations may be *structures*, e.g. wings for flying; *chemicals*, e.g. antibodies against diseases; *features of the life history*, e.g. high reproductive rate; and even *behaviour*, e.g. phototaxis in fly adults (see Unit 13.13). The majority of adaptations are *inherited*.

Artificial selection occurs when *Man* selects, for his own purposes, certain varieties of organism. These are frequently 'unfit' for survival in the wild, being suited only for the special conditions he puts them in, e.g. farms, greenhouses, gardens and homes (see Unit 19.5).

19.2 Examples of natural selection

A Industrial melanism

Peppered moth *Biston betularia*
Selection by: predatory birds, e.g. thrushes
Adaptation: camouflage

Before 1840 the light-coloured (peppered) moth survived by camouflage on lichen-covered tree trunks in unpolluted woods (Fig. 19.2). Dark mutant moths did not survive predation – they were easily seen.

Examiner's tip

Look carefully at information given and explain any figures in terms of how well camouflaged organisms are or how easily they are seen by predators.

Fig. 19.2 The two forms of the peppered moth, camouflaged

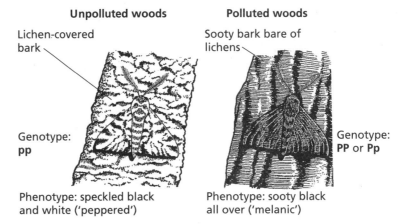

Unpolluted woods   **Polluted woods**

Lichen-covered bark   Sooty bark bare of lichens

Genotype: **pp**   Genotype: **PP or Pp**

Phenotype: speckled black and white ('peppered')   Phenotype: sooty black all over ('melanic')

When industrial pollution killed lichens and blackened bark the dark mutant moths (dominant gene, **P**) became camouflaged and survived. The light-coloured moths (**pp**) became obvious to predators. By 1900 few light moths survived in industrial areas and 98% were **PP** or **Pp**. As pollution is being reduced, these mainly dark populations are becoming peppered again; the dark moths are being predated in the cleaner woods and light ones are now surviving better.

B Sickle-cell anaemia and human survival

Selection by: disease
Adaptation: type of haemoglobin

Normal red blood cells are plate-like (see Unit 9.2) and carry O$_2$ well. If haemoglobin is abnormal the red blood cells change to half-moon or sickle shapes in capillaries; and O$_2$ is not supplied properly to cells. A mutant gene is responsible for this fatal condition (Table 19.1).

Table 19.1

	Normal person	Sickle-cell trait	Sickle-cell anaemia
Haemoglobin	Normal	Nearly normal	Abnormal
Diseases	Not anaemic but can die of malaria	Very mildly anaemic and malaria resistant	Severely anaemic (dies)
Genotype	*HH*	*Hh*	*hh*

Thus the homozygote *HH* is at a slight advantage in countries without malaria, and the heterozygote *Hh* is at an advantage in malarial areas.

C Shortage of food

Deer on the Kaibab Plateau, Arizona
Selection by: competitors for the food
Adaptation: ability to get enough food (including standing up on hind legs to browse trees)

In 1900, about 4000 well-fed deer roamed the plateau. Predators, e.g. wolves and pumas, kept deer numbers steady. In 1907, the majority of the predators were killed by Man. Unchecked, the deer population rose to over 100 000 in 20 years. Severe competition for food on an over-grazed plateau resulted in a rapid fall in population.

Note: Before 1907, deer able to outwit predators had been selected. The new conditions of 1907–1927, however, selected for deer able to compete successfully for the scarce food.

D Pesticides and medicines

These (produced by Man) are also agents of 'natural' selection (see Unit 18.16). Certain mosquitoes in South America are now adapted to surviving five major insecticides, and many kinds of disease bacteria have become resistant to certain antibiotics.

Note how mutation and new combinations of genes in all the examples A–D provide the basis for adaptation (and thus survival).

19.3 Evolution by natural selection

Tests of natural selection	1 The environment provides tests of survival. These include climate, soil type, predation, disease and competition (see Unit 19.2).
Variety	2 Of the variety of types in a population, only certain types will survive these tests.
Survival by adaptation	3 These 'selected' types survive because they are adapted to the environmental conditions. They breed, passing on their genes for these adaptations.
Mutation (*'new genes'*)	4 Any mutation which helps an individual organism to survive also gives it a better chance to breed.
Mutants survive and multiply	5 By breeding, these new genes are spread in the population.
	6 The numbers of mutant organisms (those having the genes helping survival) rises. So the population as a whole changes its characteristics, i.e. it evolves (see Unit 19.2A).
Distinct varieties...	7 In two *different* environments, the mutations that help survival are also likely to be different (see Fig. 19.3). So two main varieties arise as they gather their own, different, mutations and become more and more different.
...interbreed less	8 As the two populations become increasingly different, less and less successful interbreeding between the two marked varieties occurs. (Any hybrids (crosses) tend not to be as well adapted to the two environments as the two specialized varieties, so they do not survive.)

Barriers to interbreeding

9 Any breeding barrier (e.g. the Pyrenees mountains between France and Spain) that prevents intermixing of genes between two populations speeds up the process of varieties becoming increasingly different.

New species

10 After many generations, the differences between the varieties become so great that they cannot interbreed. Two new species have been formed.

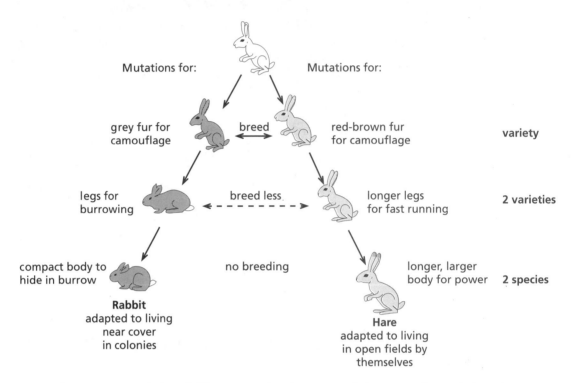

Fig. 19.3 Accumulation of different mutations in two populations over a large number of generations leads to the evolution of new species

---

19.4 Charles Darwin (1809–82)

As naturalist on *HMS Beagle* (1831–36), Darwin collected much evidence around the world of 'modification of species by descent' (see Unit 19.3).

In 1839, Darwin read *An essay on the principle of population* by the Reverend T. Malthus. This suggested that:

(*a*) the human population could increase exponentially (e.g. 2, 4, 8, 16, 32);

(*b*) but the resources, e.g. food, for it could only increase arithmetically (e.g. 2, 3, 4, 5, 6). As the population's needs could not be met by the resources, there would be a struggle to survive. Famine, disease and war would control the population, unless 'moral restraint', e.g. late marriage, were practised (whose modern equivalent could be contraception).

This idea of struggling to exist provided Darwin with the idea that in similar circumstances in nature the fittest organisms would survive. Darwin's ideas on the 'Origin of Species' are summarized below:

Observation 1	All organisms could, theoretically, increase in numbers exponentially, i.e. **organisms produce more offspring than could possibly survive.**
Observation 2	Populations of organisms, in fact, remain reasonably constant.
Deduction 1	Organisms must have to **struggle for survival** against factors that check their increase in numbers.

Observation 3	In any population there is a variety of types. Much of this variation is inherited by future generations.
Deduction 2	Those best adapted to their environment will survive, i.e. **survival of the fittest**.
Observation 4	Some species have more than one distinct variety.
Observation 5	Anything hindering interbreeding between two varieties will tend to make them even more different because each variety will accumulate mutations, many of which will be different between the two varieties.
Deduction 3	New species arise when **divergence of the two varieties** is great enough to prevent interbreeding between them.

Darwin recognized that evolution is a *branching* process. Modern types of ape, e.g. gorillas, did *not* give rise to Man, but both Man and gorilla are likely to have had common ancestors in the distant past (Fig. 19.4).

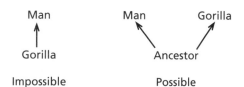

Fig. 19.4 Origins of Man

19.5 Artificial selection

Selective breeding by Man has produced:

Plants

by *cross-breeding* strains with desirable characteristics;
by increasing the *mutation* rate in stamens, using radioactive materials;
by vegetative propagation of new strains thus obtained;
by *genetically engineering* microorganisms (see Unit 18.17).

- Climate-adapted crops, e.g lettuce for cool and for hot conditions.
- Disease-resistant crops, e.g. strawberries resistant to viruses.
- High-yielding crops, e.g. rice plants that do not blow over in wind, so spoiling the rice grains (they also grow fast enough to allow two or three crops per year instead of one); wheat and apples (see Unit 18.16).
- Nutritious crops, e.g. maize strains containing *all* the essential amino acids, so helping to fight kwashiorkor (see Unit 5.7).
- Purpose-selected organisms, e.g. yeasts for brewing, for baking and for SCP; bacteria 'engineered' to make insulin (see Units 4.12 and 18.17).
- Attractive plants, e.g. roses, chrysanthemums and appetizingly coloured fruits.

Animals

by breeding from selected useful strains and from interesting mutants:
- Dogs as different as bulldogs, dachshunds, St Bernards and Afghan hounds.
- Horses such as Shetlands, shires, racehorses and mules.
- Cattle for milk (Jerseys), for beef (Herefords) and for resistance to trypanosome diseases in Africa (Zebu × Brahmin);

and by improving not only genetic stock but also the means of feeding and care:
- Hens laying more eggs per year (180 in 1920, 280 in 1980).
- Cows producing more milk per year (2500 kg in 1920, 4500 kg in 1980).
see also Units 15.5 and 15.6

19.6 Evidence for evolution: fossils

Fossils are the remains of organisms from the distant past whose hard parts are preserved in sedimentary rocks. Fossils are rare finds, since most dead organisms disintegrate by decay. Ancient organisms (buried by early sediments) are below more recent organisms (buried by later sediments). By huge compression these layers of sediments are turned to rock.

In the sides of the Grand Canyon, USA, the sedimentary rocks reveal invertebrates at the lower levels and the range of vertebrates shown in Fig. 19.5 above them. Fish are lowest down, amphibia above them and so on.

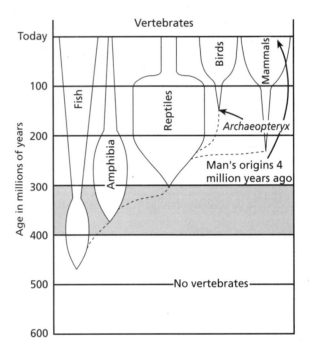

Fig. 19.5 Selected features of the fossil record. Width of areas representing groups named relates to increase or decrease in abundance

The fossil record shows that:

- The variety of life today did not arise all at once – as told in *Genesis* ('special creation').
- First life was aquatic; terrestrial life came later.
- As each new 'improved' kind of vertebrate evolved, the older, less well adapted, groups declined in importance, and many became extinct (e.g. dinosaurs).

Some particular fossils give clues as to how new groups evolved. *Archaeopteryx* (now extinct) had mainly reptile features like those of a lizard. However, its body was covered with feathers and its 'arms' were wings that allowed gliding, but not flapping. It had advantages over reptiles but became extinct when birds with flapping flight evolved.

19.7 The pentadactyl limb

Most vertebrates (except fish) have limbs to a common basic plan: one upper bone, two lower bones, wrist/ankle bones and five fingers. This is surprising in view of the different functions they perform (see Fig. 19.6) – unless they have arisen by modification, i.e. evolution.

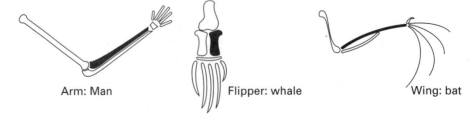

Fig. 19.6 The skeleton of three mammal limbs (simplified)

Arm: Man   Flipper: whale   Wing: bat

19.8 Lamarck's theory and the Bible

① **Lamarck** suggested that ancestors of giraffes (with short necks) achieved longer necks by striving to reach up to the foliage of trees. This change, he said, was passed on to offspring. Conversely, humans achieved their vestigial tail (coccyx) by failing to use it enough. Weissmann prevented mice from using their tails for one hundred generations by cutting their tails off at birth but the one-hundred-and-first generation had tails as long as the first.

The theory of use and disuse is *wrong*: organisms inherit genotypes, not phenotypes.

② **Biblical views** (added to by theologians)
- The variety of organisms was specially created, all at once – Bishop Ussher (17th Century) put the date at 4004 BC. Fossil evidence disproves this.

Summary

1 Evolution is the change in a species that leads to the formation of new, different, species over a large number of generations.

2 Those organisms in a species that are best adapted to the environment will survive, breed and accumulate new advantageous mutations that ensure change to new variants.

3 When new variants can no longer breed with other varieties in the species, a new species has been formed.

4 Charles Darwin was the originator of the ideas behind the 'Origin of Species through Natural Selection'.

5 Fossils provide evidence that organisms evolved.

6 The pentadactyl limb, common to most vertebrates, suggests that they have evolved.

7 Artificial selection is selection by humans (and not nature) of variants in crops and animals that they wish to use.

8 Lamarck's theory that use or disuse of parts of organisms was responsible for evolution has been disproved.

9 The theory of special creation – that the various kinds of organisms were created all at one time – is disproved by the evidence of fossils.

Quick test 19

1 What is natural selection?

2 What is the original source of variation?

3 What selective advantage do people heterozygous for sickle cell anaemia have?

4 In the evolution of two new species from a single species, when are the two new variants regarded as distinct species?

5 Who outlined the theory of evolution in a book entitled *The Origin of Species*?

6 If one looks at the fossil evidence, what is the sequence for the appearance of the vertebrate groups?

7 What was Lamarck's theory of 'Use and Disuse'?

8 How did Weissmann disprove Lamarck's theory?

Chapter 20
Ecology

20.1 The biosphere – its limits and organization

Ecology: the scientific study of organisms in relation to their environment.
Environment: the influences acting upon organisms. Two kinds:
(*a*) **biotic:** other organisms such as predators, competitors, parasites.
(*b*) **abiotic:** nonliving influences, such as climate, soil structure and water currents.
Habitat: the particular type of locality in an environment in which an organism lives, e.g. among weeds in a pond (stickleback) or among rotting leaves or wood in woodland (woodlouse).

Usually every species of organism exists as a **population** in its environment and not just as a single individual. Together, all the populations of all the species interact to form a **community** within their ecosystem. The role each species plays in the community is its **niche**, e.g. an earthworm's niche is to affect soil fertility by its activities and provide food for shrews, moles and some birds.

Ecosystem: any area in which organisms interact both with each other *and* with their abiotic environment, to form a self-sustaining unit (Fig. 20.1).

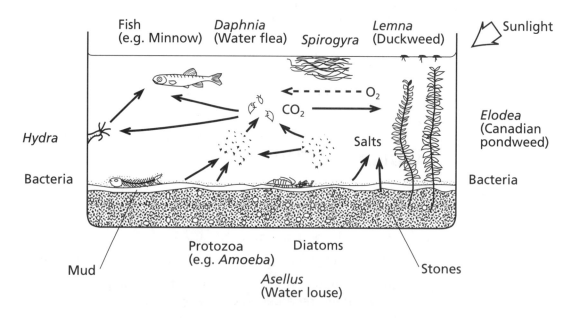

Fig. 20.1 A simple pond ecosystem in an aquarium (arrows represent feeding)

Examples of ecosystems: ponds, jungle, ocean or even a puddle. Ecosystems are not actually distinct, they interact with others. Thus dragonfly nymphs in a pond emerge as flying predators which catch their insect prey over both pond and meadow, so linking both these ecosystems. Even ecosystems in the UK and Africa are linked – by the same swallows feeding on insects in both areas according to the time of year.

Biosphere: the earth's surface that harbours life – a very thin layer of soil and the oceans, lakes, rivers and air (Fig. 20.2). The biosphere is the sum of all the world's ecosystems and is isolated from any others that may exist in space. However, other celestial bodies influence it:

(*a*) life depends on solar energy (from the sun);

(*b*) other radiations (e.g. cosmic rays) from various sources cause mutations;

(*c*) gravitational fields of sun and moon cause tides;

(*d*) at least 200 tonnes of cosmic dust arrive on earth daily.

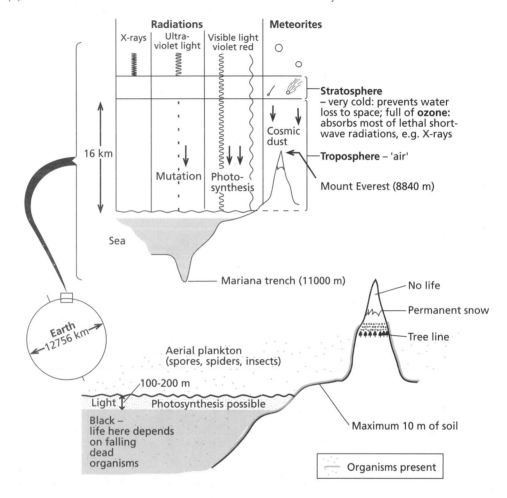

Fig. 20.2 The biosphere in relation to the earth

20.2 Food chains and food webs

Food chains, webs and cycles are units composing a community.

1 Food chain: a minimum of three organisms, the first always a green plant, the second an animal feeding on the plant, and the third an animal feeding on the second (Fig. 20.3).

All life depends on green plants (**producers**). They alone can trap sunlight *energy* and make organic *food* from water, carbon dioxide and mineral salts. Animals (**consumers**) get their energy and materials for growth from the food that producers make. In food chains:

(*a*) the number of species in a food chain rarely exceeds five;

(*b*) the biomass of each species is limited by the capacity of producers (plants) to produce food;

(*c*) an omnivore gains more food by being a vegetarian than by eating meat. Man would do better to eat grain rather than eat cattle fed on the grain (assuming first class protein needs are met – see Unit 5.7 (kwashiorkor)).

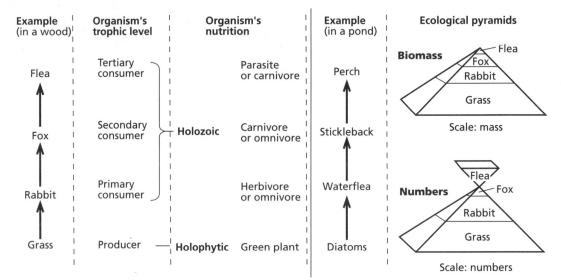

Fig. 20.3 Food chains and their properties

2 **Food web:** a number of interlinked food chains. In an ecosystem that includes foxes and rabbits, the diet of consumers is usually more varied than a food chain suggests. Foxes eat beetles, voles, chickens and pheasants as well as rabbits; and rabbits eat a great variety of green plants (Fig. 20.4).

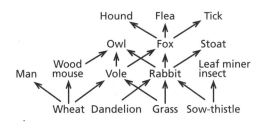

Fig. 20.4 Food web: a number of interrelated food chains

20.3 Pyramids of numbers and biomass

Every transfer of food up the chain results in a great loss in mass (**biomass**) – anything up to 90 per cent (Fig. 20.5). This is because a lot of food consumed by animals is lost owing to respiration, excretion and indigestibility (faeces), and never reaches the next member of the chain. Thus food chains can be expressed quantitatively as **pyramids of numbers** or, more usefully to farmers and game-wardens, as **pyramids of biomass** (Fig. 20.3):

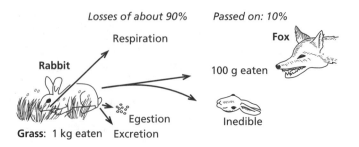

Fig. 20.5 Loss in biomass at each step in a food chain

20.4 Food cycle

Food cycles: food chains with **decomposers** added:

(a) *Detritivores:* animals which eat dead and decaying organisms, e.g. water louse, woodlouse, earthworms, springtails.

(b) *Saprophytes:* fungi decay plant materials; bacteria decay protein especially. Thus, dead organisms and excreta (organic matter) are turned into mineral salts and CO_2 (inorganic matter) – which producers need for food but could not otherwise obtain.

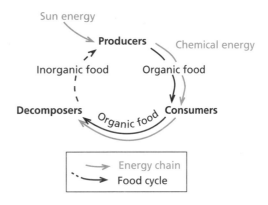

Fig. 20.6 The energy chain in a food cycle

20.5 Energy chain

Energy chain: the passage of energy from the sun along a food chain and on to decomposers. Energy is *not* cycled (Fig. 20.6). It is progressively lost along the chain, e.g. as heat from respiration.

The units making up the biosphere may be summarized as in Fig. 20.7.

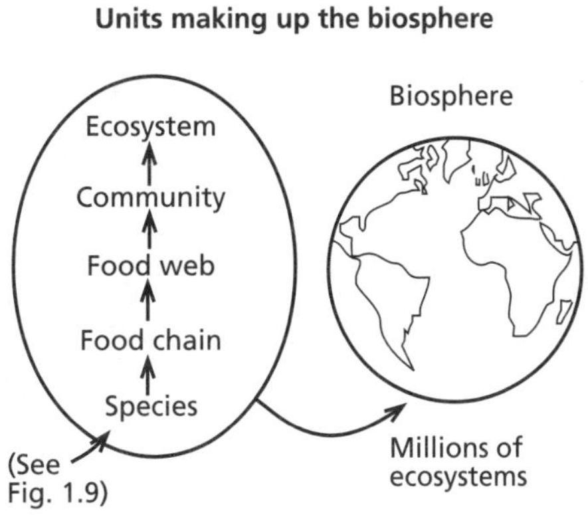

Units making up the biosphere

Ecosystem

↑

Community

↑

Food web

↑

Food chain

↑

Species

(See Fig. 1.9)

Biosphere

Millions of ecosystems

Fig. 20.7 Units making up the biosphere

20.6 Feeding relationships between species

① Predation: a *predator* is usually larger than its *prey*, an organism it kills for food, e.g. fox kills rabbit; heron kills perch. *Note:* Both organisms are animals, never plants.

'Symbiosis' is now used to describe the very close association of individuals of two different species, principally for reasons of feeding. Symbiosis includes parasitism and mutualism.

② Parasitism: a *parasite* is an organism living on or in another organism called its *host*, from which it gets its food, usually without killing it.

Examples: mosquito (see Unit 23.3), greenfly (ectoparasites) (see Unit 22.4); leaf-miner caterpillar (endoparasite).

③ Mutualism: a *mutualist* and its partner (also a *mutualist*) live very closely together, mutually helping each other. Examples:

Mutualist	Nitrogen-fixing bacteria	Mycorrhiza fungi (around roots)
Exchange	Give nitrates ↓ ↑ Give sugars	Phosphate ions absorbed from soil ↓ ↑ Sugars
Mutualist	Legumes, e.g. clover (See Fig. 22.1)	Trees, e.g. oak, pine (See Fig. 20.11)

Table 20.1 Summary comparison of feeding relationships between organisms (+ = benefits, – = harmed, ○ = unaffected; A > B means A is larger than B)

	Organisms		Size relationship
	A	B	
Predation	Predator +	Prey –	A > B
Parasitism	Parasite +	Host –	A < B
Mutualism	Mutualist +	Mutualist +	Any
Competition	Competitor –	Competitor –	Any

20.7 Competition

Competition occurs between two organisms (*competitors*), both attempting to obtain a commodity which is in *short supply* in the environment. Examples:

Commodity	Competitors (may be members of *own* species; or of *different* species)	
Light	Waterlilies out-shade diatoms	Oaks out-shade hawthorns
Food	Stickleback and minnow (for water fleas) Water fleas (for diatoms)	Squirrels and wood pigeons (for acorns) Tits (for caterpillars)
Nesting sites	Sticklebacks for nest materials	Tits for tree-holes
Mates	Frogs	Blackbirds

See also Unit 19.2C – shortage of food.

The planting density for crops is determined so as to minimize competition between individual plants. Weeds are successful competitors of crops (see Unit 22.1).

20.8 Factors controlling natural populations

A population is the number of individuals of a species in a locality, e.g. number of blackbirds in a wood. Its size depends on the availability of **resources** for living and breeding (see Fig. 20.8).

- **Plants** need light for photosynthesis, water and mineral salts for food and space to grow and respire.
- **Animals** need food and water and space in which to feed, breed and respire.

The size of a plant species population, e.g. dandelion, depends initially on the climate and soil conditions. The size of an animal species population depends initially on the size of the plant population at the bottom of its food chain, since those plants are the source of its food. The maximum population size for an animal species, e.g. in a game reserve is called its **carrying capacity**.

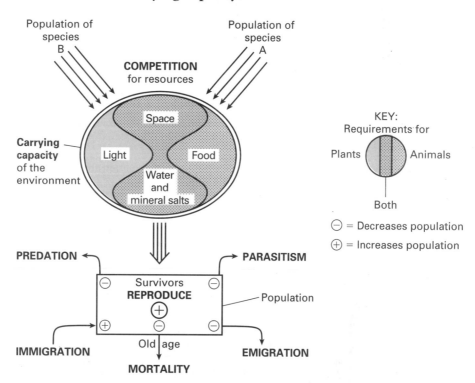

Fig. 20.8 Factors controlling population size in nature

Population size is checked by factors that limit reproduction or that kill:

① **Competition** for resources (see Unit 20.7) is fiercest between members of a *single* species because every individual requires the same things. Competition between *two different* species can be equally fierce, but is for fewer identical needs.

② **Predators** or **herbivores** reduce the populations of animals and plants respectively.

③ **Parasites** cause disease and this can lead to their host's death; or reduced capacity to compete or reproduce (through illness).

④ **Emigration** and **immigration** can, respectively, decrease or increase populations.

⑤ **Mortality** due to old age reduces the potential for increase in population by *reproduction*.

20.9 Pond ecosystem

Although Fig. 20.9 shows some features of ponds, you are unlikely to see them all. Figure 20.10 suggests how a class study may be carried out, but you may not have a flat-bottomed boat or pier to work from.

Much useful information can be got by using a dipping net (wide mesh) from the bank and establishing an aquarium with mud and plants in week 1, and representative animals (not fish) in week 2. Fish, e.g. stickleback, can be kept separately in their own aquarium and fed separately.

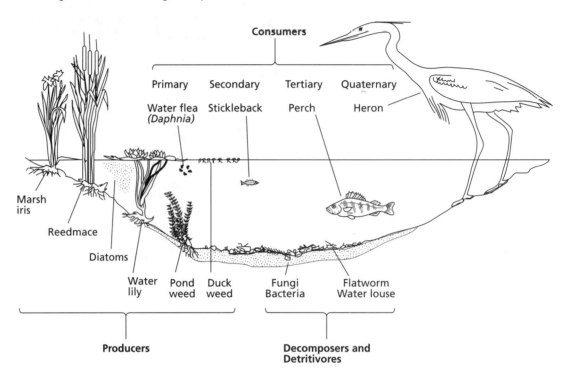

Fig. 20.9
Diagram of a simple pond ecosystem

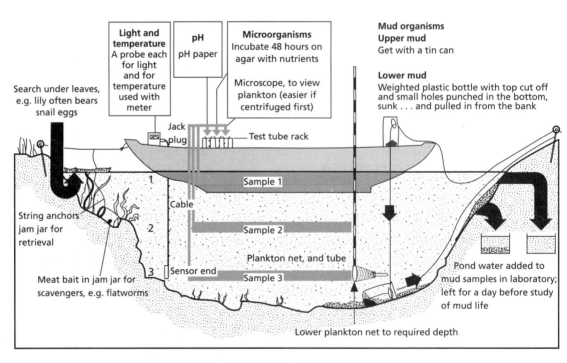

Fig. 20.10 Some methods for studying the ecology of a pond

20.10 Woodland ecosystem

Figure 20.11 gives some idea of the general structure of a wood, but the one you study will have differences. A wood is really two related ecosystems: woodland above and soil below. Figures 20.12–20.13 suggest how you may set about a class study of a wood.

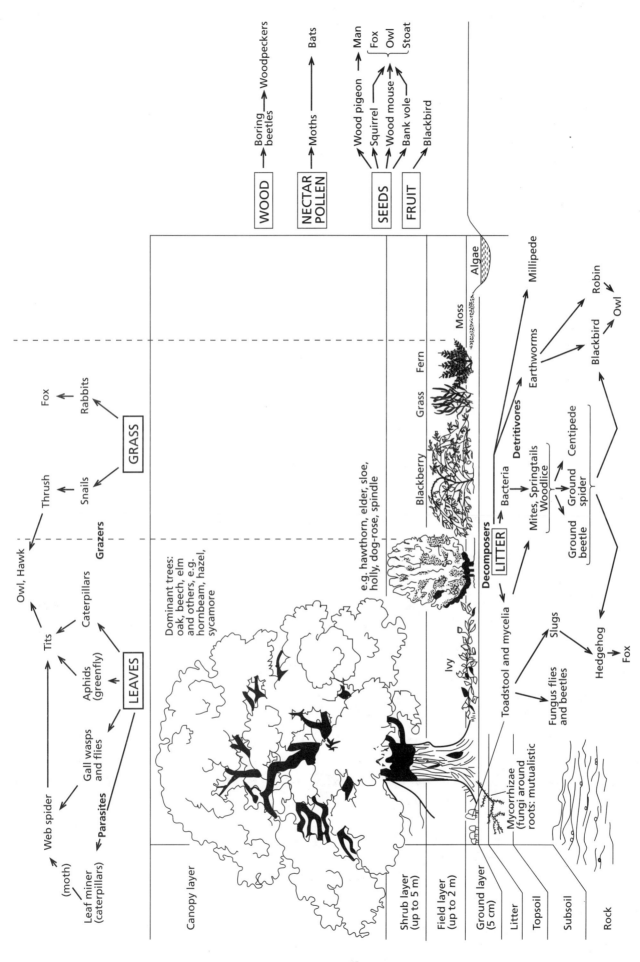

Fig. 20.11 Structure of a deciduous woodland ecosystem showing some food webs

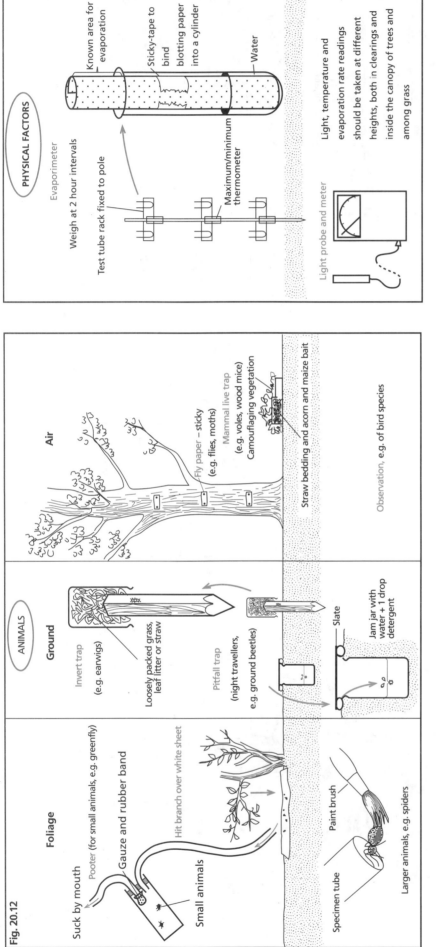

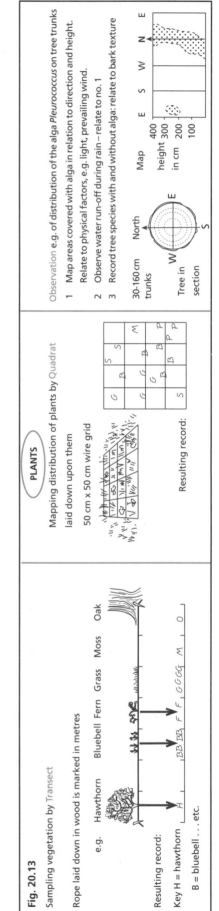

Fig. 20.12 Some methods for studying the ecology of a wood above ground
Fig. 20.13 Some methods for mapping vegetation in a wood

20.11 Keys

Keys are a means of identifying organisms in *local* situations, e.g. in a pond or woodland. The user of the key selects one of two *contrasting* descriptions, choosing the one that fits the organism being identified. The chosen description leads to a number, alongside which are further descriptions from which to choose. The final choice leads to the organism's name.

Example: Choose one of the organisms in Fig. 20.14 and use the key below the diagram to identify it.

Fig. 20.14
A variety of organisms

With wings	**1**	(*Now look at descriptions by **1** below*)
Without wings	**2**	(*Now look at descriptions by **2** below*)

1 { Two legs   C –   Bat
    { Six legs   B –   Butterfly

2 { With legs   A –   Woodlouse
    { Without legs   3 –   (*Now look at descriptions by **3** below*)

3 { With eyes   D –   Fish
    { Without eyes   E –   Earthworm

In the example above, use of internal characteristics (e.g. vertebrae) or confusing ones (e.g. hairiness) would delay identification – some butterflies are as hairy as bats!
  Your key of the organisms above could be different but still be 'correct' – if it works.

20.12 Nitrogen cycle

Green plants need nitrates for protein synthesis.
Nitrates are available to green plants from four sources:

1 **man-made fertilizers**, e.g. ammonium nitrate;

2 **lightning** – causes oxides of nitrogen to form in the air; these become nitric acid in the rainfall.

3 **nitrogen-fixing bacteria** – the only organisms capable of converting nitrogen gas into compounds of nitrogen;

4 **nitrifying bacteria** – oxidize ammonium compounds to nitrites and then nitrates, if there is air for them to use.

Nitrates are turned into nitrogen gas by **denitrifying** bacteria if the soil lacks air, as in waterlogged conditions. Nitrogen gas is useless to green plants.
  In green plants, nitrates and sugars form amino acids; these become proteins. Animals convert plant proteins into their own, but in doing so waste some, e.g. as urea, which is excreted.
  Decomposers break down dead organisms and their wastes. Nitrogen compounds in them, e.g. proteins, end up as ammonia and then ammonium compounds.

Examiner's tip

Remember clearly where the helpful and unhelpful bacteria fit into the cycle.

Examiner's tip

Use this diagram to help you explain about changes in CO_2 levels in the atmosphere and the greenhouse effect.

(a) The nitrogen cycle
N₂ (Nitrogen – 79% of air)
Denitrifiers
Nitrogen fixers
Fertilizers
Lightning
NO₃⁻
(Nitrate)
Nitrifiers
Absorbed at roots and combined with sugars to form
Plant protein
NH₃ (Ammonia)
Death
Eaten
Animal protein
(Mineral salts)
Decomposers
Waste
(CO₂)
Excreta, e.g. urea
Note that the two cycles link up
CO₂
The same decomposers
Sugars
for making protein
(b) The carbon cycle
Decomposers
Respiration (in plants and animals)
Sugars in animals
Eaten
0.04% of air
CO₂
Combustion (e.g. of wood)
Sugars in plants
boxes refer to types of bacteria
Photosynthesis (in green plants)

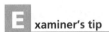

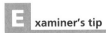

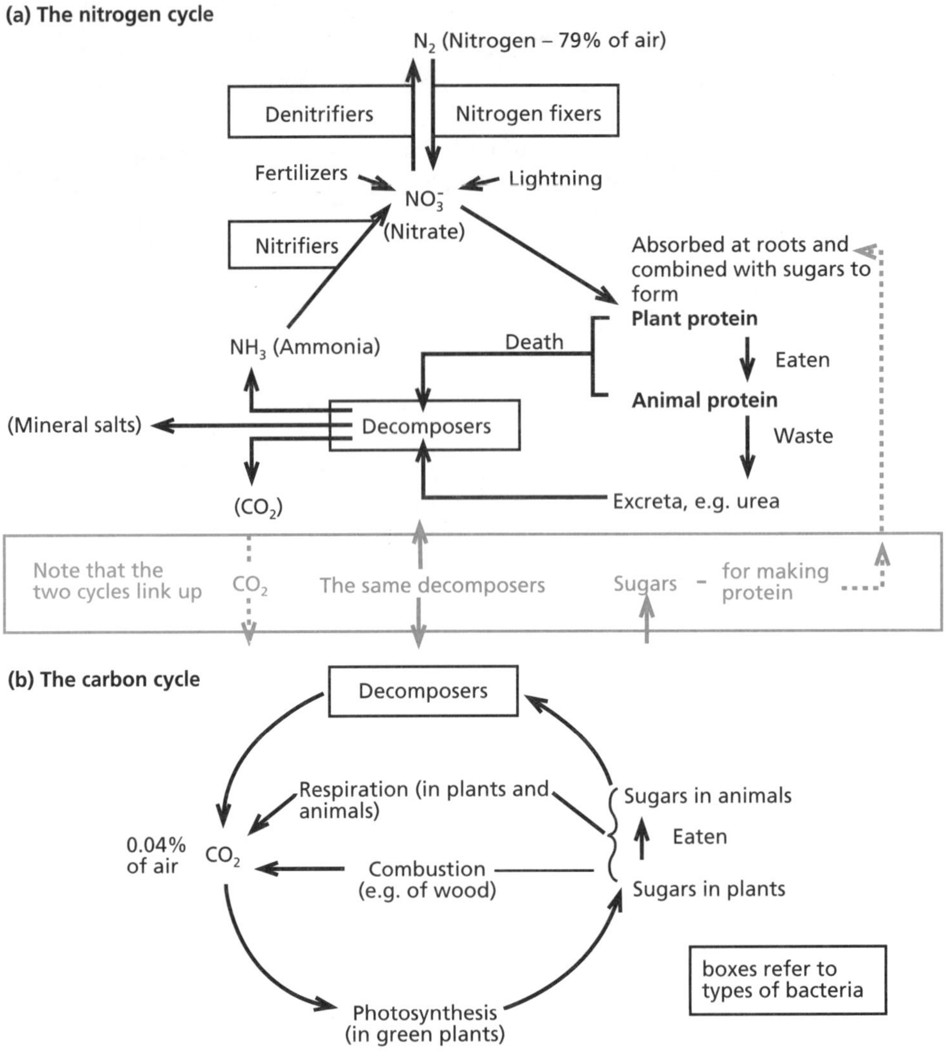

Fig. 20.15
(a) The nitrogen cycle,
(b) the carbon cycle

20.13 Carbon cycle

Examiner's tip

Notice how the nitrogen and carbon cycles are really linked in nature.

Green plants *photosynthesize* CO_2 into sugars. Most other organic molecules are made using sugar; e.g. cellulose in wood, or proteins and oils in seeds and leaves. When these are eaten by animals, the digested products are turned into animal carbohydrates, fats and proteins.

This variety of organic molecules is returned to air as CO_2 during respiration in plants and animals, in bacteria of *decay*, or by *combustion*.

Fuels include wood and the 'fossil fuels' coal, petroleum and natural gas. Fossil fuels were formed by the partial decay and compression of plants by earth-forces millions of years ago.

20.14 Water cycle

In the *water cycle* most of the water circulated does not go through organisms (Fig. 20.16). It has long been suggested that cutting down forests decreases rainfall in that area.

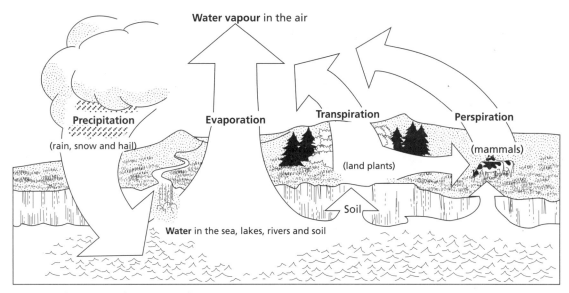

Fig. 20.16 The water cycle

Summary

1 An ecosystem is the interaction between the community of organisms and its non-living environment.

2 The biosphere is the total world ecosystem.

3 Feeding relationships in an ecosystem are represented by a food web.

4 The parts of a food web are food chains. Each food chain starts with a green plant, which provides food for a herbivore, which is then eaten by a carnivore. This is the simplest possible food chain.

5 The flow of energy along a food chain involves massive losses at each trophic level, mainly as heat.

6 Food chains can be expressed as pyramids of numbers or of biomass to give an idea of quantity.

7 Food in an ecosystem is cycled from plants to animals and from their dead bodies to saprophytes – which return inorganic food to plants by their decay activities.

8 The cycling of the elements carbon and nitrogen is particularly important to life.

9 Types of feeding relationship include predators, parasites, mutualists and competitors.

10 Studies of natural ecosystems should include measurement of abiotic factors, e.g. temperature and pH, and estimation of the numbers and distribution of species of organisms in the area studied.

11 Species can be identified by means of keys.

12 Ponds, woods and the soil are complex ecosystems, each requiring their own special methods of study.

Quick test 20

1   What is a niche?

2   What is an ecosystem?

3   What is the source of energy for all food chains?

4   What do decomposers do?

5   What is a parasite?

6   In what form do plants absorb nitrogen?

7   Why are denitrifying bacteria undesirable?

8   In what way is the passing of nutrients and of energy through ecosystems different?

9   Give two reasons why cutting down trees and burning them increases carbon dioxide levels in the atmosphere.

10   What are the three sources of water vapour going into the air?

Chapter 21
Man, his environment and the biosphere

21.1 Human population explosion

Bacteria on an agar plate show exponential growth in population. This leads to exhaustion of food and self-pollution by wastes resulting in mass death (crash phase, see Fig. 21.1) Similarly, Man's exponential growth in population (see Fig. 21.2) is resulting in both pollution of the biosphere and reduction of its resources. Unlike bacteria, Man has the ability to avoid the crash phase by using a variety of solutions.

Examiner's tip

elate changes in
opulation size to changes
 the conditions in the
nvironment.

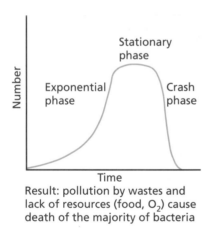

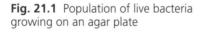
Result: pollution by wastes and lack of resources (food, O_2) cause death of the majority of bacteria

Fig. 21.1 Population of live bacteria growing on an agar plate

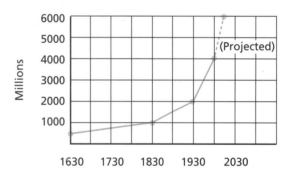

Fig. 21.2 Growth of the human population in the world

Causes of population explosion

In a natural environment many factors control plant and animal numbers (see Unit 20.8). Similar factors once controlled the population of Man's ancestors – until Man worked out ways of avoiding their controlling influence (Table 21.1).

Table 21.1. Man's avoidance of the factors controlling populations in nature

Factors controlling populations in nature	Man's methods of avoiding natural population control
1 Climate	Shelter (homes), clothes, fire
2 Predators	Tools – allowed Man's ancestors to overcome other animals with weapons
3 Food supply	Agriculture, animal and plant breeding, increase food supply Biotechnology creates new foods
4 Water supply	Reservoirs, irrigation, piped supply Filtration and chlorination eliminate disease
5 Pollution	Disposal of excreta by sewage treatment reduces disease Disposal of domestic refuse
6 Disease	Immunization, antibiotics, medicines. Public health measures

21.2 Depletion of resources

Resources are of two types: non-renewable (non-living) and renewable (living).

(*a*) **Non-renewable,** e.g. *minerals*; and natural gas which will be used up within 50 years (from *known* sources).

Soil is being lost by erosion because of unwise land use, e.g. over-grazing or clear felling of forest (thus removing the binding action of roots), particularly on sloping land, e.g. in Amazonia, Philippines and the Himalayas. New soil takes centuries to form through weathering of rock and the action of organisms. Without fine soil, many producers cannot grow and whole ecosystems may be destroyed.

(*b*) **Renewable,** e.g. *foods:* herring and whales have been over-fished. Cutting down of forests exceeds planting. Harvesting should not exceed replacement rate.

Destruction of wild-life: Agricultural needs destroy natural habitats; pesticides, poison, and hunting for 'sport' or fashionable items, e.g. skins, ivory, may all lead to extinction of species, e.g. dodo, Cape lion.

Food shortage: Two-thirds of the world population lack either enough energy foods or protein or both in their diet. Poor nations are unable to pay for the surplus food of rich ones.

Reduced living space: Overcrowded populations lead to greater chance of epidemic diseases and social diseases, e.g. vandalism, child abuse, drug-taking, alcoholism. In Britain every year about 10 000 children are registered as abused, of whom about 200 die.

21.3 Pollution

Pollution: waste substances or energy from human activities which upset the normal balances in the biosphere. Anything from noise (aircraft) and heat (atomic power stations) to various substances in excess (sewage, DDT). Industrial melanism in the peppered moth (see Unit 19.2A) is an example of the effect that pollution can have on animals.

Laws: the Clean Air Acts (1956 and 1968) have prevented the sooty smogs of industrial and city areas. Smogs caused death by bronchitis and traffic accidents, and dirtied and damaged stone buildings. In 1988 Britain encouraged widespread use of lead-free petrol, a common measure in the EC. CFCs are being replaced by other gases worldwide.

Table 21.2 Air pollutants

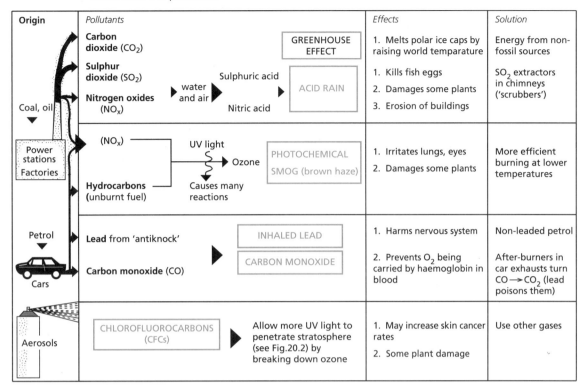

21.4 Greenhouse effect

Rising levels of CO_2 (from combustion) and methane (from ricefields, cattle and sheep) in the air have raised global temperature by slowing loss of heat from earth to outer space. This has melted ice, so raising sea level by about 25 mm in the last 50 years. If this trend continues, large areas (where a third of mankind lives) will be flooded, e.g. Bangladesh, Holland, London, New York. Burning fossil fuels (which produce extra CO_2) and felling tropical forests (which absorb CO_2) are largely responsible (see Unit 21.12, no. 6).

21.5 Acid rain

Contains nitric and sulphuric acids, with known effects (see Table 21.2). It cannot be the sole reason for serious damage to forests in Europe and the US. While SO_2 levels are falling in Europe, ozone levels are rising. Ozone damages chlorophyll. This ozone has *nothing* to do with the stratosphere (see Unit 21.6) but can cause photochemical smog.

21.6 Ozone holes in the stratosphere

A progressive **thinning of the ozone layer** (see Table 21.2) over Antarctica has been detected each winter since 1979. The rate of thinning, which occurs in the northern hemisphere too, has been ten times that previously estimated. Rich nations have been alarmed into banning the use of CFCs (in aerosol sprays, refrigerators and foam plastics), which destroy ozone. Unfortunately CFCs are stable, taking about a century to break down.

21.7 Cars

Lead, carbon monoxide, unburnt hydrocarbons (fuel), oxides of nitrogen and tiny soot particles all come from cars using leaded petrol. Diesel cars are less polluting but unsatisfactory for soot. Cars and buses driven by electric batteries or hydrogen fuel (waste is H_2O) are being designed.

Table 21.3 Land and water pollutants

	Land pollutants	Origin	Effect	Solution
	(a) Insecticides	Crop protection; control of disease vectors, e.g. mosquito	May kill top consumers; may lower photosynthesis rate of marine algae	Ban undesirable ones, e.g. DDT, as UK has done
	(b) Radioactive wastes	Nuclear reactor accidents and wastes; atom bombs	Mutations	Nuclear waste silos – but some have leaked
	Water pollutants			
	(a) Sewage Cattle slurry Silage effluent	Human	Eutrophication (see Unit 22.1)	Sewage treatment (see Unit 4.4)
	(b) Artificial fertilizers	Excessive agricultural use	Eutrophication (see Unit 22.1)	Use of organic manures (Unit 22.1)
	(c) Petroleum	Tanker accidents	Oiled sea birds, beaches	Effective accident prevention
	(d) Mercury (organic)	Chemical works; fungicides on seeds and wood	Minamata disease (paralysis, idiots born)	Effluent purification

21.8 Mercury and pesticides

Tiny amounts of pollutants absorbed by producers are concentrated along a food chain into the top consumers. Thus in the 1950s eagles had very high DDT levels and laid thin-shelled eggs that broke easily. Their population fell. Similarly, plankton in Minamata Bay, Japan, absorbed small amounts of mercury waste in a factory's effluent. This was concentrated in predators – crustaceans, then fish – and finally got into the human fish-eating population. Many people died or became paralysed. Mothers gave birth to idiot and malformed children.

Poor countries often cannot afford to ban cheap, effective insecticides, e.g. DDT – famine or disease would result.

21.9 Oil pollution

Petroleum on the sea can be removed by:

- soaking up the oil using polystyrene, peat or straw
- sinking the oil by adding powdered chalk
- surrounding it with floating booms and then sucking it up
- spraying detergents on the oil to disperse it.

However, detergents have a harmful effect on cell membranes and affect aquatic life seriously. They often harm marine life more than the oil slicks they are being used to disperse. Older-type detergents used to release phosphates on break-down – encouraging eutrophication. Modern detergents do not and they break down easily.

21.10 Radioactive waste

Radioactive waste is a form of pollution. Most of the radiation humans are exposed to comes from the sun but small amounts are due to radiation from nuclear power stations, medical equipment, nuclear explosions, and natural sources in some rocks.

Radiation can interfere with cell division and cause cancer (see Unit 17.6). There is evidence that there is an increase in skin cancer due to greater exposure to radiation caused by a depletion of the ozone layer (see Unit 21.6). Cells that are rapidly dividing (e.g. in a fetus) are more likely to be damaged by radiation so doctors are reluctant to X-ray pregnant women. People who work in areas where there is a risk of higher levels of radiation wear protective clothing and have regular medical checks.

21.11 Domestic refuse

The way waste is disposed of varies. In Germany there are separate collections of paper, plastic, glass, metal and household refuse. Treatment includes:

1 **Composting:** waste organic matter can be placed in compost bins and recycled. This produces a rich fertilizer and soil aerator for the garden; reduces cost of municipal rubbish disposal. To promote decay, the principles in Fig. 21.3 should be practised.

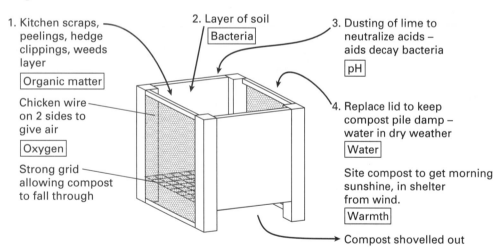

Fig. 21.3 A simple compost maker that avoids rat access

2 **Recycling:** materials such as paper, rags, glass, metals when binned separately, can be recycled. This reduces use of the world's natural resources and creates less waste to dispose of. It is, however, expensive to run recycling plants.

3 **Burning waste:** Sometimes refuse is burnt to produce heat which supplies hot water and heating to housing estates. However, toxic waste gases and smoke need removal.

4 **Burying:** Most refuse is dumped and then buried. Large areas such as old quarries are often used. They are lined and filled with layers of rubbish, compressed and covered with soil. This makes it more difficult for rats, etc. to eat the waste. Decay causes the release of methane, so vent pipes are required. When the site is covered it is seeded with grass and landscaped. It is the Environmental Health Officer's job to check refuse sites (see Unit 23.4).

21.12 Conservation, new foods and energy sources

❶ Conservation of minerals: use of substitutes for metals, e.g. carbon fibre plastics; reversing the throw-away mentality by making durable products, e.g. cars that last; recycling metals in discarded items (see also Unit 21.11).

Note: These policies would lead to lowered industrial production (and fewer jobs).

❷ Conservation of wildlife and natural scenery: strict guardianship of nature reserves; acceptance that minerals in a mountain may be less valuable than the beauty it affords. Man's need for recreation and enjoyment of nature is as necessary for health as meeting his material needs. Reclamation of gravel pits and of mining tips by suitable planting and landscaping can provide amenity areas, e.g. for sailing and as parks. Endangered species can be bred in zoos and, when they have been re-educated to live in the wild, can be reintroduced into suitable areas.

❸ Conservation of genes: wild animals and plants may not be of direct use to Man but can provide useful genes for introduction into his breeding programmes, e.g. genes for disease resistance from the small inedible potato of South America, genes for hardiness in Soay sheep, and genes for high vitamin C content in wild tomatoes (see Unit 19.5).

❹ Conservation of renewable resources: by never taking more than can be replaced (by reproduction). Reforestation is thus a priority worldwide. Meanwhile, recycling paper helps reduce tree-felling.

❺ New sources of food: greater dependence on microorganisms, e.g. 'SCP' and mycoprotein (see Unit 4.10), and soya bean meat-substitutes. Farming wild animals on their natural land supplemented by cattle feedstuffs produces high quality lean meat quickly, e.g. red deer (Scotland), wildebeeste (Africa).

❻ Finding new (acceptable) energy sources, e.g. solar, wind and tidal power and biomass. Fast breeder nuclear reactors will produce very much more dangerous waste than conventional reactors – a possible mutation hazard. But using fossil fuels (coal, oil) to a greater extent raises CO_2 levels in air causing a *greenhouse effect* (see Unit 21.4). Biomass from fast-growing willow or poplar clones is a cheap and environmentally sound fuel source. The CO_2 produced from burning the chipped wood in high-efficiency burners is simply recycled by growing new trees. To produce the same energy from coal costs almost three times, and from oil four times, as much. To recycle metals, produce substitutes for them, and make artificial fertilizers is very energy consuming.

Examiner's tip

It is easy to go off the point with this type of question. Use the mark allocation to help you and explain all the points you make.

Summary

1 The growth of the human population has been exponential.

2 World resources are finite and must be used wisely and where possible recycled, if non-renewable, e.g. minerals.

3 Renewable resources must be harvested at a rate that allows replacement, e.g. forests and fish.

4 Wildlife is being destroyed wantonly. Not only its beauty but its usefulness as a source of drugs and of genes for introduction into domestic breeds should be conserved.

5 Pollution is the spilling of harmful substances or energy into the environment.

6 Pollution knows no national boundaries: the greenhouse effect, thinning of the ozone layer and acid rain are of concern globally.

7 Air, land and water are being polluted by industry, agriculture and power generation.

8 Car engines produce large amounts of carbon monoxide that affects the blood.

9 Lead pollutants can cause brain damage in young children.

10 High levels of nitrates in water may lead to eutrophication.

11 Chemicals and non-biodegradable pesticides may become more concentrated up a food chain.

12 Radioactive waste can increase the risk of cancer.

13 Composting, recycling, burning and burying can all be used to dispose of domestic refuse.

14 Humans are making natural ecosystems unstable by their activities, e.g. deforestation and pollution.

Quick test 21

1 What four things have improved to allow a population explosion?

2 Why does overgrazing lead to soil erosion?

3 What is pollution?

4 What are the main greenhouse gases?

5 How is acid rain formed?

6 What harm can lead pollution cause?

7 Why do oxygen levels fall in water containing excessively high levels of mineral salts?

8 What is the link between aerosols and harmful radiation?

9 What conditions are needed for successful composting?

10 What are the advantages of recycling waste materials?

Chapter 22
Food production

22.1 Maximizing the crop or flock

Food production requires the artificial management of ecosystems to maximize productivity. No matter whether it is management of plant crops, land animals such as cattle or poultry or the farming of fish, the principles are the same:

- improve conditions for feeding and growth
- remove competitors, predators, and disease (parasites)
- selectively breed to suit the crop environment (see Unit 19.5)
- consider the environmental effects of farming

In addition, the cost of the 'improved' method of cultivation must be less than the increased revenue it brings to the farmer.

Table 22.1 Five factors needing control to maximize food production

Plants	Factor	Animals
Improve conditions for photosynthesis Supply needed minerals (fertilizers)	Feeding	Provide a balanced diet Supply mineral and vitamin feed supplements
Healthy soil, support, shelter from wind	Growth conditions	Shelter from harsh conditions including wind and temperature
Remove weeds	Competitors	Exclude or kill other herbivores
Kill pest herbivores especially insects	Predators	Exclude by fences, netting
Use fungicides and insecticides	Parasites	Use antibiotics on bacteria and other protective drugs

Traditional farming practices require particular attention to the soil as a basis for good plant growth: ploughing, liming, fertilizing and rotation of crops.

❶ Ploughing
   (*a*) Aerates and drains soil by creating ridges and furrows (thus discouraging denitrification).
   (*b*) Brings leached salts up to near the surface for roots.
   (*c*) Brings pests, sheltering deep down, up to the surface for frost to kill.
   (*d*) Allows frost to break up the ridges of soil.
   (*e*) Turns organic matter, e.g. wheat stubble, into the ground to decay.

❷ Liming
   The addition of powdered $CaCO_3$:
   (*a*) neutralizes acidity;
   (*b*) allows efficient application of fertlizers;
   (*c*) flocculates ('clumps') clay particles together into larger groups ('crumbs') with air spaces between them.

❸ Fertilizing
   Fertilizers supply mineral salts deficient in soil. They can be applied in organic or inorganic form (see Table 22.2).

Examiner's tip

You can explain the need for fertilizers because the natural cycles, e.g. nitrogen are disrupted by harvesting the crop.

Table 22.2 Comparison of organic and inorganic fertilizers

	Organic: e.g. clover ploughed in to decay and animal dung + urine	**Inorganic:** factory products, e.g. $(NH_4)_2SO_4$ or wastes, e.g. basic slag
Cost	Cheap	Expensive
Composition	Not known	Precise amounts can be applied
Application	Difficult (bulky, sticky)	Easy (powders, granules)
Action	Slow but long-lasting	Quick but short-lasting
Soil structure	Improved by 'humus'	Not improved
Earthworms	Encouraged	Can harm them
Water retention	Improved	No effect

Excessive use of fertilizers can pollute freshwater with nitrates. These may kill freshwater animals by eutrophication (see Table 21.3);

Eutrophication (the enrichment of natural waters with mineral salts) works in the following way:.

(a) *Mineral salts* drain off recently over–fertilized fields; or are formed by bacterial breakdown of sewage, cattle slurry or silage effluent in the water.

(b) *Algae multiply* exponentially, given this excess of food (water goes green). They crash in numbers as their food runs out.

(c) *Bacteria multiply* exponentially, given an excess of dead algae to decay.

(d) Bacterial respiration sharply *reduces* O_2 in the water – *killing aquatic animals* by suffocation. This worsens the situation as even more bodies decay.

④ **Rotation of crops**

Crop rotation enables the growth of different crops on the same land in successive years without manuring each year. The two harvested crops have different mineral requirements and often obtain them from different soil depths. In the 'fallow year':

(a) **legumes**, e.g. clover, are sown to restore *nitrogen compounds* to the soil when the plants decay after being ploughed in (Fig. 22.1). Other minerals (removed in crops) are restored by fertilizing.

(b) **parasites**, e.g. rust fungi, hiding in soil, die (no host plants available).

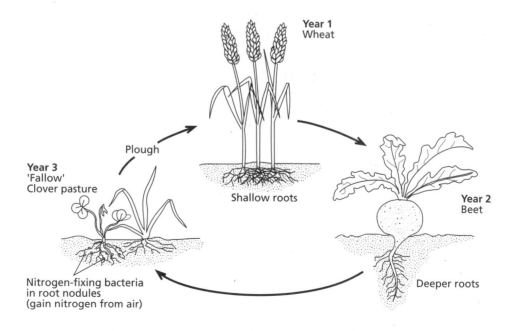

Fig. 22.1 Rotation of crops

22.2 Pest control

Pests are created by humans. They are organisms whose numbers are normally kept under control naturally in their ecosystems. But given the opportunity of abundant food (crops and animals) their population rises enormously, causing crop damage. Pest control can be achieved in three ways:

1. **Environmental management:** e.g. crop rotation (see Unit 22.1); breaking pest life cycles (see mosquito Unit 23.4).

2. **Chemical control:** expensive to buy and apply; often harms innocent species; can get into food chains, causing harm. Examples:
   - 2:4 D – a herbicide (see Unit 13.16) sprayed onto leaves, kills broad leaved weeds leaving cereal crops unharmed – this chemical is biodegradable.
   - DDT (an insecticide, now banned) was widely used in the 1950s. It is not easily broken down (biodegraded). Tiny amounts on sprayed pests, e.g. caterpillars, were concentrated up the food chain and affected birds of prey. These laid thin-shelled eggs that broke easily and their populations fell dramatically.
   - copper sulphate (a fungicide) can be used to control potato blight (see Unit 22.3).

   Disadvantages
   - Pests become resistant to chemicals by mutation.
   - Organisms other than the intended target (including humans) may be affected.

3. **Biological control:** artificial breeding and release of natural enemies (predators and parasites) onto affected crops. It is cheap and self perpetuating (the enemies breed); and controls the pest only – not other harmless species, e.g. Myxoma virus controls rabbits through myxomatosis; Guppy fish eat mosquito larvae in water (see Unit 23.3); ladybirds eat aphids (see Unit 22.4). Sometimes, however, the control organism changes its food preference to a harmless species.

New methods include irradiating male pests (bred in the lab) with X-rays to make them sterile and releasing them into the wild. Eggs laid are therefore unfertilized.

22.3 Plant diseases

Plants suffer disease mainly from viruses and fungi. Important ones include:

Virus: Tobacco mosaic virus, transmitted by greenfly, attacks leaves of tobacco and tomato plants.

Fungi: *Phytophthera,* causing potato blight which resulted in millions of Irish deaths by starvation in the potato famine.
Puccinia, the 'rust' fungus which seriously damages leaves of cereal crops.
Ceratocystis, transmitted by bark beetles, causing Dutch elm disease which has killed millions of elm trees.

Potato blight (see Fig. 22.2) can totally destroy a potato crop in weeks, reducing foliage and tubers to a brown stinking mass. Spores landing on the plant germinate to form branching hyphae within the tissues and feed by penetrating and digesting the contents of cells with enzymes. Once established, the fungus produces sporangia outside the plant but only in very humid (>85%) weather. These release spores that are distributed to other plants and tubers by wind or rainwater.

Control of plant diseases is by
1. Using disease-free plants: e.g. using seed potatoes from Scotland where conditions for potato blight are unsuitable.
2. Plant breeding: crossing cultivated plants with wild ones containing genes for disease resistance. Some resulting plants are disease-tolerant, i.e. continue to give good yields although infected.

3 Crop rotation (see Fig. 22.1): spores from the previous year's crop have no new plants to infect and so die out.
4 Crop management: delaying sowing times to avoid transference of pathogen from one crop to the next one.
5 Killing vectors: e.g. greenfly using ladybirds or insecticides.
6 Using fungicides: these often contain copper, as in Bordeaux mixture for vine mildews, and are sprayed on foliage at regular intervals.
7 Notification of diseases to Agricultural Offices to prevent epidemics by providing advice and help.

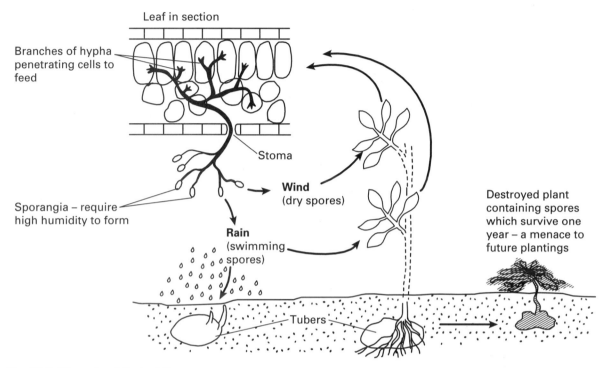

Fig. 22.2 Life cycle of *Phytophthera*

22.4 Greenfly (aphids) – parasites of plants

Greenfly get sap under pressure from the phloem of plants by piercing the stem with a sharp proboscis. Through this they also transmit virus diseases, e.g. TMV (see Unit 3.1); deform the growth of leaves; and encourage sooty-fungi to grow on honey-dew exuded from the greenfly onto leaves, where the blackened surface reduces photosynthesis. Aphids are serious agricultural pests.

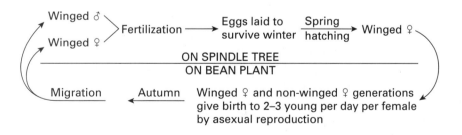

Fig. 22.3 Life cycle of the bean aphid

Control methods

1 Remove spindle trees growing near fields (over-wintering sites).
2 Liberate laboratory-grown ladybirds on crop (aphid predators), i.e. biological control.
3 Spray crop with insecticide, e.g. permethrin (does not affect Man) or systemic insecticides (see Unit 8.9).

22.5 Glasshouses

Almost all crop yields in the UK would increase if grown in glasshouses but costs would exceed rewards in most cases. Only of advantage for some sub-tropical crops; gaining earlier harvesting than in fields; or for decorative plants or those with a high cash return, e.g. tomatoes.

The glasshouse environment provides:

① **Factors increasing photosynthesis**
  - Warmth – thermostatically controlled heaters; cooling by fans, ventilation, blinds when temperature rises above optimum.
  - Light – additional lighting to increase hours of photosynthesis.
  - Carbon dioxide enrichment – by burning fuels, CO_2 cylinders.

② **Mineral salts and water** supplied in electronically controlled amounts. Some crops are grown in flowing solutions alone (hydroponically) – no soil.

③ **No competitors**

④ **Pest control** by biological and/or chemical means (see Unit 22.2).

⑤ **Physical assistance** by protection from wind, rain, hail; supports where needed. Air filters prevent entry of fungal disease spores.

Examiner's tip

Explain how changing these factors affects the rate of photosynthesis.

22.6 Battery farming and fish farming

Poultry

Poultry reared for egg production yield far more in their controlled conditions than free-range hens. Those reared for meat are ready for market sooner. More birds are reared per unit area. Their environment includes:

① **A balanced diet** provided by automation (saving costs).

② **Cages** allowing only restricted movement – movement uses energy, diverting some food from creating growth and eggs.

③ **Warmth** to prevent use of food for energy purposes and not growth.

④ **Shelter** from wind, rain, etc.

⑤ **Controlled light** period to keep hens laying for longer.

⑥ **Predators and disease organisms** are excluded.

⑦ **Waste control** by automation.

Concerns over battery farming include
1 De-beaking to prevent hens pecking each other.
2 Their restricted living space for an originally jungle-living bird.
3 Unnatural food.

Such principles can also be applied to rearing cattle and pigs – in sheds.

Fish farming

This is a less controlled situation (e.g. water temperature and contents of sea or river) but otherwise similar. Controlled amounts of pellets, formulated to give a balanced diet, often with additives to colour muscle and antibiotics to fight disease are given at set times to fish in cages/tanks. These cages also exclude predators.

Examiner's tip

Remember to write about how controlling the environment will have a beneficial effect. You may sometimes need to write about the costs of the control methods and the possible environmental harm they may cause.

Summary

1 Agriculture involves keeping the soil in good condition and providing water and mineral salts for plant growth.

2 It also requires selection of good plant or animal stock and the reduction of their competitors, diseases and species feeding on them to maximize production in this artificial ecosystem.

3 Soil needs ploughing, liming and fertilizing.

4 Fertilizers can be applied in organic or inorganic form.

5 Crop rotation prevents 'exhaustion' of soil and helps control pests.

6 Pests may be kept in check by biological or chemical control – each with its own advantages.

7 Glasshouses can be used to provide an artificially modified environment to increase plant growth.

8 Animals can be reared in controlled environments to improve productivity, e.g. fish farms and battery hens.

Quick test 22

1 Why are carbon dioxide levels artificially increased in glasshouses?

2 What are the dangers of chemical control of pests?

3 Why are biological control methods particularly successful in glasshouses?

4 Why are glasshouse crops particularly susceptible to attacks by microorganisms?

5 What conditions favour the spread of potato blight?

6 Which part of the plant do greenfly (aphids) feed from?

7 What three factors are controlled in a glasshouse to increase the rate of photosynthesis?

8 Why is meshing/netting used around fish farms at sea?

Chapter 23
Disease

To function effectively the body needs to maintain a constant internal environment (achieve homeostasis). Any change from normal is called disease.

23.1 Types of disease in humans

1. **Genetic:** since these diseases are inherited, they are *incurable*.
   Examples: **haemophilia** – a gene mutation; **Down's syndrome** – baby has an extra chromosome, i.e. 46 + 1, owing to abnormal meiosis in the mother. Person has retarded development and usually dies before the age of 40 (see Unit 18.16).

2. **Diet deficiency:** curable by eating a balanced diet.
   Examples: lack of vitamin C (**scurvy**, see Unit 5.6); or protein (**kwashiorkor**, see Unit 5.7); or overeating (obesity, See Unit 5.7).

3. **Hormonal:** curable by artificial supply of hormone.
   Examples: lack of thyroxine (**cretinism**) or insulin (**diabetes**) (see Unit 13.9).

4. **Environmental:** often preventable by wise precautions.
   Examples: skin cancer (excessive sunbathing); asbestosis (not wearing face masks against asbestos dust).

5. **Degenerative:** caused by ageing.
   Example: arthritis.

6. **Pathogenic:** entry of parasites (pathogens) into body which upsets its metabolism.
   Examples: viruses (see Unit 3.1), bacteria (see Unit 3.2) fungi (see Unit 22.3), protozoa (see Unit 23.2).

Diseases (1)–(5) cannot be 'caught' (non-infectious). Infectious diseases (caused by organisms) are transmitted from human to human. Malaria and rabies (transmitted by vectors) are therefore also non-infectious. Contagious diseases are transmitted by touch alone, e.g. syphilis.

23.2 Pathogenic diseases – entry and control

The body comes into contact with large numbers of microorganisms that cause no harm. These are non-pathogenic. The majority of human pathogens are bacteria and viruses. There are a few others including fungi (e.g. athlete's foot) and protozoa (e.g. sleeping sickness). These pathogens enter the body either through natural openings or through the skin. If they are **virulent** they cause disease; **non-virulent** strains cause only mild symptoms.

Table 23.1 How microorganisms enter the body despite the body's protective measures

Entry site	Method of transmission	How entry site is protected	Examples of pathogens	
Mouth and Nose	Airborne	Mucus in nasal passages, mucus and ciliated lining of trachea	Virus / Bacteria	Measles, chicken pox common cold, influenza TB, whooping cough, pneumonia
	Food	Hydrochloric acid in stomach	Bacteria	Salmonella
	Water	Hydrochloric acid in stomach	Bacteria / Protozoa	Dysentery, cholera / Dysentery amoeba
Eyes	Airborne contact	Salty, mildly antiseptic tears	Bacteria	Conjunctivitis
Vagina, penis and anus	Sexual contact	Acidic secretions in vagina	Virus / Bacteria	HIV (AIDS), Hepatitis B / Syphilis
Skin	Vector bites	Keratin in layer of dead cells on surface, and sweat (antiseptic)	Virus / Protozoa / Bacteria	Rabies / Malaria / Typhus
	Piercing/scratching	Blood clotting provides temporary barrier while new skin grows	Virus / Bacteria / Fungus	HIV (AIDS), Hepatitis B / Tetanus / Athlete's foot

xaminer's tip

n't try to remember all of e pathogens. Select an ample of each.

23.3 Malaria and mosquitoes

The mosquito lays its eggs *on* stagnant water. The aquatic larvae breathe air through spiracles at the surface of the water; so do the pupae. The adults may emerge within a week after egg-laying in tropical countries. The females need a meal of blood to ensure proper egg development before fertilization. They tend to 'bite' humans at night, sheltering by day in dark places in houses. These habits give opportunities for **controlling mosquitoes**:

- drain marshes or otherwise remove stagnant water (prevents egg laying);
- spray light oils containing insecticide on water that cannot be removed (oil blocks spiracles, suffocating the aquatic stages; the insecticide kills females landing to lay eggs);
- introduce 'mosquito fish', e.g. *Gambusia* or guppy, into the water (to eat larvae and pupae);
- spray walls of houses with long-lasting insecticides, e.g. DDT (kills adults sheltering there).

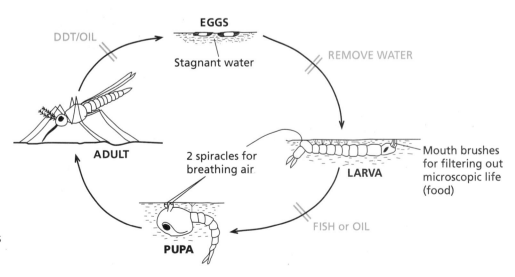

Fig. 23.1 Life cycle of the Anopheline mosquito and methods of controlling it (in green)

Mosquitoes do not *cause* **malaria**. They only *transmit* it, if they are given the opportunity to suck up the parasites of an infected person. When mosquitoes 'bite' they inject saliva to prevent the blood clotting. It is with this saliva that the parasites enter healthy people.

Despite precautions, millions of people are affected by malaria in the tropics. Millions die of the high fevers it produces. Those with sickle-cell anaemia trait (see Unit 19.2B) survive better.

Drug-resistant strains of *Plasmodium* and insecticide-resistant strains of mosquitoes arise by mutation (see Unit 18.16) making control of malaria a continuing problem.

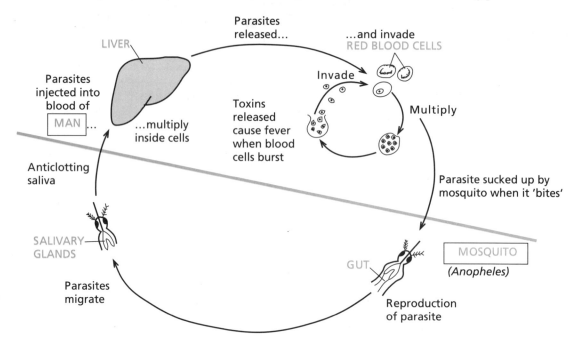

Fig. 23.2
Life cycle of *Plasmodium*, the malaria parasite

E xaminer's tip

Remember the difference between controlling and preventing.

Modern methods of malaria control include:

① Controlling the mosquito (see above).

② Preventative medicine (prophylaxis), i.e., regularly taking drugs which kill the parasites on entry, e.g. mepacrine.

③ Quarantine (isolating) those who become diseased, away from other people and under mosquito nets (to prevent infecting mosquitoes).

④ Curing diseased people with Artemisin (to which *Plasmodium* is not resistant).

⑤ Impregnating mosquito nets with Permethrin, which both repels and kills mosquitoes.

⑥ Vaccinating against *Plasmodium* at present gives 50–75% protection in trials in Colombia and Venezuela.

Various mosquito species also infect Man with:

● **Elephantiasis:** enormous enlargement of limbs caused by blockage of the lymph vessels by millions of tiny worms (nematodes). Incurable.

● **Yellow fever:** severe jaundice (yellow skin) caused by liver damage from a virus which may cause death.

23.4 Personal and community hygiene and health

Prevention of disease is preferable to cure.

Personal hygiene

Requires daily attention to body (see Fig. 23.3) and clothing.

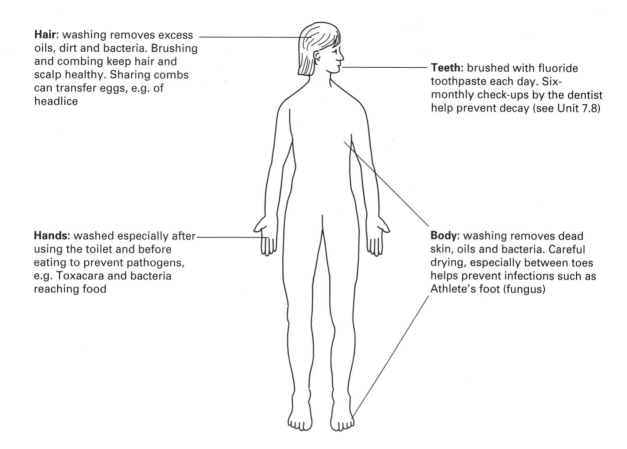

Hair: washing removes excess oils, dirt and bacteria. Brushing and combing keep hair and scalp healthy. Sharing combs can transfer eggs, e.g. of headlice

Teeth: brushed with fluoride toothpaste each day. Six-monthly check-ups by the dentist help prevent decay (see Unit 7.8)

Hands: washed especially after using the toilet and before eating to prevent pathogens, e.g. Toxacara and bacteria reaching food

Body: washing removes dead skin, oils and bacteria. Careful drying, especially between toes helps prevent infections such as Athlete's foot (fungus)

Fig. 23.3 Personal hygiene

Clothes: washed and dried to remove breeding sites for pathogens. Handkerchiefs sneezed or coughed into, prevent spread of pathogens by droplets in air.

Domestic hygiene

- Clean homes reduce disease transmission.
- Kitchens: free of dust; food vessels, utensils washed and dried after use.
- Food: stored to preserve it uncontaminated, e.g. in freezers.
- Cooked meats stored separate from fresh; cooked correctly, e.g. adequate thawing of poultry before cooking.
- Wastes: correct disposal including food and sewage.

Community hygiene

Environmental Health Officers ensure:

- **refuse** is correctly disposed of and rats are controlled
- **sewage** is correctly disposed of (see Unit 4.4)
- clean **drinking water** is provided; public swimming pools are clean (see Unit 4.4)
- **food shops** and eating places comply with health regulations, e.g. fly control
- **certain diseases** are notified to them to prevent spread, e.g. TB
- **quarantine:** isolating infected patients when necessary
- **vaccination** and immunization programmes are carried out (see Unit 23.6)

E xaminer's tip

emember to include things your answer even if they st seem common sense; t do explain why they are portant to prevent sease spread.

23.5 Defences of the body against pathogens

If the body's defences are penetrated, the body responds to the infection in three main ways:

❶ **Blood clotting:** If the skin is pierced, clotting prevents further blood loss and prevents bacteria entering. The dry, protective scab which then forms allows the wound to heal beneath it.

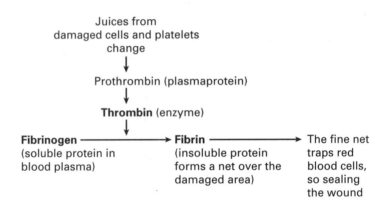

Fig. 23.4 How blood clots

First aid to someone bleeding: apply *pressure* to the wound with a cloth to stop blood flow, so promoting clotting.

❷ **Phagocytes:** White blood cells that move quickly to the site of infection and ingest microbes.

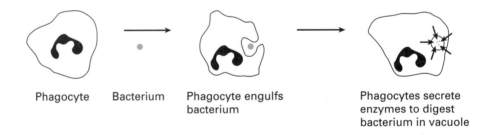

Fig. 23.5 Phagocytosis

Phagocytes are not specific and will ingest *all* cells that are recognized as 'foreign'.

❸ **Lymphocytes:** White blood cells that respond to **antigens** (foreign proteins on invading cells or the chemicals they produce). Lymphocytes recognize only one antigen from a particular pathogen and produce an **antibody** to it. This attaches to and destroys the antigen or pathogen. When an infection occurs, the rapid reproduction of lymphocytes in the lymph nodes (see Unit 9.7) can cause them to swell, become hot, and feel tender.

There are two types of lymphocyte:

1 **T cells** keep antibodies on their surface and migrate to 'foreign body' sites. They kill, e.g. tissue transplants ('rejection').

2 **B cells** release antibodies into blood plasma. These destroy toxins or attach to blood parasites or 'foreign' body cells to destroy them (see Unit 18.3).

Examiner's tip

Remember phagocytes and lymphocytes are effective only after microorganisms have entered the body. The other mechanisms are to prevent entry.

23.6 The immune system, vaccines and transplants

Immunity

Immunity is protection against pathogenic disease by antibodies. Antibodies are produced by lymphocytes (see Unit 9.2). A particular antigen is destroyed by its own *specific* antibody produced by *one* clone of lymphocytes and no other. When a pathogen enters the body for the first time it takes weeks to produce a clone of lymphocytes with enough antibodies to kill off that pathogen. So the body shows the signs and symptoms of that particular disease. On recovery, some of the clone of lymphocytes are stored in lymph nodes, remembering the antigen ('memory cells'). On subsequent re-infection, that pathogen is quickly recognized by its memory cells. They reproduce rapidly, secreting enough antibodies to kill the pathogen, so preventing illness (see Fig. 23.6).

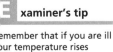

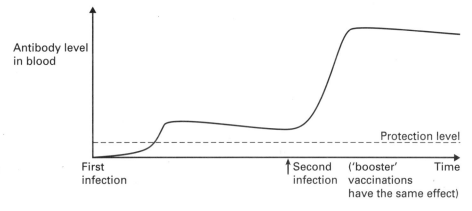

Fig. 23.6 Antibody production by the body when infected

Immunity can be gained by the body in a variety of ways.

Table 23.2. Methods of gaining immunity

	Passive immunity (body is not involved)	Active immunity (body is involved in producing antibodies)
Natural	Antibodies are given directly to the person, e.g. mother passes antibodies to fetus via the placenta and to baby via breast milk.	The body is infected by a pathogen. This causes lymphocytes to produce antibodies.
Acquired (artificial)	The body is injected with antibodies produced by other organisms.	Weakened or dead strains of the pathogen are introduced into the body (vaccination).
Protection	'Shortlived' Immediate protection, e.g. against rabies.	'Long lasting' because of memory cells. Takes weeks to be achieved.

Vaccines

Provide antigens which, when injected or scratched into the skin, stimulate the body to become actively immune. There are five kinds:

1. **Killed virulent** pathogens, e.g. whooping cough, polio.
2. **Live non-virulent** strain of the pathogen, e.g. tuberculosis, measles.
3. **Toxin** molecules from the pathogen chemically modified so that they are no longer toxic but still resemble the toxin antigenically, e.g. diphtheria, tetanus.
4. **Antigens** separated from the pathogen used as a vaccine, e.g. influenza.
5. **Antigens** produced by genetically engineered bacteria (see Unit 18.7), e.g. Hepatitis B virus.

Some pathogens have many different strains, e.g. viruses causing common cold. This makes it very difficult to produce one effective vaccine for all of them.

Examiner's tip

Questions about transplants may also ask you about the effects on people's lives of having or needing a transplant.

Transplants

All cells have antigen sites on them. The body accepts its own antigens and therefore does not produce antibodies against them. When an organ is transplanted from another person, e.g. kidneys, heart, liver, etc., this has 'foreign' antigens on the cells. The body may produce antibodies to reject the transplanted organ.

To reduce the risk of rejection:

1 Careful **tissue matching** is done between the donor and recipient.
2 **Immuno-suppressant drugs** are given to suppress reproduction of lymphocytes. This suppression of the immune system increases the risk of infections from other pathogens so recipients are kept in sterile conditions to reduce the risks.
3 **Irradiation** of the transplant area of the body also reduces white blood cell activity.

23.7 Drugs, antibiotics, antiseptics and disinfectants

Drugs are chemicals made by humans or other organisms. Some are harmful and possession of them is illegal, e.g. LSD – which has no medical purpose. Others (in the right doses) assist medically, e.g. sulphonamides for curing bacterial infections, aspirin for headaches, belladonna for helping people with ailing hearts and mepacrine for malaria. The term 'drug' is thus too vague to be very useful.

Antibiotics are chemicals secreted by bacteria or fungi and extracted by humans for their own use in killing microorganisms (but not viruses) in the body. *Examples*: penicillin, aureomycin. Accurate choice of antibiotic to treat an infection depends on taking a swab (see Unit 3.6).

Antibiotics work by interfering with the metabolism of bacteria, so they do not affect human cells or viruses. When a 10-day course of antibiotics is given, it is important that it is taken for the full length of time. Otherwise some bacteria may survive and develop resistance to the antibiotic.

Antiseptics are chemicals used in such a dose that they kill microorganisms but *not* human cells with which they make contact. May be diluted disinfectants, e.g. weak 'Dettol' for gargling or bathing cuts.

Disinfectants are chemicals made by chemists to kill microorganisms, e.g. neat 'Dettol' in toilets.

23.8 Notable contributions to health and hygiene

● **Edward Jenner** (1749–1823): practised *vaccination*. He scratched cowpox material (spots on cows caused by the vaccinia virus) into the skin of humans. The patients also developed mild spots, but became protected against the disfiguring or lethal disease smallpox. Smallpox has now been eliminated from the world.

● **Louis Pasteur** (1822–1895): father of *bacteriology*. Discovered the bacterial nature of putrefaction and many diseases. Saved silk industry (pebrine disease of silkworms), brewers ('ropy' beer), poultry farmers (chicken cholera) and cattle farmers (anthrax) from severe losses by developing sterile techniques and vaccines. Finally, developed a rabies vaccine to protect humans.

- **Joseph Lister** (1827–1912): developed *antiseptic surgery*. Used fine phenol spray to kill bacteria during operations, dramatically reducing hospital deaths. Today *aseptic surgery* is used – sterilization of all equipment before use, in autoclaves (see Unit 3.4).
- **Alexander Fleming** (1881–1955): discovered lysozyme (natural antiseptic in tears and saliva) and the *antibiotic* penicillin – secreted by the mould *Penicillium*.
- **Howard Florey** (1898–1968) and **Ernst Chain** (1906–1979) developed commercial production of penicillin in the US in 1941 having isolated the active principle from the cultivated mould

Summary

1 There are six major kinds of disease, each with its own problems for control.
2 Mosquitoes transmit the disease malaria (they are vectors) but do not cause it.
3 Personal and domestic hygiene reduce risk of disease.
4 Environmental Health Officers monitor community health.
5 Natural defences of the body include the skin, blood clotting and white blood cells, but antibodies are particularly useful.
6 The immune system produces antibodies in response to antigens on the cells of invading microorganisms.
7 Immunity may be natural or acquired.
8 Vaccination enhances the body's protection against disease, before exposure to pathogens.
9 The immune system has to be suppressed when organ transplants are done.
10 Medicines, antibiotics, disinfectants and antiseptics all play their part in controlling diseases.

Quick test 23

1 Give two types of disease that are not infectious.
2 Give four ways of controlling mosquitoes.
3 How is *Toxacara* transmitted?
4 What is the difference between fibrinogen and fibrin?
5 Why do phagocytes gather at cuts in the skin?
6 Why is it better for a person to have active rather than passive immunity to pathogens?
7 What is the difference between T cells and B cells?
8 Why do organs given in transplants sometimes get rejected?
9 What are antiseptics?
10 What is Alexander Fleming famous for?

The examination

Technique

Students should not be entered for an examination that is beyond their ability. Success in examinations for which you have been entered (which assumes that you *do* have the ability) lies in good 'examination technique'. The only way to develop this technique is by practising lots of exam questions. Such questions follow in this section, and even more can be found in the Letts *GCSE Questions and Answers Biology* book. Your teacher will usually advise you on the type of examination you will sit by showing you past question papers. But certain principles of technique apply to all methods of examination:

1. **Arrive in plenty of time** – avoid worry over missing the start of the exam.

2. **Come fully equipped** with pen, pencil, rubber, ruler, calculator, watch and coloured pens or pencils.

3. **Read the exam instructions carefully.**

4. **Plan your time for answering** according to the marks allocated to each part of the question. If you are stuck on part of a question, leave it and come back to it at the end.

5. **Do the maximum number of questions.** Usually, modern exams allow you plenty of time to complete all the questions. But always check your answers right through for any that you may have missed.

    Where you have left an answer-space blank you can be certain of one thing: a *blank* scores *no* marks. So look again at the question and write *something*. That 'something' has a better chance of scoring you marks than a blank. Think positively!

6. **Understand what the question asks.** Never twist the examiner's words into a meaning that was not intended. It is no use answering a completely different question from that written on the examination paper. In an examination, mis-information of this kind earns you no marks.

7. **Plan before writing** your paragraph and experimental answers. Organize key words into a *logical order* or pattern. This is particularly important when you have been asked to design an experiment. Use *short*, clear sentences, each one explaining a single step in the procedure (see the section below).

    The number of marks available for each part of a question gives an indication of the number of different points you should make. The space provided is usually more than enough for the length of answer required.

8. **Use large labelled diagrams** in your answers if they make your answer clearer. Descriptions of experiments are almost always clearer, and certainly much shorter, when diagrams are used. Diagrams save words.

9. **Set out your work neatly.** An examiner is human. If your written answers are neatly set out he is much more likely to give you the benefit of the doubt where your answers are not entirely clear. Illegible answers gain no marks.

10. **Check your spelling, punctuation and grammar.** This may affect your marks.

11. **Keep a cool head.** You can only do this by getting plenty of sleep, regular meals and some exercise over the examination period. Exercise each day so that you are tired enough to sleep well and get up refreshed. Do *not* stay up all night revising.

Tackling various types of question

1 Short answer questions

Short answer questions are usually easy questions requiring only writing one or two words, choosing words from a list, finishing a table or labelling a diagram. They give good coverage of the syllabus. As the syllabuses for GCSE require two-thirds of the questions to consist of non-short answer questions, the number of these questions will be limited.

2 Structured questions

A structured question consists of some information given in the question and a number of questions based upon the information given. Usually there are spaces or lines for you to write the answers. Bear in mind the amount of space you are given for the answer. If you are given three lines the examiner is expecting more than one or two words. Also, the number of marks for each part is given. If two marks are allocated for a part of a question, more than a single word is required in your answer.

In both Foundation and Higher tier examinations at least 25% of the marks must be allocated to questions requiring either **Extended** or **Continuous** writing. Continuous writing is defined as an answer needing one or two sentences. Extended writing is defined as an answer needing three or more consecutive sentences. The balance between extended and continuous writing is different in the two tiers.

Foundation tier 5% extended writing

20% continuous writing

Higher tier 10% extended writing

15% continuous writing

Although the specification for questions mentions numbers of sentences, you will not be penalized if you do not write in sentences. Particularly if you are short of time near the end of the examination, concise notes will be acceptable.

The important thing to remember is that your answer must be well structured. When you have written your answer, read it through critically. Do not be tempted just to add extra words to make your answer look longer. Your answer can still score full marks if it is short, providing it correctly answers all aspects of the question

Exam jargon

- **'State'** or **'list'** means put down as simple facts – nothing else. **'Name'** is a similar instruction: no explanations are required.

- **'Explain'** requires not only the facts or principles but also the reasons behind them. When you are thinking out the answer to an 'explain' question, ask yourself 'which?', 'what?', 'where?', 'why?' and 'when?' about the subject. These questions will help you to avoid leaving out information that you know. You *must*, however, only give the information that is asked for – for example 'which?' and 'when?' may be irrelevant (unnecessary) in a particular question.

- **'Calculate'** usually means not only give the answer but *show your working*. Often marks are awarded for correct method even if the answer is wrong.

- **'Suggest'** means there may be a variety of 'correct' answers that require you to reason or to apply scientific knowledge to the information given. You may not have been taught the answer: an hypothesis is required.

Graph, diagram and experiment questions

- **Graphs:** If you are asked to put information onto a graph, it is vital that on both axes you state the relevant *units*, e.g. 'g' or 'cm^3/h' or 'numbers of live insects'. Usually the title of the graph is supplied by the question – but sometimes it is important that *you* should provide it. All plots must be precise and ringed. You will avoid wrong plots by using a ruler to lead your eye to the precise spot. You should now plot a line of best fit either by eye or with a computer's help.

- **Diagrams:**

  1 *Draw in pencil* – in case you need to use an eraser.

  2 *Draw large* – for clarity and easy labelling; then put down your pencil.

  3 *Rule your labelling lines* in biro, avoiding crosses. Biro does not smudge against the ruler. Neither can the straight biro labelling lines be confused with being part of the detail of the drawing (which is in pencil). The lines should end *on* the part indicated and not stop short.

  4 *Label* in ink or biro neatly and add a *title*.

  If you follow the drill *in sequence* you will save time. And time is often marks!

- **Experiments**

  Experiments must be written up in a logical order under subheadings. The account usually includes a diagram which *saves* words. Do not duplicate the information in a diagram by also giving a *written* account of what it shows. Only write what the diagram does *not* say.

  Questions asking you to *describe* experiments are usually asking you to *design* an experiment. These answers require only the Planning (P) part (see Coursework table on page 238).

Relevance in answers

Sadly, a large number of reasonably knowledgeable students do not do themselves justice because they write irrelevant answers. Sheer length of an answer will not gain any marks. It is only the key facts and principles that the examiner is looking for, *whatever* the length of the answer. So do not 'pad out' your answers.

If you highlight key words in the question as you read it, that may help you to cover each point required.

Common errors when answering Biology questions

(*a*) In a question worth 2 marks, giving 5 answers and hoping that the examiner will give you marks for the correct ones and ignore the wrong ones.

(*b*) Imprecise answers, e.g. 'you will sweat' rather than saying 'you will sweat more'.

(*c*) Imprecise language, e.g. 'you will go to the toilet more' rather than 'the volume of urine produced increases'.

(*d*) Inaccurate spelling, e.g. 'urether' does not get the mark either for 'ureter' or for 'urethra'. Know the spelling of technical terms.

(*e*) When listing similarities and differences of two organisms or processes

    (i) not stating clearly which is which

    (ii) not stating which of the two has which differences, e.g. one is black, the other red.

(*f*) Inaccurately labelled diagrams (see above, no. 2).

(*g*) Not labelling axes of graphs, nor putting in units.

(*h*) Not showing working in calculations or including units.

(*i*) Not using clear layout in genetics problems (see p. 159) nor giving a key to the symbols used, e.g. the male is Dd.

(*j*) Common confusions include:

    (i) mitosis with meiosis

    (ii) acid rain with greenhouse effect and with ozone depletion.

(*k*) Areas proving difficult to explain: the workings of the kidney; homeostatic control mechanisms.

Practice exam questions

Chapter 1 (answers – page 225)

1   (a)   The nucleus controls the cell's activities.

Using the terms: gene   enzyme   RNA   DNA   ribosome   amino acids
explain how the nucleus does this.   (6)

(b)   Explain how a student who has obtained a strip of onion cells could prepare
this for microscopic examination. Be careful to explain the function of the
coverslip and of a stain used in preparing the slide.   (4)

(c)   Figure 1 shows a double strand of DNA splitting to make 2 strands. The
nucleotides are shown as C, G, A and T. These only assemble in particular
pairs.

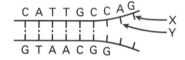

Fig. 1

(i)   During what process of life does this splitting and reassembling of DNA
take place?   (1)

(ii)   Name (by letter) the nucleotides that would occupy the positions X
and Y   (2)

(iii)   When the process of DNA assembly is complete would you say that the 2
strands are 'similar', 'identical', or 'dissimilar'?   (1)

Chapter 2 (answers – page 225)

2   Figure 2 shows a 'sea-food' dish.

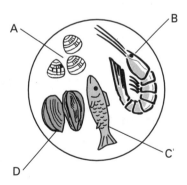

Fig. 2

(a) Identify, in a table, the groups to which A, B, and C belong and give two features that each would have to prove your identification.

	Group	Two characteristics of the group
A	Mollusc	1.
	....	2. ....
B		1. Exoskeleton of chitin
	....	2. ....
C		1. Gills
	....	2. .... (6)

(b) Which organism, A, B, C, or D is a vertebrate? (1)

(c) Name a group of animals that
   (i) is single celled
   (ii) gives milk to its young
   (iii) has no vertebrae
   (iv) has feathers
   (v) collects nectar and pollen for its young (5)

Chapter 3 (answers – page 225)

3   Figure 3 shows the structure of a simple virus.

   (a) Name the labelled parts X and Y. (2)

Fig. 3

   (b) State three ways in which a bacterium differs in structure from a virus. (3)

   (c) How and where do viruses get their food? What do they do with it once it is obtained? (3)

   (d) Name a virus that is (i) helpful and (ii) harmful to humans. (2)

   (e) Describe how you would obtain bacteria from soil and then culture them. Explain any safety procedures you would use (6)

Chapter 4 (answers – page 225)

4   Figure 4 shows a fermenter that can be used to grow microorganisms.

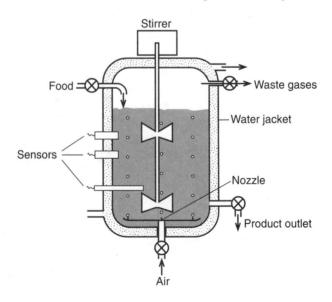

Fig. 4

(a) (i) Name three things that are monitored by sensors in the fermenter. (3)
    (ii) Why is a stirrer used in the fermenter? (1)
    (iii) Give two reasons why air is bubbled through a fermenter. (2)
    (iv) When might methane be bubbled through the fermenter instead of air? (1)
    (v) How are fermenters sterilized before they are set up? (1)

(b) (i) The fungus *Penicillium* is grown in a batch fermenter. What does batch fermenter mean? (1)
    (ii) Describe briefly how *Penicillium* can be grown in the fermenter so that it produces the antibiotic penicillin. (4)

(c) When a person needs penicillin the instructions on the bottle say that it is important to complete the course. Why? (2)

Chapter 5 (answers – page 225)

5   Read the following passage and then answer the questions.

'Your diet should provide you with energy, materials for growth and metabolism, enough water and sufficient indigestible bulk to help you pass food along the gut.'

(a) (i) Name the two classes of food that provide the most energy. (2)
    (ii) How do we release energy from these foods? (1)

(b) (i) What main class of food is required for muscle growth? (1)
    (ii) What disease would a person who is undernourished with this class of food suffer from? Describe the symptoms of the disease. (3)
    (iii) What main mineral element is required to help make bones? (1)
    (iv) Which of the three choices, steak, cheese or potatoes would you choose as being best for promoting growth? Explain your answer. (3)

(c) Give three reasons for needing water in your diet. (3)

(d) What is the 'bulk' quoted in the passage and from what do we get most of it in our diet? Give two reasons why 'bulk' is good for us. (4)

Chapter 6 (answers – pages 225–6)

6 (a) Complete the following equation for photosynthesis:

$$(B) \ \text{..................}$$

$$6CO_2 + (A) \ \text{.....................} \longrightarrow (D) \ \text{....................} + 6O_2 \qquad (4)$$

$$(C) \ \text{..................}$$

(b) Explain fully how product (D) above:
    (i) is stored in the leaf (2)
    (ii) is moved to a growing point (2)
    (iii) provides for energy and growth at a growing point. (3)

(c) Figure 5 shows a long green leaf. Pieces of coloured plastic film that allow only one colour of light to pass through were placed on the leaf. The leaf was then left in the dark for two days. The plant with this leaf was then placed in the light. After six hours the leaf was tested for starch. Part of the result is shown in Fig. 6.

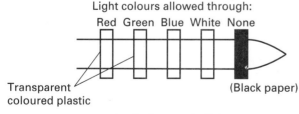

Fig. 5

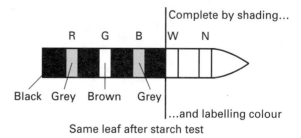

Fig. 6

    (i) Complete the shading and colour labelling on Fig 6 to show what you would expect when the leaf was tested for starch. (3)

    (ii) What conclusions can you make about the effect of different colours of light on the amount of photosynthesis? (4)

    (iii) Why was the leaf placed in the dark at the start of the experiment? (1)

    (iv) Describe how you would carry out the starch test on the leaf. (6)

Chapter 7 (answers – page 226)

7 The flow diagram in Fig. 7 represents the passage of a meal and its major chemical components through the human digestive system.

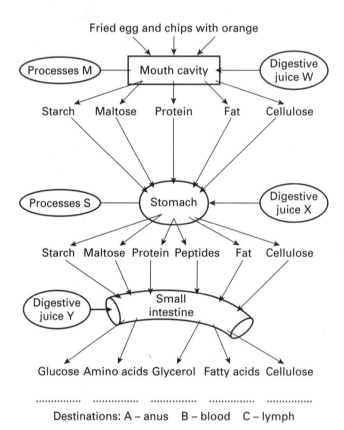

Fig. 7

Destinations: A – anus   B – blood   C – lymph

(a) What are the processes occurring at M? (2)

(b) What are the processes occurring at S? (2)

(c) What two parts of the meal contain:
    (i) protein   (ii) cellulose? (2)

(d) One digestive juice entering the small intestine contains enzymes that are capable of digesting almost all of the meal. Name the juice. (1)

(e) Place one letter A, B or C from the destinations below the flow diagram under each of the five substances in the small intestine to indicate where each of them will next go. (5)

(f) Digestive juice X was found to be pH 2.5 and juice Y to be pH 9.

    (i) Explain how you would test whether the extracted enzyme from juice X would work in both pH conditions. (6)

    (ii) The enzyme in juice X does not in fact digest protein in alkaline conditions. Suggest how proteins are digested in the small intestine. (2)

Chapter 8 (answers – page 226)

8   Figure 8(a) shows an ancient evaporimeter. It measured the rate of loss of water by evaporation from a porous pot in different environmental conditions.

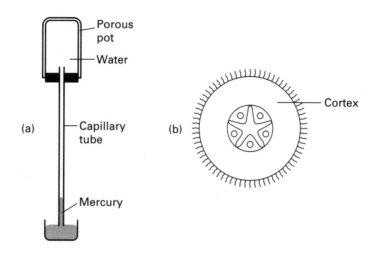

Fig. 8

(a)   (i)   What is evaporation of water from a plant called?   (1)
      (ii) What organ in a plant would the porous pot correspond with?   (1)
      (iii) What tissue in a plant would the capillary tube correspond with?   (1)

(b) Name three environmental conditions that would increase the rate of evaporation of water from a plant.   (3)

(c) Figure 8(b) shows a cross-section of a young root.
      (i)   In what two ways can you tell that it is a root and not a stem?   (2)
      (ii) Label the phloem.   (1)
      (iii) What materials does the phloem transport?   (1)

(d) In a potato plant, in which direction do materials in the phloem pass between tuber and leaf
      (i) in spring?   (ii) in summer?   (2)

(e) Explain how 'systemic insecticides' work in getting rid of greenfly pests.   (3)

(f) Explain how guard cells may influence:
      (i) loss of water vapour   (ii) photosynthesis, in a leaf.   (4)

Chapter 9 (answers – page 226)

9   'Blood vessels provide cells with energy sources, substances for growth and a removal system for wastes.'

(a) By reference to named substances in the blood, explain:
      (i)   how the energy is obtained from the energy sources by cells   (2)
      (ii) how the blood promotes growth in cells   (2)
      (iii) what wastes are removed and the organs which excrete them.   (4)

(b) ·Smoking increases the quantity of harmful substances in the blood. Name two of these, and explain what harm they do via the blood.   (4)

(c) Coronary heart disease is a major cause of death in the UK. Explain how people die from CHD.   (3)

(d) Some young women are anaemic, i.e. have fewer red blood cells than normal.
      (i)   What effect does this have on them?   (1)
      (ii) Suggest how the condition can arise.   (2)

Chapter 10 (answers – page 226)

10 (a) Complete the following equations for respiration in humans:

    (i)   .... + oxygen ⟶ carbon dioxide + ... + energy   (2)

    (ii) .... + no oxygen ⟶ .... + energy   (2)
    (iii) Under what circumstances would equation (i) take place?   (1)
    (iv) Under what circumstances would equation (ii) take place?   (1)
    (v) How does the body remove the product in equation (ii) and deal with it? (3)
    (vi) The energy released in equation (ii) is much less than in equation (i).
        Explain why this is so.   (1)

  (b) Yeast can also respire without oxygen.
    (i) When it does so what are the two chemical products?   (2)
    (ii) How does Man use each of these products in commercial processes?   (2)

  (c) The breathing rate of a person after exercise can be used as a measure of their fitness. How would you compare the fitness of two similar people using this means?   (4)

Chapter 11 (answers – page 226)

11 Figure 9 shows a kidney nephron and a collecting duct.

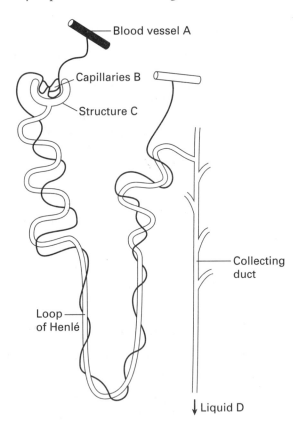

Fig. 9

  (a) (i) Name A, B, C and D.   (4)
      (ii) In which region of the kidney are B and C to be found?   (1)

  (b) A clear fluid arrives in structure C. Its volume is reduced by 80% by the time it reaches the loop of Henle. Liquid D is only 1% of its original volume in C.

    The composition of blood plasma at B, the clear fluid in C and of the liquid D are shown in the Table in mg/l.

Substance /Fluid	Plasma at B	Fluid in C	Liquid D
Proteins	82.5	0	0
Amino acids	0.8	0.8	0.8
Glucose	1.5	1.5	0.0
Urea	0.4	0.4	20.0
Salts	8.0	8.0	16.5

    (i)   Explain how a clear fluid comes to arrive in structure C. (2)

    (ii) Why is there no protein in this fluid? (1)

    (iii) From the data given, what are the two main functions of the nephron tubules? (2)

(c) Name in sequence the three structures through which liquid D will now pass before it leaves the body. (3)

(d) The amount of urine a person produces after exercise is less than normal. Explain the changes that occur to cause the kidney to produce less urine. (4)

Chapter 12 (answers – page 226)

12 Figure 10 is an incomplete drawing of a section through the eye

(a) Complete it by drawing in (i) the pupil (ii) the ciliary body. Label them. (2)

(b) Label (i) the retina (ii) the fovea. (2)

(c) Explain the eye's response to:
    (i)   bright light suddenly shone into it
    (ii) dust landing on it. (6)

(d) How does the eye focus on the words in a book? (3)

(e) What does the choroid do? (2)

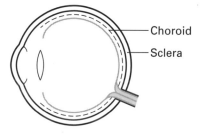

Fig. 10

Chapter 13 (answers – page 226)

13 Figure 11 shows an incomplete reflex arc.

(a) (i)   What two types of tissue may the motor neurone send impulses to? (2)

    (ii) If the sensory cell is sensitive to light, where precisely in the body would it be situated? (2)

    (iii) Describe simply how an impulse is transmitted from a sensory to a relay neurone. (3)

    (iv) How is a voluntary action different from a reflex action? (2)

(b) How would a person be affected if (i) the sensory neurones in the leg were damaged and (ii) the motor neurones to the leg were damaged? (2)

(c) If a person had a damaged cerebellum, what physical symptoms might they show? (2)

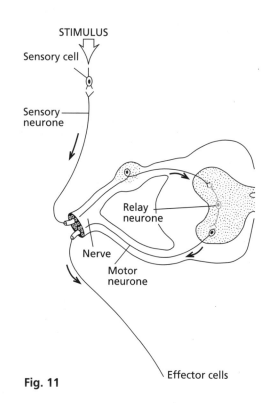

Fig. 11

Chapter 14 (answers – pages 226–7)

14 Figure 12 shows structures in an arm.

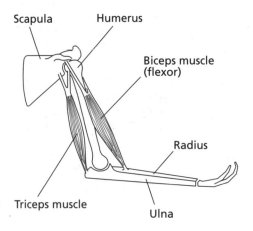

Fig. 12

- (a) (i) Name the tissue that attaches the biceps muscle to the radius. (1)
  - (ii) The tissue that holds the ulna close to the humerus. (1)
- (b) Explain how the fore arm is raised. (3)
- (c) Why do muscles always occur in pairs? (1)
- (d) (i) What type of joint is found at the elbow? (1)
  - (ii) How is the type of joint at the shoulder different from the elbow? (1)

- (e) Figure 13 shows more detail of the joint.

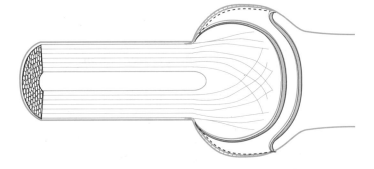

Fig. 13

Explain how it is designed to move smoothly (4)

- (f) State two functions of mammalian skeletons, other than for movement. (2)

Chapter 15 (answers – page 227)

15 Figure 14 shows a cutting taken from a plant.

- (a) Explain why each of the following is done.
  - (i) a large piece of the plant is used
  - (ii) the cutting is placed in a mixture of sand and peat
  - (iii) most of the leaves are removed
  - (iv) rooting hormone is added to the cut end (4)

Fig. 14

- (b) (i) An alternative method of asexually producing plants is to use tissue culture. Outline the procedure used to produce plants by this method. (5)
  - (ii) Give **two** advantages of producing new plants by tissue culture or cuttings (2)

Chapter 16 (answers – page 227)

16 Figure 15 shows a simplified diagram of a villus in the placenta.

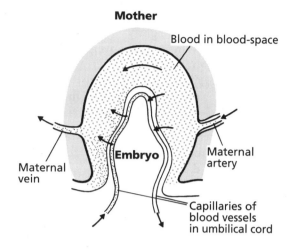

Fig. 15

(a) (i) Name two substances passing from the mother's blood to fetal blood and two substances passing from the fetal blood to mother's blood. (4)

(ii) Explain how the structure of the placenta allows efficient exchange of materials. (3)

(b) What are the functions of the amnion? (2)

(c) (i) Explain the changes that take place during childbirth in the uterus. (4)

(ii) What two things must be achieved soon after the birth of a baby? (2)

Chapter 17 (answers – page 227)

17 Figure 16 shows seeds placed in four different conditions.

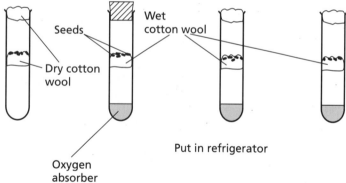

Fig. 16

(a) In which tube will the seeds germinate? (1)

(b) Figure 17 shows a section through a seed.

Describe the early changes that occur inside the seed as it germinates. (3)

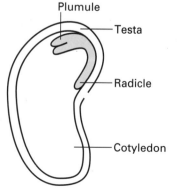

Fig. 17

(c) The graph in Fig. 18 shows the changes in dry weight of a plant starting with germination.

(i) How would you measure dry weight? (3)
(ii) Why is there a weight loss initially? (2)
(iii) What will happen to produce the increase in mass? (3)

(d) After germination explain how the root will start to grow down into the soil. (3)

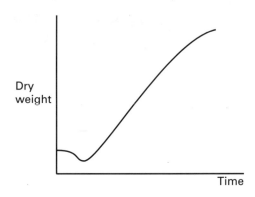

Fig. 18

Chapter 18 (answers – page 227)

18 (a) Complete the diagram below to show how a woman and a man have an equal chance of producing a boy or a girl baby. (3)

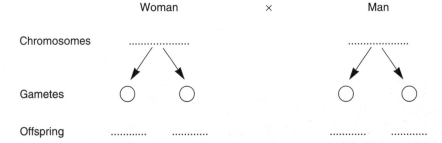

(b) Cystic fibrosis is caused by a recessive gene. Using the symbols F for normal gene and f for cystic fibrosis gene, show how two people who do not show symptoms of cystic fibrosis can have a child who is affected. Explain your answer fully (you are advised to draw a Punnett square.) (4)

(c) Haemophilia is a sex linked gene. What are the five possible genotypes and phenotypes? (5)

(d) (i) A student crossed a white flowered plant with a red flowered plant. When they grew, the seeds all produced plants with pink flowers. Explain how this happened, using a genetic diagram in your answer. (3)

(ii) Explain, with the help of a diagram, what offspring would result from crossing two pink plants. (4)

Chapter 19 (answers – page 227)

19 Figure 19 shows the forelimb of a human, a bat and a whale.

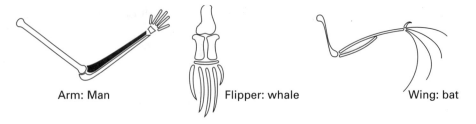

Fig. 19

(a) A bone is shaded on the human forelimb. Shade the same bone on the bat and whale forelimb. (2)

(b) How do the structures of these forelimbs support the theory of evolution? (2)

Chapter 20 (answers – page 227)

20 (a) Figure 20 shows a food web at the edge of an oak wood.

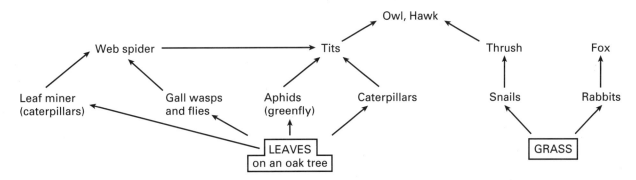

Fig. 20

Write down **one** food chain with five organisms in it. (1)

(b) Pyramids of number and pyramids of biomass can be constructed from a food chain.
   (i) When studying a food chain what are the advantages of measuring the numbers of organisms? (1)
   (ii) When studying a food chain what are the advantages of measuring the biomass of the organisms? (1)
   (iii) What are the disadvantages of measuring the biomass of organisms? (1)
   (iv) For the food chain ending with 'fox' draw a pyramid of numbers and a pyramid of biomass. (2)
   (v) Describe the effects on the food web of spraying the area with an insecticide. (3)
   (vi) Decomposers are not shown on the food web. Explain the role of decomposers in an ecosystem. (3)

Chapter 21 (answers – page 227)

21 (a) Coal and oil can be burnt in power stations and factories to release energy. They produce two major pollutants, carbon dioxide and sulphur dioxide.
   (i) Explain how carbon dioxide may lead to a melting of the polar icecaps. (4)
   (ii) Explain how sulphur dioxide may kill fish eggs. (4)

(b) Oil for refineries may be delivered by sea in tankers. Sometimes the oil escapes into the sea.

Explain the use of (i) powdered chalk and (ii) detergents to treat oil pollution. (2)

(c) Recycling reduces the use of natural resources. Figure 21 shows a compost maker used for recycling organic material.

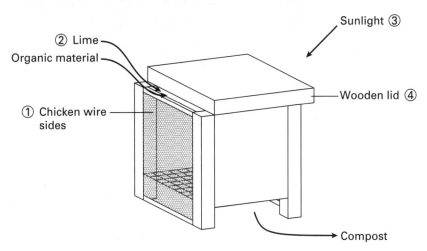

Fig. 21

Explain how the labelled features 1 to 4 help bacteria in the compost maker to produce the compost. (4)

Chapter 22 (answers – page 228)

22 Food production can be increased by artificially controlling environments. The temperature, light period and carbon dioxide levels can be controlled in a glasshouse.

(a) For each factor explain how it can help to improve food production. (3)

(b) The diagram shows two food chains.

A: Wheat ⟶ Humans

B: Grass ⟶ Sheep ⟶ Humans

Why does **A** give humans more food? (2)

(c) The diagram shows another food chain involving humans

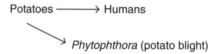

(i) Why does *Phytophthora* pose a problem? (1)
(ii) *Phytophthora* has branching hyphae. What kind of organism is it? (1)
(iii) How can *Phytophthora* be controlled? (1)

(d) The numbers of birds of prey have decreased in this country over the last 100 years. Part of the reason for this is the way farmers have controlled pests on their crops. Explain how controlling pests of crops could lead to a decline in the number of birds of prey. (4)

(e) An alternative method of pest control is biological control. Explain what is meant by biological control and explain any two advantages (3)

Chapter 23 (answers – page 228)

23 Figure 22 shows two types of white blood cell A and B.

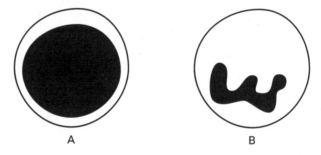

Fig. 22   A   B

(a) Name each and explain briefly how they protect the body against microbes. (4)

(b) Figure shows an incomplete mechanism for blood clotting.

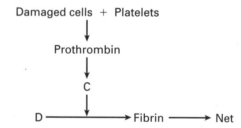

Fig. 23

(i) Complete the missing labels C and D. (2)
(ii) How is chemical D different from fibrin? (1)
(iii) Explain how the net helps to seal the wound. (2)

(c) A person receiving an organ transplant is given immuno–suppressant drugs.
(i) Explain why these drugs have to be given. (3)
(ii) Explain how these drugs work. (2)

Answers to practice exam questions

In the answers, the statements between 2 semicolons are worth 1 mark. The slash sign (/) denotes alternative answers for the mark.

In the longer questions, there are often more possible answers than there are marks available. Any combination of correct answers up to the maximum indicated by the marks in brackets, will give full marks.

1 (a) A part of a **DNA** strand called a **gene** is copied into a strand of **RNA**. This passes to a **ribosome** in the cytoplasm. Together they control the linking of **amino acids** into protein. The protein is often an **enzyme** and enzymes **control** a cell's metabolism (any 6 of 7 terms used correctly)
   (b) Place object on slide; add water drop (or stain) to show up cell parts; support coverslip on edge; lower to exclude air bubbles and keep wet
   (c) (i) Growth/asexual reproduction/ mitosis/meiosis
        (ii) X: C Y: T
        (iii) identical

2 (a) A Mollusc **chalky shell**; **soft body** B **Arthropod Many-jointed legs**; **segmented body**; **or Crustacea** exoskeleton of chitin (any 1) C **Fish Fins; scales**; gills (any 1)
   (b) C
   (c) (i) Protozoa
        (ii) Mammals
        (iii) Invertebrates (or any invertebrate group)
        (iv) Birds
        (v) Bees

3 (a) X: protein; Y: DNA or RNA
   (b) Larger; a cell; DNA in a loop; any correct parts of a cell e.g.. cell wall (any 3)
   (c) From inside; cells; reproduce
   (d) (i) e.g. myxomatosis
        (ii) any viral disease

   (e) sterile loop (and soil-water); streak on agar; shielded by lid/tape lid on; incubate in oven (any 4); safety – sterilize loop in flame; do not cough/sneeze on agar; do not open culture (any 2)

4 (a) (i) pH; O_2 levels; food levels; product levels; temperature Any 3
        (ii) to bring cells into contact with substrate
        (iii) to agitate/mix cells; create aerobic conditions/for bacterial respiration
        (iv) when anaerobic conditions are needed
        (v) by blowing steam through system
   (b) (i) nothing added or removed until the end of process
        (ii) fungus + glucose + minerals + air added; nutrients used up as fungus grows; when nutrients fall to critical level; fungus begins secreting antibiotic
   (c) Bacteria that survive longest are likely to have some genes for resistance; they may survive and pass on genes for resistance to their offspring

5 (a) (i) carbohydrate; fats
        (ii) respiration
   (b) (i) protein
        (ii) Kwashiorkor; pot belly; stick legs
        (iii) calcium
        (iv) cheese; contains calcium and protein; fat for energy
   (c) removing wastes (urine); heat loss (sweating); for digestion (hydrolysis); lubrication (e.g. gut, joints); transporting absorbed food, CO_2 (in blood), etc. (any 3)
   (d) cellulose/fibre; fruit/veg.; helps peristalsis; prevents colonic cancer

6 (a) (A) $6H_2O$ (water) (B) and (C) sunlight and chlorophyll (D) $C_6H_{12}O_6$ (glucose)
   (b) (i) turned into starch; by enzymes
        (ii) turned into sucrose; transported in phloem

(iii) respired (for energy); combines with nitrates; to form amino acids / protein (for growth)

(c) (i) white → black; none → brown; in between → black

     (ii) white: good; red and blue: quite good (any 2); green: useless

     (iii) to de-starch leaf

     (iv) boil; extract chlorophyll in boiling ethanol; safety (no flame); rinse in hot water; add iodine; 1 mark for correct sequence

7 (a) Chewing; digesting by enzyme

    (b) Churning; digesting by enzyme

    (c) (i) egg

        (ii) chips

    (d) Pancreatic juice

    (e) B B C C A

    (f) (i) water bath at 37 °C; protein, e.g. egg strips; + enzyme 'solution'; control with protein alone in water; digested if egg disappears

       (ii) different enzymes/at least two enzymes used

8 (a) (i) transpiration

       (ii) leaf

       (iii) xylem

    (b) Warmth; wind; low humidity

    (c) (i) root hairs; wide cortex; central xylem; phloem islands between xylem arms (any 2)

       (ii) label (see Unit 8.10)

       (iii) organic / sugars / amino acids

    (d) (i) tuber → leaf

       (ii) leaf → tuber

    (e) Sprayed on leaf; pass to phloem; sap sucked up by greenfly

    (f) (i) increase if wider / in light; decrease if closed / in dark

       (ii) increase entry of CO_2 in light / open; decrease if in dark / shut

9 (a) (i) oxygen + glucose react (respiration); in mitochondria of cells

       (ii) supplies amino acids → grow cells (protein); growth hormones

       (iii) CO_2; removed at lungs; urea; at kidneys; mineral salts; at kidneys/skin (any 2)

    (b) CO; reduces O_2 carrying capacity; nicotine; carried to brain, causes addiction

    (c) Fatty material (atheroma); blocks coronary arteries; prevents O_2 / food supply to heart muscle (dies)

    (d) (i) less O_2 carried / 'tired'

       (ii) lack of iron in diet; heavy menstruation; genetic (any 2)

10 (a) (i) glucose; water

       (ii) glucose; lactic acid

(iii) normal activity

(iv) strong exertion

(v) panting to get O_2; to oxidize some lactic acid to CO_2 and water; turn most of lactic acid back into glycogen

(vi) incomplete breakdown of glucose

    (b) (i) ethanol + CO_2

       (ii) ethanol – alcoholic drinks /gasohol; CO_2 – baking

    (c) Measure breaths per min. at rest; give them same exercise; for same time; time how long before breathing rate returns to normal

11 (a) (i) A: renal arteriole; B: glomerulus; C: Bowmin's capsule; D: urine

       (ii) cortex

    (b) (i) blood pressure; filters (tissue fluid) from plasma

       (ii) protein molecules too large to pass through capillary walls

       (iii) reabsorb soluble foods; most water (from filtrate)

    (c) Ureter; bladder; urethra

    (d) Water lost by sweating; osmoreceptors in brain register more concentrated blood; ADH secreted; more water absorbed from filtrate

12 (a) Two drawings, labelled (see Fig. 12.1)

    (b) Correct labels

    (c) (i) circular muscle; of pupil; contracts (less light enters)

       (ii) conjunctiva; causes blinking; weeping (to remove it)

    (d) Ciliary muscle contracts; allowing lens to collapse (fatten); become of short focal length

    (e) Nourishes cells (capillaries); stops internal reflection (melanin)

13 (a) (i) gland; muscle

       (ii) retina; inside back of eye

       (iii) electrical impulse arrives at end of sensory neurone; stimulates secretion of transmitter/ acetylcholine into synaptic gap; acetylcholine generates electrical impulse in relay neurone

       (iv) impulses go to brain; impulses generated by brain pass to motor neurones (for action)

    (b) (i) would have no feeling but could move

       (ii) would have feeling but could not move

    (c) Poor balance; lack of coordination

14 (a) (i) tendon

       (ii) ligament

    (b) nerve impulse reaches biceps; biceps muscle contracts/shortens and thickens; forearm pivots at elbow

    (c) muscle can only contract (antagonistic muscle contracts to extend it again)

    (d) (i) hinge joint

       (ii) can move in more than one plane

(e) Cartilage; smoother than bone so surfaces slide easier; synovial fluid; lubricates joint

(f) Support; shape; protection; manufacture red blood cells; transmit sound (any 2)

15 (a) (i) large food supply available

(ii) to provide water/nutrients support/ air for respiration in roots

(iii) to reduce transpiration

(iv) to promote cell division in tissues at cut surface

(b) (i) cells obtained and placed on nutrient agar; auxins added to promote cell division; transfer callus and add other plant hormones (cytokinins); to promote specialization of cells into different tissues; transplant out

(ii) large numbers produced; identical to parents; without having to resort to sexual reproduction

16 (a) From mother – O_2; glucose; amino acids; antibodies; vitamins; from fetus – CO_2; urea

(b) (i) large surface area; short diffusion distance; blood replaced constantly at both sides of placenta

(ii) protection; constant temperature

(d) (i) uterus wall contracts; amniotic cavity ruptures/waters break; muscle at neck of uterus thins/cervix dilates; uterus contracts to force baby out

(ii) cut umbilical cord; birth of placenta; get the baby breathing (any 2)

17 (a) The tube where the conditions include water, warmth and O_2 i.e. D

(b) Water enters seed; enzymes/amylase; converts starch to maltose; maltose used to produce energy; by respiration (any 3)

(c) (i) heat plants at 60 °C; measure mass; repeat until mass constant

(ii) food store/carbohydrate; used up in respiration to provide energy for growth

(iii) leaves will be formed; photosynthesis will begin; carbohydrate will be produced and stored

(d) Cells at tip divide rapidly/ by mitosis; cells behind tip increase in size; by water being absorbed and cells swelling; geotropic responses cause root to grow down (any 3)

18 (a) woman XX; man XY; gametes Ⓧ Ⓧ Ⓧ Ⓨ; offspring two males XY and two females XX

(b)

Parents		Ff	×		Ff	(1)
Gametes	Ⓕ	ⓕ		Ⓕ	ⓕ	(1)
Offspring		Ⓕ		ⓕ		
Ⓕ		FF		Ff		(1)
ⓕ		Ff		ff		

identify ff as child suffering from cystic fibrosis (1)

(c) $X_H X_h$; $X_H X_H$; $X_h X_h$;
carrier   normal   haemophiliac
female   female   female

$X_H Y$; $X_h Y$
normal   haemophiliac
male   male

(d) (i) codominance/neither white nor pink dominant; parents WW where W = white allele and RR where R = red allele; offspring all WR = pink

(ii) Parents WR × WR (1)

Gametes Ⓦ Ⓡ Ⓦ Ⓡ (1)

Offspring		Ⓦ	Ⓡ	
Ⓦ		WW	WR	(1)
Ⓡ		WR	RR	

ratio: 1 white: 2 pink: 1 red (1)

19 (a) correctly shaded bones (see Fig 19.6)

(b) The same pattern of bones in the forelimb of all three; suggests a common ancestor/ modification of one structure for different purposes

20 (a) Chain beginning with leaves via leaf miner or gall wasps and on to owl or hawk

(b) (i) relatively easy to obtain numbers of organisms

(ii) takes account of an organisms size/ used in agriculture/carrying capacity of reserves

(iii) have to destroy the organism to weigh the dry mass

(iv) a pyramid with a large base and two decreasing layers on top for both parts

(v) oak growth increases as fewer insects to feed on it; animals that feed on the insects will die; or find alternative food elsewhere

(vi) break down dead plants and animals; release minerals into the soil; so they are now available for plants to absorb

21 (a) (i) carbon dioxide levels rise in atmosphere; light energy from sun penetrates atmosphere and hits earth; converted to heat; CO_2 retains heat which normally escapes, so melting ice

(ii) sulphur dioxide in air dissolves in rain; to form sulphuric acid; falls as acid rain into lakes; pH of lake becomes more acidic; fish can't breed and survive (any 4)

(b) (i) it causes the oil to sink

(ii) it disperses the oil

(c) the wire allows air in for respiration; the lime maintains the pH at a level to help bacteria to grow; the sun allows it to warm up; the lid stops moisture escaping

22 (a) Temperature increases the rate at which enzymes in photosynthesis work; carbon dioxide allows photosynthesis to occur faster; light allows photosynthesis to occur faster/longer

(b) The more trophic levels the less energy/food is transferred

(c) (i) reduces the potato yield for humans
(ii) fungus
(iii) spraying plants with a fungicide/pesticide; uninfected seed potatoes, etc.

(d) Animals feeding on plants absorb pesticide and retain it; predators eat herbivores and the pesticide they contain; levels get higher and higher up the food chain; birds of prey get such high levels of pesticide that it interferes with their breeding

(e) Using a predator or parasite to control a pest; no pollution/effects on other organisms in ecosystem; highly specific; self-perpetuating (controller breeds)

23 (a) A: lymphocytes – produce antibodies;
B: phagocytes – digest pathogens

(b) (i) C: thrombin; D – fibrinogen
(ii) D is a soluble protein; fibrin is an insoluble protein
(iii) net traps red blood cells; these dry out to form hard protective scab

(c) (i) transplanted organs have antigens on cell surface; recipient's white cells recognize foreign antigens and produce antibodies to attack/reject organ
(ii) reduce white blood cell sensitivity to antigens and stop antibody production

Answers to quick tests

Quick test 1

1 Cell membrane, cytoplasm, nucleus.
2 Excretion: elimination of wastes of metabolism. Egestion: elimination of indigestible waste.
3 Receive sunlight energy; turn it into chemical energy in bonds of glucose.
4 Respire it into CO_2, water and energy (ATP) to power vital functions.
5 Cell wall, large vacuole and chloroplasts.
6 To control the cell's activities; pass on genes to its descendants.
7 Bases, sugar and phosphate.
8 DNA is copied into RNA; RNA message passes to ribosome; ribosome assembles amino acids into an enzyme.
9 A protein catalyst that speeds up chemical reactions in organisms.
10 **BDCEAF.**

Quick test 2

1 <u>Homo sapiens</u> (capital H, small s, all underlined).
2 Not cells, no metabolism of their own.
3 No true nucleus, very small cells.
4 Bacteria, fungi.
5 Mosses, ferns.
6 Exoskeleton of chitin, segmented body, many-jointed legs.
7 Insects: 6 legs, wings, 3-part body; spiders: 8 legs, no wings, 2-part body.
8 Mammals, birds.
9 Amphibia.
10 Egg, larva, pupa, adult.

Quick test 3

1 Protein and DNA or RNA.
2 Inside cells, as parasites.
3 Water, organic food, suitable temperature, suitable pH, no UV or γ radiation

4 Binary fission.
5 (a) chlorine (b) disinfectants (c) antibiotics
6 Place discs of filter paper impregnated with different antibiotics (and a plain control) on the culture; incubate; the disc with the widest clear ring around it indicates the best one.
7 Secrete enzymes onto food; absorb the digested products via rootlet hyphae.
8 Gets rid of dead organisms; turns them into food for plants – CO_2 and mineral salts
9 Green plants without roots stems or leaves.
10 Bottom of food chain; provide a lot of the world's oxygen.

Quick test 4

1 Batch: a single charging of the fermenter with nothing added. Continuous: nutrients contiinually added.
2 Temperature, pH, nutrient levels, oxygen levels, waste, e.g. carbon dioxide levels.
3 To sterilize the fermenter.
4 Methane and carbon dioxide.
5 A mixture of sewage and useful microorganisms with air bubbled through it.
6 To allow starch reserves to be broken down into maltose.
7 Heated to 85 °C for 30 minutes.
8 Water, glucose, nutrients and possibly heat.
9 Bacteria.
10 Proteases break down proteins into amino acids; lipases break down fats into fatty acids and glycerol.

Quick test 5

1 Organic molecules contain carbon and are complex.
2 CO_2, water, mineral salts.
3 Have no chlorophyll.
4 Magnesium.

5 (a) red blood cells (haemoglobin)   (b) bones and teeth   (c) tooth enamel

6 Fats, oils.

7 Organic food required in minute quantities to maintain health.

8 Disease caused by deficiency of protein in the diet.

9 Benedict's

Quick test 6

1 Carbon dioxide + water $\xrightarrow[\text{chlorophyll}]{\text{sunlight energy}}$ glucose + oxygen

2 Enzymes link large numbers of glucose molecules into starch.

3 Ethanol or acetone.

4 Variegated one.

5 Red, blue, (white).

6 One that reduces the possible rate of photosynthesis, e.g. (lack of) light at dawn.

7 Palisade, spongy mesophyll, guard cells.

8 Water – via xylem in veins; CO_2 – via stomata into air spaces.

9 Sugar and nitrates

10 Active transport, diffusion.

Quick test 7

1 Mechanical and chemical breakdown (digestion), absorption, egestion.

2 Emulsify fats in the small intestine.

3 Temperature, pH and enzyme concentration.

4 Small intestine: absorbs glucose, amino acids, fatty acids and glycerol. Large intestine: none.

5 Dehydration and loss of food.

6 Provides bulk to food so intestine wall muscles have something to grip on for peristalsis.

7 Storage, excretion, export and destruction (detail in Fig. 7.9).

8 Incisors – single long sharp edge to cut off bits of food.
Canines – pointed to pierce, rip and tear food or help kill prey.
Molars and premolars – large ridged surfaces to grind food.

9 Sugar and bacteria, which turn it into acids (to erode enamel).

10 To grind up cellulose cell walls of plant material they eat.

Quick test 8

1 Solvent, reactant, lubricant, provides support, coolant.

2 The random movement of substances from a region of high concentration to a region of low concentration.

3 Requires cell membrane, respiration (i.e. living cell) and is selective.

4 (a) vacuole   (b) cell membrane.

5 A plant cell inflated by osmosis.

6 Enters root hairs; leaves via leaf stomata.

7 Warmth, wind, low humidity, light.

8 Phloem.

9 No protoplasm, only cell wall.

10 Our kidneys.

Quick test 9

1 Need a more rapid transport system for food and wastes than diffusion allows.

2 The liquid part, without blood cells.

3 Haemoglobin.

4 White blood cells – phagocytes and lymphocytes.

5 They plug cut capillaries; help the clotting process.

6 Thinner walled, with valves; carry blood under low pressure, towards heart.

7 Heart pumps blood to lung, returns; to body, returns, i.e. twice through heart.

8 Coronary arteries blocked.

9 Left ventricle.

10 Tissue fluid.

Quick test 10

1 To release energy for vital functions.

2 glucose + oxygen $\xrightarrow{\text{enzymes}}$ carbon dioxide + water

3 Without oxygen.

4 (a) lactic acid   (b) ethanol

5 Great exertion; by rapid breathing afterwards, to deal with accumulated lactic acid aerobically.

6 Orange or yellow.

7 Large surface area, wet, thin.

8 Raising ribs, lowering diaphragm – which increases volume and decreases pressure in chest cavity.

9 Paralyses ciliated cells in trachea; increases mucus secretion; emphysema; lowers athletic ability; stunts baby's growth in uterus

10 ATP.

Quick test 11

1 CO_2, urea, water (**not** faeces).
2 Lungs, kidneys, liver, skin.
3 Excretion, water regulation (osmoregulation).
4 Ureter, bladder, urethra.
5 Water, urea, salts, bile pigments, (broken down toxins and hormones).
6 Glucose in the urine; injections of insulin.
7 Ensures water conservation from the urine.
8 Radiates heat from surface capillaries; sweats; hairs lowered (little insulation).
9 Maintenance of constant composition of tissue fluid around cells – stable metabolism.
10 Sensitive, waterproof, barrier against pathogens, physical protection, camouflage.

Quick test 12

1 Detectable changes in the environment.
2 They change the energy of a stimulus into nerve impulses.
3 Nose, tongue.
4 Thermostat of the hypothalamus; breathing centre of the medulla oblongata.
5 Fovea.
6 Radial muscles of iris.
7 Cornea, lens, ciliary muscles.

Quick test 13

1 Synapse.
2 Acetylcholine.
3 Sensory cell → sensory neurone → relay neurone → motor neurone → effector cell(s).
4 Muscle and gland.
5 Balance and coordination of muscle action.
6 Hallucinogen.
7 Insulin and glucagon.
8 Raises blood glucose level; increases heart and breathing rate; diverts blood to skeletal muscles from elsewhere.
9 Auxin.
10 Positive geotropism.

Quick test 14

1 Support and locomotion.
2 Muscles only contract; so a second muscle is required to extend the first after it has contracted.
3 Ligaments attach bone to bone; tendons attach muscle to bones.
4 Shoulder; hip. Allows movement in more than one plane.
5 By turgor on its cellulose cell walls; by lignified cells, e.g. xylem.
6 Involuntary muscle.
7 Transmit sound.
8 Swollen joints.

Quick test 15

1 They are all identical to the original parent.
2 To start cells dividing to form roots.
3 Scion controls quality of product; stock controls vigour of growth.
4 To cause cells to grow into a callus.
5 Pollination is the transfer of pollen from the anther to the stigma; fertilization is the fusion of the male nucleus of the pollen tube with the egg cell nucleus to form a zygote nucleus.
6 Insect: larger, spiky or sticky; wind: smoother and lighter (some with wing sacs).
7 Pollen germinates; pollen tube containing a nucleus grows down style; pollen tube enters the ovule; the two nuclei fuse.
8 Ovary forms the fruit; ovule forms the seed.
9 Fruits catch on fur; fruits are eaten.
10 By nuclear transplantation or embryo division and putting their results into the uteri of foster mothers to grow into young.

Quick test 16

1 Oviduct.
2 Head provides the genetic material; middle contains mitochondria to produce energy; tail is for swimming.
3 To promote ovulation.
4 To increase the surface area for exchange of materials between the mother's and fetus's blood.
5 Protection and support of the embryo/fetus.
6 Luteinizing hormone (LH) from the pituitary.
7 To secrete progesterone to maintain the uterus wall intact.
8 Stop implantation of fertilized eggs.
9 Progesterone.
10 Their blood contains antibodies to the HIV virus but they do not display the symptoms of AIDS.

Quick test 17

1 Irreversible increase in size or mass.
2 Apical meristem.

3 Vacuolation followed by differentiation.

4 Genes, climate and nutrients.

5 Radicle (root).

6 Starch in the cotyledons or endosperm.

7 For aerobic respiration to give energy for growth.

8 The organisms are destroyed.

9 Growth cells, out of control.

Quick test 18

1 Protein and DNA.

2 Gene controls production of an enzyme; one or more enzymes control a series of chemical reactions.

3 Genotype – the genetic make up of the individual; phenotype – appearance (characteristics) of the individual.

4 Tt and Tt where T = allele for tall and t = allele for dwarf.

5 X_hX_h; X_HX_h; X_HX_H; X_HY; X_hY.

6 Mitosis is used in asexual reproduction when identical offspring are produced; meiosis occurs in sexual reproduction to form the gametes.

7 Discontinuous are usually controlled by a single gene; continuous are usually controlled by several genes.

8 A mutation is a change in the genetic information of an individual.

9 Bacteria and fungi.

10 Pattern of bars created after an autoradiograph of a treated DNA sample has been made. A genetic fingerprint is unique for each human individual.

Quick test 19

1 Elimination by the environment of those least adapted to it so permitting only those best adapted to survive.

2 Mutations.

3 Resistance to malaria.

4 When they can no longer interbreed.

5 Charles Darwin.

6 Fish; amphibians; reptiles; mammals; birds.

7 Features used frequently were improved and passed on to subsequent generations, e.g. giraffe ancestors grew longer necks to reach high foliage.

8 Cut off mice tails for many generations so they could not be used. Tails of the final generation were as long as those of first generation parents (and not shorter, through disuse).

Quick test 20

1 The role a particular species plays in the community.

2 An area where living things interact with one another and their environment as a unit.

3 Sunlight.

4 Break down dead plants, animals and excreta.

5 An organism living on or in another organism from which it obtains food.

6 As nitrates from soil through roots; some have nitrogen fixing bacteria in roots to absorb nitrogen.

7 Convert nitrates in soil into nitrogen.

8 Nutrients are cycled round and round; energy flows through the food chain and leaves as heat.

9 Felling trees reduces photosynthesis and burning them produces CO_2.

10 Evaporation from physical surfaces (seas, rivers, lakes, soil); transpiration from plants; perspiration from mammals.

Quick test 21

1 Agriculture; sanitation; water supply; medicine; (education).

2 No roots to bind soil together; less cover on surface to prevent soil being washed away.

3 Waste substances (or energy) from human activities that upset the normal balances of the biosphere.

4 Carbon dioxide; methane.

5 Sulphur dioxide and nitrogen oxides dissolve in water vapour in the air to form sulphuric and nitric acids.

6 Damage to the nervous system especially to young children.

7 A population explosion of algae leads to their death. Their decay by bacteria ensues. Large numbers of bacteria use the oxygen for aerobic respiration.

8 Aerosols may release chlorofluorocarbons (CFCs) into the atmosphere; these break down ozone in the stratosphere allowing more UV radiation to reach the earth's surface.

9 Warmth; moisture; oxygen; suitable pH; microorganisms that cause decay.

10 Less use of natural resources; less waste to dispose of.

Quick test 22

1 To increase the rate of photosynthesis.

2 Organisms other than the intended one may be affected.

3 Predator and pest are in close contact; often no alternative food source for predator.

4 Conditions that favour plant growth also favour growth and spread of microorganisms.

5 Warm and rainy.

6 Phloem cells in the stem and leaves.

7 Temperature; carbon dioxide; light intensity and duration.

8 To prevent entry of their predators or competitors that eat their food; to prevent escape of fish (crop).

Quick test 23

1 Genetic; diet deficiency; hormone; environmental; degenerative.

2 Remove stagnant water; cover water surfaces with layer of light oil; biological control with 'mosquito fish'; insecticides.

3 On dirty hands.

4 Fibrinogen is a soluble blood protein; fibrin is an insoluble blood protein in the form of strands.

5 To digest bacteria that may get through the damaged area.

6 Immunity is long lasting when gained actively.

7 T cells have antibodies on their cell surface; B cells release antibodies into blood plasma.

8 The recipient's body produces too many antibodies against the antigens on the surface of the transplanted organ.

9 Chemicals that kill microorganisms but not human cells.

10 He discovered antibiotic penicillin.

Coursework

From 1998 there is a new coursework system for all GCSE Science courses. The same system applies to all GCSE Examination Boards.

During your Biology course you will be expected to complete a coursework assessment that includes a **whole investigation**.

A whole investigation involves you scoring marks in four separate skill areas. These are:

- Skill Area P – Planning experimental procedures.
- Skill Area O – Obtaining evidence.
- Skill Area A – Analysing evidence and drawing conclusions..
- Skill Area E – Evaluating evidence.

In addition you can score marks by carrying out assessments which test only one or two of these skill areas. Your final mark must include **at least two pieces of work** of which **one must be a whole investigation**.

For each of skill areas P, O and A, there is a maximum of eight marks and skill area E has a maximum of six marks, making a possible total of 30 marks.

A single final total mark out of 63 is obtained which includes three marks allocated for your spelling, punctuation and grammar (SPaG). This mark out of 63 is calculated by adding together the best marks awarded for each of the four skill areas, doubling the total, and then adding a further mark out of three for spelling, punctuation and grammar.

For example, if you are awarded four marks for skill areas P and O, three for skill area A, two for skill area E and two for SPaG, your overall mark is

$$2 \times (4 + 4 + 3 + 2) + 2$$

A total of 28 is obtained for the coursework assessment.

The marks awarded by your teacher, and samples of the work from your school or college will be checked (moderated) by an expert from outside your school to make sure the marking is the same as in all other schools and colleges. The moderator may add marks to your total, if your teacher has been harsh, or deduct marks, if your teacher has been generous in the marking.

There follows some helpful advice on each of the skill areas P, A, O and E which should help you get the highest marks in each of these skill areas. One word of warning at this stage: sometimes the maximum mark you can achieve in a skill area is limited by how complicated the investigation is.

Skill Area P Planning experimental procedures

The table on page 235 shows the Programme of Study requirements for Skill Area P.

The first point to make about this skill area is perhaps a very obvious one. If you are being entered for a Biology examination, the subject of your coursework must be biological. You cannot use coursework which is about the motion of a pendulum, even though it has been marked using the same criteria. You might, however, use an investigation about rates of reaction using enzymes in Chemistry and Biology.

Programme of Study Requirements

You should have been taught the following:

- To use scientific knowledge and understanding, drawing on secondary sources such as textbooks, databooks, computer simulations, the work of other students, etc., to turn your ideas into a form that can be investigated.

- To carry out preliminary work where this helps to carry out what you have to do. For example, some quick experiments at different temperatures may help you decide which range of temperature you should investigate in an enzyme experiment.

- To make predictions where it is appropriate. If you want to score high marks, your prediction should be quantitative. *Note:* the previous Coursework system, operating up to 1997, required a prediction to be made for every investigation and without a prediction the investigation was invalid.

- To consider the key factors in situations where a number of factors apply.

- To plan how to vary or control key variables.

- To consider the number and range of observations or measurements to be made.

- To recognize contexts, for example field work, where variables cannot readily be controlled and to make judgements about the amount of evidence needed in these contexts.

- To select apparatus, equipment and techniques, taking into account safety.

Your investigation should use your factual knowledge of Biology. If your investigation involves a prediction, this should be based upon factual knowledge. You need to say something like:

I think ....will happen because ....

To help you get a suitable 'because', it may be best to include a section of theory which you consider relevant. You are allowed access to any resources available, including books, to find out the information.

At this stage we must consider the topic of **variables**. Suppose you are measuring the volume of oxygen produced by a plant in five minutes at different light intensities at room temperature. Clearly the light intensity and the volume of oxygen are related. The more light you use (up to a maximum), the more oxygen will be produced. The light intensity is an **independent variable**. This means it can be what you choose it to be. The volume of oxygen is a **dependent variable**. This is because it depends upon the light intensity used.

There are other variables in this investigation which you have fixed:

1. The amount and type of plant.
2. The temperature – room temperature.
3. The length of time the oxygen is collected for.

When you are planning, it is important to identify all your variables and decide which ones you are going to vary and which ones you are going to keep unchanged. It is very unwise to vary too many variables at the same time. When you start varying a new variable, compare the new results with your previous ones. If you are making predictions about the effects of different variables, try to predict the effect before you start and try to give a scientific reason why. It does not matter if you are wrong.

Ensure that your planning is clearly written in a form which your teacher and the external moderator can follow. Remember marks can only be given for what is written down. You cannot get marks for thoughts you had but did not write down.

At this stage your teacher will look at your plan and may even make suggestions, especially for your safety!

Skill Area O Obtaining evidence

The following table shows the Programme of Study requirements for Skill Area O.

Programme of Study Requirements
You should have been taught the following: ● To use a range of apparatus and equipment safely and with skill. ● To make observations and measurements to a degree of precision appropriate to the context. ● To make sufficient relevant observations and measurements to give reliable evidence. ● To consider uncertainties in measurements and observations. ● To repeat measurements and observations where appropriate. ● To record evidence clearly and appropriately as you carry out the work. Usually this requires you to record your results in a suitable table.

In this skill area you carry out the plan you made. As you do this you will make detailed observations and/or measurements. To gain the highest marks, there must be measurements.

Make sure you write down your observations straight away. Use a suitable table or tables if possible. There are two reasons why you should record your observations and measurements immediately:

1 In case you lose them. This is not as silly as it seems. It does happen.
2 The table enables you to see possible errors or gaps in your results and helps you to see patterns that exist in them.

Make sure your observations are detailed. If you are observing the breakdown of starch using iodine indicator, record the colour changes accurately, for example different intensities of blue/black and olive. Or simply stop at when blue–blackness disappears.

If you are taking measurements, are you taking them to the right degree of accuracy? If you are measuring the rate of oxygen production from a plant is it sufficient to count the *number* of oxygen bubbles produced or should you collect the gas in a measuring cylinder or syringe to get *volume*? Are the bubbles the same size?

Is it sufficient to do the experiment once, or should you do the experiment a number of times and average the results? Your results are likely to be more accurate if, for example, in the photosynthesis experiment you repeat your results at each light intensity three times. You will then be more confident about your conclusions. But is the plant you use photosynthesizing as well at the end of the experiment as when you started? Is the amount of CO_2 available to the plant at the beginning the same as that at the end of the experiment?

Before you analyse your results, show them to your teacher. If you do not have all the information that you need you can be given other results to work from.

Do not be afraid to modify or change your plan.

Skill Area A Analysing evidence and drawing conclusions

The following table shows the Programme of Study requirements for Skill Area A.

Your measurements are usually best displayed in some kind of graph. You can put your results into a computer to help you plot the graph. If you draw a graph on a piece of graph paper, choose your scales and axes carefully. Try to fill the piece of graph paper and use simple scales, e.g. 1 small square represents 1 °C, rather than a complicated scale, e.g. three small squares represent 2 °C. Label the axes and draw a line of 'best-fit'. This may not go through all the points plotted. Put an appropriate title on your graph.

Programme of Study Requirements

You should have been taught the following:

- To present qualitative and quantitative data clearly. Often recording your results in a logical order helps in analysing your results.
- To present data as graphs, using lines of best fit where appropriate.
- To identify patterns or trends in results.
- To use graphs to show patterns and relationships between variables.
- To present numerical results to an appropriate degree of accuracy.
- To check that conclusions drawn are consistent with the evidence.
- To explain how results support or undermine the original prediction when one has been made.
- To try to explain conclusions in the light of your knowledge and understanding of science.

Having got all your observations and measurements, now is the time to try to make sense of them. Go back and remind yourself of your original plan and any prediction you made. Look objectively at your results. Do they support your prediction?

If you have altered two or more variables, what effect does each one have on your experiment? You may find that altering one variable has much more effect than varying the other. If your prediction is not right, try to suggest why not.

Draw a conclusion from your results and try to explain your conclusion using your scientific knowledge and understanding.

Skill Area E Evaluating evidence

The following table shows the Programme of Study requirements for Skill Area E.

Programme of Study Requirements

You should have been taught the following:

- To consider whether the evidence is sufficient to enable firm conclusions to be drawn.
- To consider reasons for anomalous results and to reject such results where appropriate.
- To consider the reliability of results.
- To propose improvements to the methods that have been used.
- To propose further investigation to test your conclusions.

This is the most difficult skill area for candidates. You have to look at your evidence and comment upon its reliability and whether it is sufficient to enable you to draw a firm conclusion. You should also try to explain any anomalous results (results that do not seem to fit in with the rest).

If you collected three results and plotted them on a graph, it is unlikely that you will be able to justify a straight line graph. You probably would need one or two more results to be able to confirm a 'straight-line' relationship.

Finally in this skill area you should suggest changes you would make, if you were repeating the experiment, in order to improve the accuracy of your results. This could involve improvements to your existing experiments or designing new experiments.

Getting the best marks in your coursework

Use the following table when planning and executing your experimental work. The checklist will tell you whether you are extracting the maximum number of marks that you can.

	P: Planning Planning my work	O: Obtaining evidence Collecting my data	A: Analysing and concluding Making my conclusions	E: Evaluating Evaluating my work	
2 marks	I can plan something to investigate. It will work safely.	I can use equipment safely. I can make some observations or take some measurements	I can show what I have found out.	I can say something about how well my plan has worked. I can say something about my results (evidence).	**2 marks**
4 marks	→ plus… I know that my plan is a fair test. I can choose the right equipment to use. I can predict what I think will happen	→ plus… I can make enough observations or measurements to be useful. I can record these observations or measurements carefully.	→ plus… I have drawn suitable simple diagrams, charts or graphs of my results. I can recognize trends and patterns in what I have found out.	→ plus… I can say how accurate my results are. I can recognize results that do not fit a pattern. I can suggest improvements to my plan.	**4 marks**
6 marks	→ plus… I can use scientific ideas to decide which are the most important factors to vary or control. I can say what observations and measurements I will need to take, and how many of them I will need.	→ plus… I can make careful and accurate observations or measurements. I can record these clearly. I can repeat my observations and measurements if this will help accuracy.	→ plus… I have drawn the right appropriate diagrams, charts or line graphs (with line of best fit) for my results I can do simple calculations to make my results meaningful. I can draw a conclusion from my results. I can relate my conclusions to my scientific knowledge and understanding.	→ plus… I can explain how good my evidence is in support of my conclusion. I can suggest improvements to obtain further evidence. I can suggest new work which would extend the investigation.	**6 marks**
8 marks	→ plus… I can use detailed scientific ideas in my plan to get reliable results. I have used information, which I quote, from books or other sources which helped me to plan.	→ plus: I can demonstrate that I used equipment skillfully to obtain high quality results. I have made enough observations and measurements (including repetitions if necessary) to obtain reliable evidence.	→ plus… I can use detailed scientific ideas to explain my conclusion. I can explain how my results support or contradict my original predictions.		**8 marks**

Remember that coursework makes up 25% of your final marks. These marks, earned before you take the written examination, can make a significant difference to your final grade.

Index